ociety

N **ducation**

Stanley William Rothstein
California State University, Fullerton

Merrill,
an imprint of Prentice Hall
Englewood Cliffs, New Jersey   Columbus, Ohio

Library of Congress Cataloging-in-Publication Data

Rothstein, Stanley William
    Schools and society : new perspectives in American education/
Stanley William Rothstein.
      p. cm.
    Includes bibliographical references and index.
    ISBN 0-02-403993-4
    1. Educational sociology—United States. I. Title
LC191.4.R69 1996   95-18739
370.19—dc20   CIP

Cover photo: R. Cord/H. Armstrong Roberts
Editor: Debra A. Stollenwerk
Production Editor: Christine M. Harrington
Text Designer: Matthew Williams
Cover Designer: Proof Positive/Farrowlyne Assoc., Inc.
Production Manager: Deidra M. Schwartz
Electronic Text Management: Marilyn Wilson Phelps, Matthew Williams,
    Karen L. Bretz, Tracey Ward

This book was set in Stempel Schneidler by Prentice Hall and was printed and
bound by R. R. Donnelley & Sons Company, Harrisonburg. The cover was
printed by Phoenix Color Corp.

© 1996 by Prentice-Hall, Inc.
A Simon & Schuster Company
Englewood Cliffs, New Jersey 07632

Printed in the United States of America

10 9 8 7 6 5 4 3 2 1

ISBN: 0-02-403993-4

Prentice-Hall International (UK) Limited, *London*
Prentice-Hall of Australia Pty. Limited, *Sydney*
Prentice-Hall of Canada, Inc., *Toronto*
Prentice-Hall Hispanoamericana, S. A., *Mexico*
Prentice-Hall of India Private Limited, *New Delhi*
Prentice-Hall of Japan, Inc., *Tokyo*
Simon & Schuster Asia Pte. Ltd., *Singapore*
Editora Prentice-Hall do Brasil, Ltda., *Rio de Janeiro*

For Our Daughter Stacy

☙

Preface

Ⓖ   Ⓖ   Ⓖ   Ⓖ   Ⓖ   Ⓖ   Ⓖ   Ⓖ   Ⓖ   Ⓖ   Ⓖ

Schools and Society presents a comprehensive review of the most recent and important social theory and research concerning modern educational systems. It analyzes the social functions of education in modern, commercial society. Multidisciplinary and social psychological in its approach, it explores important questions such as: *What are the functions of schooling in American society? How do classroom practices help in the fulfillment of those functions? Why are the schools organized as they are and what can be done to change them? What are the social and psychological costs of schooling youth in mass institutions?*

Using a cross-cultural perspective and a structural-functional theoretical orientation, this book considers educational systems as they have developed in England, France, and the United States. Schools are perceived as bureaucracies that developed in the post-feudal period, emerging from new forms of commercialism and the death of the monarchical system. The authority of modern governments and school systems derives from laws and not from age-old traditions. Teachers themselves derive their authority from such governments, becoming agents of the modern state and society. *Schools and Society* examines the thinking of the great social scientists who witnessed the wrenching transition from agrarian to industrial culture during the nineteenth century.

Schools are shown to be reproductive agencies that are concerned with maintaining the status quo in an Information Age that is changing at a dazzling pace. Along with the family, the church, and the state, schools present children with a series of lessons and beliefs that endorse the recent past while preparing youth for an increasingly unknown and unpredictable future.

Patterns of social mobility in commercial systems are explored and related to the educational experiences of youth from different sectors of modern society. Children's academic successes or failures appear to be related to their speech and language and to the variance that exists between such verbal abilities and those of educational systems. Classroom experiences of children are linked to those of teachers, who often have views of themselves that are quite different from those of the public they serve. The social-psychological conse-

v

quences of classroom life seem distressing for both groups—but must be viewed against the background of one of the most noble experiments in human history: the decision of American society to educate all youth no matter what their economic or intellectual condition.

Chapter 1 studies the modern world in transition, harkening back to the work of the great sociologists and psychologists of the nineteenth and early twentieth centuries. Chapter 2 examines the social functions of schooling in modern society and links education to other sectors of commercial life. Chapter 3 presents the evidence for the relationship that appears to exist between the family background of students and their success or failure in schools. Chapter 4 discusses educational knowledge as a socially constructed body of learning containing strong elements of ideology and propaganda in it. Chapter 5 analyzes the sociology of school curriculum and its relationship to institutions of higher learning and the labor market. The role of schoolteachers is discussed in Chapter 6, along with differences that exist between their self-perceptions and the way they are viewed by the public. Chapter 7 analyzes schools as bureaucracies, relating them to the rise of modern representative governments in the nineteenth and twentieth centuries. Chapter 8 describes the social relations that develop in classroom life; and Chapter 9 investigates the social and psychological consequences of present-day instructional practices. Chapter 10 sums up the condition of educational systems as they operate in commercial society; and Chapter 11 provides the reader with the problems and possibilities for school reform we prepare to enter the twenty-first century.

ACKNOWLEDGMENTS

This book has benefitted greatly from the patience shown to me by my editor, Debbie Stollenwerk. The author is also indebted to Christine Harrington for her project management, and to Professors Walt Beckman, William Callison, and Louise Adler for their years of continuing encouragement and support. Many others were kind enough to share their thoughts and work with me. Among them, I can only mention Professors Richard Altenbaugh, Frank Lutz, David Drew, Joseph Weeres, Antonia Darder, and Con Briner.

The reviewers of this text provided helpful suggestions for which I am grateful: Richard Altenbaugh, Slippery Rock University; Barbara L. Jackson, Fordham University; Thomas H. Jones, University of Connecticut; Frank W. Lutz, East Texas State University; P. Rudy Mattai, State University of New York at Buffalo; Fred Muskal, University of the Pacific; and Robert C. Serow, North Carolina State University

And finally, a note of thanks to Vice-President Mary Kay Tetrault, whose continuing interest and concern allowed me to focus my attentions on this book.

Contents

Chapter 1 ⑥ *Introduction: A World in Transition*   **1**

Community and Society: Ferdinand Tonnies   2
The Individual in Modern Life: Georg Simmel   5
Anomie and Normlessness: Emile Durkheim   9
The Human Predicament: Sigmund Freud   10
Projects   12

Chapter 2 ⑥ *Schools in Transition*   **15**

Functionalism   17
Socialization or Indoctrination   19
Assimilation and Social Control   21
Projects   24

Chapter 3 ⑥ *Knowledge and Ideology*   **27**

Definitions of Ideology   29
Ideologies in Schools   30
The Nature of Educational Production   34
Pedagogic Authority and Work   38
Pedagogic Action: The Teaching Process   39
Projects   42

Chapter 4 ⑥ *The Sociology of School Curriculum*   **47**

Knowledge and Culture   51
Power Systems in Schools   52
Curriculum Development and Reform   56
Can Changes Be Made?   58
Projects   61

Chapter 5 ❻ *Schoolteachers*   **67**

Teacher's Self-Perceptions   68
Society's Perception of Teachers   70
The Teacher-Pupil Relationship   73
The Feminization of the Teaching Profession   75
Teacher Organizations   77
Teacher Militancy: A Case History   79
A Final Note   81

Chapter 6 ❻ *The School as a Bureaucracy*   **87**

Capitalism and the Rule of Law   88
Bureaucracy   89
The School As a Bureaucracy   91
Bureaucratic Structures and Personal Needs   95
Projects   100

Chapter 7 ❻ *The Social Relations of Classroom Life*   **103**

The Framework of Classroom Life   106
The Instructional Act   108
The Language of Devaluation   111
Resistances and Failures   113
The Instructional Situation   114
Projects   117

Chapter 8 ❻ *Family Background and Academic Achievement*   **121**

Causes of School Failure   126
European Perspectives   130
The G. I. Bill: A Case History   133
Projects   136

Chapter 9 ❻ *Social Psychological Perspectives*   **139**

Human Nature and the Social Order   140
Dominance and Submission: The Paramount Relationship   142
Psychological Consequences   145
A Struggle for Dominance   148
Projects   153

Chapter 10 ❻ *Urban Education and the Significance of Race*   **157**

Definitions   158
The African-American Experience: A Special Case   161
Integrating Urban Schools   163
Hispanic Americans: A Brief Sketch   165
Projects   167

Chapter 11 ⑥ *Possibilities* *171*

    John Dewey's Legacy   173
    Social and Educational Knowledge   176
    Reforming the Schools   177

Glossary *181*

Selected Bibliography *185*

Index *197*

1

Introduction:
A World in Transition

⊚   ⊚   ⊚   ⊚   ⊚   ⊚   ⊚   ⊚   ⊚   ⊚   ⊚   ⊚

OBJECTIVES

In this chapter you will learn the answers to these questions:

- ⊚ *Why did the classical sociologists feel uneasy about the shift from agrarian to industrial society?*

- ⊚ *What did Ferdinand Tonnies mean when he spoke of Gemeinschaft (community) and Gesellschaft (society)?*

- ⊚ *How did commercial society create a new kind of person?*

- ⊚ *What did Durkheim mean by the term **anomie**, and how did it affect the intense desires of people living in commercial society?*

- ⊚ *How did Freud define the conflict between society and the individual in modern life?*

We cannot understand schooling apart from its relationships to other social and economic forces in modern life. Nor can we fully grasp it by focusing solely on its present-day practices and functions. Any systematic study of educational systems must pay attention to the social transitions of the past few centuries. For this, the work of the classical sociologists—Ferdinand Tonnies, Georg Simmel, Emile Durkheim, and Sigmund Freud—is paramount. These authors, whose writings span a period from approximately 1880 to 1930, witnessed the final stages of the shift from agrarian to industrial society with concern for the apparent breakdown in social controls and community. They were uneasy about the effects of these new conditions, which were producing increasing numbers of alienated individuals. Some of this anxiety was brought on by the collapse of the old order and the uncertainties created by capitalism, world trade, and the rise of mass society. Men and women seemed much more aware of the world they had lost and the imbalances that were developing during this period of change. Neither the new conditions nor the faltering institutions of the past seemed able to restrain the insatiable greed of individuals now that communities had been split asunder and megalopolises were becoming the centers for modern life and education. The classical sociologists saw that the free labor of the industrial world led inevitably to a freedom from communal restraints and values of the past, causing individuals to experience higher levels of social isolation, loneliness, and despair. They were also aware of the personal and mental anguish that accompanied the urbanization of modern life. In the past, beliefs had been supported by the collective efforts of people living in close proximity to one another. Now the mobility of individuals made the old ways seem impractical as men and women made themselves more comfortable with the demands of bureaucracy and mass institutions. Personal maladies and psychological trauma seemed to be greater in urban centers, with their conflicting and ambiguous moral values and standards. In spite of the development of educational systems throughout Europe, there seemed to be a collapse of social values and conduct and a general feeling of despair.

COMMUNITY AND SOCIETY: FERDINAND TONNIES

According to Ferdinand Tonnies,[1] modern society is characterized by an estrangement and separation between individuals that is unique in the history of humankind. This **alienation** of human beings from themselves and from others can be traced to imperialism and the increased competition for world markets and world trade. More and more, people find themselves in a world of rapid transition they cannot live in nor understand. Increasingly, the fate of the solitary individual living in isolation in the midst of expanding urban centers seems to have become a world fate.

Writing in 1880 near the end of these social upheavals, Tonnies was able to distinguish two principal types of social relationships: the **Gemeinschaft**, where family and community values were cherished, and the **Gesellschaft**, where they were not.[2] He was able to describe how the rapid transitions of industrial and commercial society were creating a new individual, one who was estranged from family and friends and at home in urban communities. The values of families and communities were being replaced by a rampant individualism and cosmopolitanism. Traditionally, agrarian society had been based on religious values and craft industries, but the new conditions created different interests, needs, and desires. The cooperativeness of the feudal period gave way to a more competitive and less friendly, mercenary society. The attitudes of avaricious money-lenders now held sway. The values of commercialism and contractual relations became dominant, creating urban centers of unlimited size and density.

The change from a collective to a more individualistic society struck at the foundations of family life, which had characterized human existence from its beginnings.[3] Family members had been bound together by ties that existed without their awareness or intention in the past. They were united by language and culture as whole persons rather than for their usefulness in particular situations. Gemeinschaft affirmed the unity of persons living and working in the same house, the same town. It grew out of a common language, culture, ancestry, and close-knit life activities. For Tonnies, Gemeinschaft included all the close friends and neighbors who shared similar languages, customs, and beliefs. It also included friends who came together through affection, similar likes and dislikes, and vocations.

During the feudal period when Gemeinschaft prevailed, people were born, lived, and died within a twenty-mile radius, centering their lives around families and communities. With the rise of commercialism, however, these strong communal ties broke down, leaving little in their place. People were freer now, but they were also more isolated and alone. Human relationships were more consensual now, but the warmth of the Gemeinschaft was being supplanted by useful associations and an increasingly impersonal world. With these changes, there was a lessening of the individual's commitment to the values, ideas, and loyalties of the precapitalist period.

Writing while many of these changes were still occurring, Tonnies made the further point that the tendencies toward Gesellschaft created a new kind of people who were only concerned about themselves and what belonged to them. These new individuals were more reflective, calculating their advantages in every relationship they entered into. "To him everything becomes a means to an end . . . his relationships to other men, and thus to associations of all kinds, begins to change".[4] In this modern era, the new individuals and their interests appear on the stage of history isolated and dissociated from family and community. They establish a contact with another person only when it is deemed useful. The close bonds of the Gemeinschaft period are replaced by the depersonalization of Gesellschaft.

The triumph of the Gesellschaft, of the contractual relationships entered into with prior calculation for the attainment of mutual ends, forces people to interact with one another fractionally, with only a part of their personality. This fragmented personality reveals only the part of itself that relates to the specific demands of organized economic or educational activities. The force that supports these types of associations is the individual's gains and aspirations in capitalist society. In such a society, people lose control of the tools of production. Mass society produces tension and isolation that shatter the sense of community people have shared since the dawn of time. Without these primary groups of family and community, the individual experiences an identity crisis, a loss of self-knowledge, and an inability to achieve meaningful associations within the void of the Gesellschaft. Individuals see themselves as buyer or seller, employer or employee, and their activities become obsessed with the process of commodity accumulation.[5]

These insights allowed Tonnies to develop two polar types of human personality: **Wesenwille**, or natural or integrated will associated with Gemeinschaft relationships, and **Kurwille**, or will shaped by rational weighing of means and ends associated with contractual or Gesellschaft relationships. Wesenwille consists of the drives, impulses, and emotions of human beings. It corresponds to their natural likes and dislikes, their natural dispositions, and signifies the individual's will as it encompasses the process of thinking. Kurwille, on the other hand, is conditioned by rational thought and the assessment of means and ends. It assesses the pros and cons and signifies the person's thinking as it includes the will as one of many elements to be considered in making a rational decision. These two forms of will are central to Tonnies' theories of personal development. Tonnies believed that most individuals were combinations of these polar types, but that in recent history Kurwille has become predominant. Commenting on the use of Kurwille and the nature of labor in capitalist society, Tonnies wrote that, to a large degree, the work of the masses of individuals has become impersonal and unsatisfying. "The satisfaction which most of us find in our work is not inherent in the occupational activities which we carry out; it is found primarily in the pay envelope . . . the equivalent for the numbers of hours put in . . . work for extrinsic end . . . to avail the individual of means which have no inner relationship to his life and its goals. Kurwille suppresses or conceals our dislikes . . . Kurwille divorces means from ends."[6]

The ascendancy of Gesellschaft has weakened the sense of community that people had always experienced in the past. It has created isolated individuals who live and work in increasingly depersonalized cities and suburbs. Gesellschaft individuals, detached from family and community, float in and out of relationships. They participate in corporate structures which they are powerless to control, and they seem incapable of replacing the traditional values of the precapitalist period with new ones that will restore a sense of meaningfulness to life.

In these ideas, there seems to be a tendency to idealize the past at the expense of modern society. A critique of Tonnies' elegant theories must deal with his glorification of the precapitalist social order as a "golden age" during which individuals lived in greater safety and security than they enjoy today. He saw serfdom or the peasant-landowner relations as beneficent social relations in which people viewed one another, not as commodities, but as whole human beings. Work was not fragmented, as it is today. Peasants and artisans were able to complete most aspects of their work and could take pride in their accomplishments. These benign pictures of the past ignore the grinding disease and poverty which characterized the lives of the peasant classes. They also ignore the military, political, and legal forces that were used to maintain the class structures of these precapitalist systems. Critiques of Tonnies' ideas have taken the following line: men and women living and working in different social systems at different times in world history cannot be compared to show that one group was better or worse off than another. True, serfs worked within a familial and kinship structure that is foreign to most modern employees. But those structures were more arbitrary and less profitable. Bondsmen and serfs may have lived in a world of Gemeinschaft, but it was a life that usually kept them impoverished and without hope. Wars may have been less destructive in this period, as Tonnies wrote, but they were often continuous. Barter may have been more simple, but only because people were not yet able to travel and communicate over long distances. The supposition that men and women who live in a Gesellschaft suffer more than people did in the past certainly needs further examination. Another criticism of Tonnies is that the ideal types of Kurwille and Wesenwille are overly functional in their construction, even though Tonnies wrote that most persons were a blend of the two, depending on the situation they found themselves in. Still, in his unification of social systems theory and psychology, Tonnies did point the way for us. Men and women in modern society have become more calculating in their thinking and less related to their familial roots. This is because, as Tonnies noted, capitalism needs certain types of individuals to hire for successful production. These people must be willing to relocate in ways that would have been difficult or impossible for serfs, peasants, and artisans.

THE INDIVIDUAL IN MODERN LIFE: GEORG SIMMEL

According to Georg Simmel, the problems of modern life center on the individual's struggle to retain autonomy and personal existence in the face of overwhelming social forces. In his study "The Metropolis and Mental Life,"[7] Simmel paints a vivid picture of the fight modern men and women must wage to maintain their sanity and security in the face of urban forces they can only vaguely understand. In more primitive times people waged a struggle with nature to satisfy their physical and psychological needs. But the transformation from agrarian to industrial society that began in the eighteenth century forced people to give up some of their most cherished beliefs and ideologies to meet the new realities of science, commerce, industry, and urbanization. People now had to work outside the home in mills and factories, where the goal of achieving greater efficiency and productivity demanded that people specialize their work. Now workers were interdependent and part of a productive process that made it possible for more and more people to congregate and live in more crowded spatial surroundings. Capitalism required workers who were as reliable as their machines, while workers themselves resisted being made into cogs in an enormous industrial system. An inquiry into the consequences of these new conditions must seek to resolve the conflict between the individual's need for autonomy and meaning in life and urban society's need to standardize all work and thought in overcrowded metropolises.

Simmel categorized the urban dweller's personality as one of intense neurotic agitation. This was a consequence of the enormous changes in culture and belief that challenged the stability of the inner and outer psychological well-being. Human beings had always been creatures who distinguished between different elements in their environment. Their minds were stimulated, as Hegel had shown, by a stream of consciousness that made one impression after another on their minds. Some impressions simply flitted across their consciousness, while others created more lasting images and ideas. The advent of urbanism caused a sharp increase in the flow of images, while people's ability to differentiate the images from one another decreased sharply. Movement in the metropolis had a tempo conditioned by the economic, social, and occupational needs of the city, in contrast with the more leisurely pace of psychic life in small towns and villages. In living patterns of the past, human beings had lived with mental images that were slower and more in consonance with traditions and the natural forces of the world. Now, the cosmopolitan character of urban life called into question all notions of religion and a psychic life based on strong emotional and family relationships. As Tonnies had written, these relationships were founded on the Gemeinschaft and the continuous associations of people who knew each other in more complete, less fragmented ways. To respond to the multifarious stimuli of the urban environment, individuals created a more detached, rational way of responding to people and situations they encountered in their daily lives. In describing this process, Simmel seemed to follow the work of Tonnies, viewing urban individuals as people who reacted more with their heads than their emotions. They were more alert to outside stimuli, using their sense of survival and rationality to protect their inner life from the overwhelming images and power of metropolitan life.

Simmel further distinguished between the conflict that exists between monetary principles and the individualism phenomenon that was so important during the craft period preceding modern mass production. Money is impersonal and available to all who can gather it into their hands. It reduces all problems between persons and things to a simple question: How much? But interpersonal relationships are always singular in nature and based on emotional affinities. Thus, the conflict is between such intimate relationship needs and the rational relations of the commercial world that make human beings into numbers to be moved about for the benefit of industrial production. For the urban world of commerce and industry, only the increase in economic achievement is important. Urban individuals deal with buyers and sellers, who may or may not have some impact on their future economic well-being. The circle of acquaintanceship is much wider than that of the small number of familial and neighborly associations of the pre-industrial era, when the Gemeinschaft was supreme and life was lived among familiar people and places. In the feudal period, buyers and sellers almost always knew one another, and they knew the conditions that produced the goods they desired. But the urban world supplies its members through mass production and a market economy, often forcing individuals to buy from producers they cannot know or fully trust. The depersonalization of this process gives to everyday urban life a matter-of-factness that differs from what human beings experienced previously. As Tonnies noted, personal relationships are now subordinated to the needs of economic calculation, and domestic production and barter become anomalies, at best.[8] The rational mode of thought and the needs of the money economy are so intertwined that it is difficult to say which is dominant. What seems apparent, however, is that the two forces feed on one another, together dominating the value systems and mores of metropolitan life.

Simmel concluded that the minds of urban individuals had become more calculating, more concerned with determining advantages for the self against all others. The world could now be comprehended in mathematical terms with each element in it given a precise value. The individual spent more time weighing decisions in terms of their economic impact, calculating the advantages of one action or another, and determining numerically the most profitable measures to pursue. Clearly, the very nature of urban life demanded many of these mental characteristics. Human beings interacted with so many more people in such complex relationships that a certain punctuality and way of doing business became necessary to avert chaos. Millions of individuals had to be integrated into this enormous urban system, which could not adequately meet their different interests and concerns. Urban life demanded an awareness of time and punctuality that was unknown in previous eras.

Simmel also suggested that this need to measure things quantitatively has depersonalized modern life while paradoxically creating the most intense forms of personal subjectivity. The blasé attitude so commonly observed as a trait of urbanites was a consequence of living and working in environments that bombarded the psyche with innumerable stimulations. An existence that emphasized the pursuit of material and sensual well-being led to this attitude and finally to the cessation of all reactions. Simmel insisted that we need look no further than the effects on the human nervous system to understand reactions to the rapidly changing and contradictory demands of urban relationships. These physiological tensions were influenced by other attitudes and demands of the money economy. Blasé individuals would have to blunt their discriminatory abilities if they were to live satisfactorily in an impersonal and machine-made world. They did not value things that did not relate directly to their economic well-being, since they tended to value everything in terms of exchange value. Money became the means through which people expressed their values and thoughts, hollowing out the center of things and reducing the modern world in the process. Everything could be assessed or explained in terms of quantitative value, seen in terms of how much money was needed to purchase and maintain certain manufactured items or historical curios. Simmel also called attention to the need for individuals to preserve themselves in the face of these demands from urban systems, developing a reserved attitude that allowed them to navigate through each day without becoming emotionally exhausted. If they were to relate to each event in an emotional way, as people had in the feudal era, their **psychic state** would soon be unimaginable. This gave individuals a personal freedom different from any that has ever existed in Western society. Early cities were comparatively small circles of close-knit individuals who banded together for trade and physical protection from enemies. Citizens had little freedom of movement or action and were governed by group mores and beliefs. According to Simmel, larger kinship groups and political parties began in this way and kept a strict control over the behavior of members. He argues that, to the degree that a group's population expands, its power to inhibit and control the personal behavior and thoughts of its members lessens. The smaller the number of people in a social situation or system, the more restricted will be the relationships that can exist there.

A final point of Simmel's theory is that the highest economic division of labor and commerce occurs in the cities.[9] People identify themselves by their affiliations with industrial and commercial establishments, using signs and cards to validate their identities. The normal human struggle against nature for food and shelter has been replaced by a competition with other people who live and work in a world defined by words and numbers. The specialization and rationalization of work processes led to greater productivity and consequently to the producer's need to create demand from the consuming public.

These, then, are the elements of urban life that transform the mental and psychic lives of individuals living in large cities. But there are other, underlying causes, too. There is the problem of asserting one's personal preferences and personality in a metropolitan life that is teeming with people. Human beings are tempted to seek pseudo-Gemeinschaft associations (e.g., joining groups or clubs) in an attempt to give greater meaning to their personal existences. Simmel reminds us that interhuman contact is quite different in these metropolises where everyone tries not to waste time and where relationships are often gauged by whether they can provide amusement or advance one's career.

ANOMIE AND NORMLESSNESS: EMILE DURKHEIM

Emile Durkheim[10] has also drawn attention to the need to examine the effects of the division of labor in modern society and the development of a more urban social system in the eighteenth and nineteenth centuries. With the advent of high-speed machinery and mass production, individual have been forced to work outside the home, causing separation from age-old familial and neighborhood associations and loyalties. Indeed, this revolution in the way people worked had profound consequences for social consciousness and individual morality. It is perhaps significant that the concept and potential for alienation first appeared and increased markedly during this period of expanded world trade and commerce when the norms of life seemed to change radically. The past was dominated by more spiritual and religious concepts and loyalties, but the new industrial system set no limit on the worldly desires of individuals. People could have heaven on earth if they worked hard enough; their strivings would be rewarded by ever-larger amounts of material goods.

In describing this transition, Durkheim seemed to echo the work of Tonnies. In one passage, he suggested that under normal conditions social systems had the capability and methods for controlling the intense desires of individuals while still providing them with ways for attaining personal happiness and success. Only society, operating through its traditions and laws, could perform these needed functions. Only society could control the insatiable desires of individual citizens. What would happen, however, if society were to lose the power and authority to control its members' appetites?

Under these circumstances, people were less and less certain about what is right and wrong. The old religious and group restraints no longer existed in sufficient strength, and the new norms of commercial society were either misunderstood or led to a state of complete normlessness, or *anomie*. The morality of the past was replaced by an uncertain morality of the majority. Individuals found themselves alienated from their roots as well as from the system in which they lived and worked. He noted an apparent lack of harmony between the desires and aspirations of individuals and their means for achieving them. People began to believe that their fate was a matter of luck or other forces outside their control. They commonly believed that no matter how hard they worked, little would come of it. Anomic responses increased as commercial society demanded that all individuals compete for economic and social success that only a few could attain.

Many others, such as Parsons, have drawn attention to the social alienation that seems to accompany the individual's integration into industrial and urban communities. They suggest that Durkheim's views of anomie and norm-lessness are a distinguishing feature of modern society. The onset of world trade, urbanization, and industrialization have destroyed the normative and structural conditions of traditional society, uprooting people from their families and neighborhoods. The local group institutions that provided stability, security, and personal identity no longer have the power to control and give meaning to human life. This is because there are no mandatory normative values to support the new industrial communities that have grown up throughout the modern world. Thus there is an absence of Gemeinschaft, an absence of familial and neighborly membership for individuals living in immensely crowded, industrial communities.

THE HUMAN PREDICAMENT: SIGMUND FREUD

No study of the struggle between the individual and society would be complete without a discussion of the works of Sigmund Freud.[11] He defined the conflict between society and the individual as an age-old struggle between personal needs and those of the group. Just as he focused his **psychoanalysis** on the experiences and mental life of individuals, so he introduced the concept of human unhappiness as a given that cannot be denied or significantly changed by societies. To explain the open hostility human beings show toward culture and the restraints of social systems, Freud looked first at history and then at the nature of human beings as they have evolved in modern times. He wrote that in the pre-industrial period Christianity sought to exercise control over its members by urging them to place a low value on the rewards and realities of earthly life, while modern civilization taught its members opposite values and orientations. Modern life was dominated, as Weber has shown, by increased rationality and science and the development of world capitalism and trade. But science proved to be a disappointment, and the mood of people in modern society seemed to be one of increasing disillusionment and unhappiness.

Still, the realization that new inventions and technologies would not create a happy society became a given in modern thought and scholarship. Freud urged us to remember, however, that such uneasiness and discomfort with civilizations and cultures was not a new phenomenon. Human beings learned how to better control nature while improving their own living standards. In spite of this increased power to control the natural world, the basic nature of human beings remained constant. As Freud described it, the individual constantly behaved as "a wolf to other men." Hence people's essential animalism had to be controlled by social compacts and institutions if civilization were to survive. In modern society, the state exercised this control, representing an important step forward in the development of human affairs. Freud noted that the first people to raise their voices instead of their hands in anger were the initiators of the kinship structures and social systems that evolved into modern civilization. Still, the demands of the group interfered with the passionate needs and desires of individuals, forcing them to suppress and repress many aggressive and erotic needs. These needs lingered in the unconscious, often erupting in explosive violence, anger, or frustration.

This aspect of social life was Freud's major contribution to this field. It brought into sharp focus the struggle that existed in all social systems between the repressed passions and drives of the human animal and the demands of culture and civilization. He postulated a powerful and clinically supported theory of human nature that gave his political and social commentaries an unusual force. *Civilization and Its Discontents* provided the basis for a social foundation of Freud's psychoanalytic theories, linking the nature of human beings to their cultural and social development. These theories were further influenced by primeval experiences that caused dynamic conflicts between the ego, id, and superego of individuals and the group to which they belonged. Human beings were besieged by unconscious needs and primeval, ardent feelings of love and hate which they could barely control. These needs and feelings, in turn, produced intimate feelings of anxiety and shame since they centered on murderous, rapacious, and incestuous desires that often emanated from the earliest moments of life.[12]

For Freud, modern society was a necessary control mechanism that caused an inevitable conflict between individuals and their cultural lives. The state and religious institutions that protected human beings from their own destructive powers also produced the feelings of alienation and discontent that the great philosophers spoke about. Utopian schemes could not cope with these conflicts since they denied the animal nature of human beings and overemphasized human rationality.

Freud's analysis comes full circle with his history of aggression. Human beings were not the gentle, rational, loving individuals of idealistic dogmas and beliefs. Aggression existed above and beyond property rights, above and beyond religious beliefs and attitudes. It provided people with pleasure as well as pain. Aggression balanced love relationships by binding members of groups together in affection while strengthening their natural tendency to mistrust and hate outsiders.

Comprehending the enormous sacrifices of civilized society makes the unhappiness of the individual more understandable. Men and women had powerful sexual and aggressive drives or instincts, which could not be eliminated without serious psychological consequences. Affection and hatred struggled with one another to control the social relationships of human beings. Freud further related the love or erotic drive to life and human aggressiveness to death. These two drives clashed in a battle between will and death, with the culture of a social system inhibiting the worst effects of aggression as best it could. Antisocial behaviors and thoughts were forced into repression, burrowing deep into the mind from which they came.

Freud saw these developments in terms of people's need to improve their condition by working and living in ever-larger social groups.[13] This was linked to the need to improve communication skills to better understand and be understood by people outside the immediate, primary group. In primeval times, people may have had ways of distinguishing their own flesh and blood and what their relationships were to one another. With the advent of larger and larger social organizations, the need for new ways of distinguishing between friends and foes became more apparent. The first families were connected in ways that were probably similar to other advanced animals around them. The development of speech and language brought with it rituals, traditions, and a cultural heritage that influenced the way people saw their lives. Freud related these new structures to a moment in history when the primal father was overpowered and murdered by his sons, creating in them a sense of anxiety and guilt that has persisted into our own times. He suggested that the totemic restrictions they later placed on themselves required written laws that they could discuss and refer to when disputes arose. This was the beginning of human civilization for Freud, the moment when the rights of individuals were codified into laws and traditions. Kinship groups were now held together by common economic activities and emotional ties. The **psychogenetic** ability to speak and use language gave human beings a new mastery and power over their physical and psychic world. Now they could live and work in stable communities, hunting and gathering in larger and larger groups, and increasing their wealth and security.

⑥ *Summary*

This introductory chapter has dealt with the emergence of new social structures in society. These formed the backdrop in which state schools were established in Europe and the United States. Of course, we will focus much of our attention on current educational practices, but subsequent chapters will reinforce the notion that it is not possible to isolate schooling from its socioeconomic context.

⑥ *Projects*

1. Interview two or three older people about what their life was like forty or fifty years ago. Write a short essay describing how people were different then. Talk also about how they were the same.

2. Study the divorce rates in your community and state. Write a short essay telling what these indicate about the strength or weaknesses of families in your area, your school.

3. Think about the many roles you play in your life. How different are you in your actions and attitudes? When you assume the role of

teacher, how does your personality change? How far is it from your "real" personal identity?

⑥ *Endnotes*

1. Tonnies, Ferdinand, *Community and Society* (New York: Harper & Row, 1957), 258–259.

2. Ibid., 1–11.

3. Ibid., 38–40.

4. Pappenheim, Fritz, *The Alienation of Modern Man* (New York: Monthly Review Press, 1959), 73–74.

5. Tonnies, *Community and Society*, 247.

6. Pappenheim, *The Alienation of Modern Man*, 69–104.

7. Simmel, Georg, "The Metropolis and Mental Life," in *Images of Man: The Classical Tradition in Sociological Thinking*, ed. C. Wright Mills (New York: George Braziller, 1960), 409–423.

8. Tonnies, *Community and Society*, 54–56, 81–84, 180–183.

9. Simmel, "The Metropolis and Mental Life," 437–448.

10. Durkheim, Emile, "On Anomie," in *Images of Man: The Classical Tradition in Sociological Thinking*, ed. C. Wright Mills (New York: George Braziller, 1960), 449–485.

11. Freud, Sigmund, *Civilization and Its Discontents*, trans. James Strachey, (New York: W. W. Norton, 1961), 46–50.

12. Freud, Sigmund, *The Ego and the Id* (New York: W. W. Norton, 1989), 26–32.

13. Rothstein, Stanley W., *The Voice of the Other: Language as Illusion in the Formation of the Self.* (Westport, Conn.: Praeger, 1993), 47–68.

2

Schools in Transition

OBJECTIVES

In this chapter you will learn the answers to these questions:

- ⑥ *Why was there a conflict between families and schools during this period of transition?*

- ⑥ *What role did educational systems play in socializing youth?*

- ⑥ *What is functionalism, and why was it used to explain schooling's purposes in modern society?*

- ⑥ *Why are schools "reproductive" agencies in industrial culture?*

- ⑥ *How have schools been used to indoctrinate students of totalitarian governments?*

- ⑥ *How did schools serve immigrant children in the United States?*

At the end of the nineteenth century, Emile Durkheim described the triumph of industrial culture and the changes it produced in living and work patterns of European society.[1] His concern focused on the conflict that occurred between families and the state during this time of explosive educational growth. Turning first to the rights of the family, Durkheim acknowledged that children belonged to their parents in the first instance.[2] The parents were the earliest teachers, giving their children social identity, language, and thought processes to use for a lifetime. Writing in a period of unprecedented change, Durkheim described how the transitions resulting from the Industrial Revolution were creating confusion and conflict between the interests of state educational systems and those of the family and community. Family and religious values were being challenged by those of the schools, creating new conditions and attitudes among the youth of the nation. The close familial relations of the past and the rights of parents to direct the intellectual and moral development of their children were being directly threatened by national educational institutions. Urban, industrialized values and beliefs were becoming dominant, undermining older ideas that viewed education as an essentially domestic and religious concern.

The advent of science, industrialism, and commercialism were only the beginning of a cultural process that systematically attacked the foundations of family and community life.[3] Reacting to these changes, French families, for example, sought to minimize the intervention and power the state could exert through its expanding educational systems. Parents wanted the state to act as an auxiliary to the education of their children but wished to maintain the ultimate power to direct their intellectual and moral development. Nevertheless, when families showed that they were less and less able to perform these duties, the state expanded its educational system to do the job.

Durkheim was quick to point out, however, that the state had a positive role to play, especially when there was a harmony of interests between the schools and the families they served. Education had always been a function of the collectivity,[4] even when families and the Church were given the major responsibility for it. Its function was to help youth adapt to the needs of the society in which they lived. For this reason, the state had always shown an interest in the way children were educated; it had, in the modern era, constantly monitored the ideas and values teachers presented to children. For Durkheim, the state played an important role in assuring parents and students that the instructional efforts of teachers would be put to the service of the entire nation and not the private beliefs of a few. It also assured that the different and conflicting interests in society would not be reflected in public school classrooms.

During this period, Durkheim wrote about education in France as a benign institution. It was, he argued, an agency that sought out the ideas and beliefs that most citizens considered valid and that were necessary for society to maintain itself. The training of the child could not be left to the arbitrary beliefs and attitudes of parents, relatives, and friends. Writing during a time when many changes from agrarian to industrial society were still occurring, Durkheim noted that education was now a social function the modern state could not disregard. No educational system could be permitted to provide children with an antisocial education, one that questioned the values and social foundations of the state that funded it. Nor could it be said that the state created the valid ideas that became the basis of educational systems. These ideas were established by communities and families living and working together over many years. The state and its educational system could only affirm these ideas, making children aware of them from one generation to the next. Despite the many differences of opinion that existed in society, according to Durkheim, there were certain primary principles necessary for people to adapt themselves to the requirements of modern life. These included a respect for reason and the science it made possible, as well as ideas and opinions at the core of democratic morality. The state's role was to insist on the teaching of these principles and ideas in classrooms throughout the nation. In this role, the state was to ensure that children everywhere would be aware of these principles and ideas and would speak about them with reverence and respect.[5]

FUNCTIONALISM

The writings of Emile Durkheim were anchored in functionalist ideas that were current during the latter part of the nineteenth century. Proponents of **functionalism** analyzed the functions of social institutions in industrial culture and viewed the social system as an organism in the Darwinian sense, possessing many of the same needs and concerns as living things. They assumed that the social system must, in every instance, ensure that its members had the food, clothing, and shelter needed to survive. Sexual and reproductive functions had to be set in place along with rules that governed family life. Institutions such as the state, the Church, and commercial corporations needed to be established along with a social and economic division of labor.[6] Such thinking found affirmation in anthropological studies indicating that social systems, no matter how primitive or advanced, needed to socialize their young to maintain themselves.[7]

A strength of the functionalist perspective has been its ability to clarify education's role in commercial society. From this perspective, schools were a benevolent but powerful force creating the social cohesion and unity that commercial society required.[8] Schooling's relationship to the social, political, and economic structures became more understandable, and the logic of the educational system related to the reproductive needs of modern society. The economy and the state, for example, took on an important place in these processes because of their role in reproducing skilled workers and loyal citizens. For Durkheim, education in modern society was fundamentally a matter of authority and social control. Its duty was to create from antisocial infants, socialized men and women who could work and function effectively in an increasingly complex world. Children had to be taught inner controls so they could carry on the work of the society, sublimating their own impulses to the demands of citizenship and labor.

Nevertheless, functionalist perspectives have certain problems to consider. The view of society as an organism is a nineteenth-century assumption that was deeply influenced by discoveries in the biological sciences. Functionalists tend to explain existing social phenomena by referring to the needs of the organism, seeing society as a giant biological entity with many of the needs and drives of living things. They recognize institutions that have no apparent function as well as others that seem to have many functions. They even call some institutions *dysfunctional* because the institutions seem to work against the social system's capacity to fulfill its fundamental needs.

These criticisms of functionalism may seem formidable enough, but there are still other problems with this approach. Underlying newer, structural-functional approaches is the need to accept the idea that teachers and students are dominated by unseen forces in the social and economic realm. But individuals may often be unaware or unconscious of these social forces and the way they affect daily life. In the Marxian or Freudian system,[9] individuals may misrecognize or repress what is happening to them and are therefore unable to see and understand certain relationships in society. The legal force that stands behind the legitimate authority of schools, for example, is not always perceived by teachers, students or parents. In these theories, the state has the primary task of reproducing itself and its economic and cultural relations in society. In Marxist theories, the state carries out the demands of those who possess social and economic power in the system.[10] The power of state agencies to reproduce themselves is a basic tenet of such systems of thought, even though recent history seems to contradict such ideas. Economic realities of wealth or poverty often do these socializing tasks better and with less conflict. Families seem to teach the lessons of status and place through language and culture, with schools merely reinforcing these first learnings. In American schools, as we shall see, these messages are not as focused as functionalists would have us believe, and both families and schools send children other messages that are meant to conflict with their formal, instructional communications.

Banks[11] has argued that Durkheim underestimated the complexities of modern society and the conflicts that would occur when children from different social origins tried to work and learn in traditional classroom settings. The division of labor and the demands of world trade and commerce meant that people would come to the schooling situation with different interests and concerns. Durkheim was overly concerned with the problems of socialization and character building, but insufficiently attentive to the problems of indoctrination as they were played out in classrooms and schools. During his time, education was highly valued by the new **burgher** class, which had assumed ascendancy at the end of the feudal period. For these people, education was a way of building moral character and industriousness in children, ensuring they would fit into the new world that was being created by capital, science, and industry.

SOCIALIZATION OR INDOCTRINATION

Researchers after World War II tended to agree with Durkheim's ideas, although they viewed the socialization function of schools in a more unfavorable light. They pointed to the educational system's use of political and economic indoctrination and its need to reproduce relationships that maintained the status quo in schools and society.[12] Education prepared children for their places in a stratified labor force that was inherently unequal. The state funded schools, in this view, to guarantee that the economic and social system of the moment would be accepted without thought or discussion. Bowles and Gintis[13] related the classroom practices of teachers in the United States to commercial society's need for certified workers, for employees who possessed the educational qualifications to function in an increasingly complex, pyramidal economic system.

Of course, the use of education to prepare students for a future place in society and the workplace is not peculiar to the modern era. The system of schooling for the common folk has a long history dating back to the monarch's desire to produce loyal and right-thinking citizens.[14] Durkheim sought to understand the nature of such educational systems by studying the early Christian tradition and its Greco-Roman heritage. He was particularly interested in the forms and practices that schools and society adopted to solve the pressing problems of their age. Mannheim, too, believed that only by examining such structures and practices could one understand the social forces that gave rise to modern educational systems.[15] Different historical situations demanded different responses from the political and educational leadership: the advent of high-speed industrial production, the development of the division of labor, and the development of a strong demand for manufactured goods created new needs and ways of doing things during and after the Industrial Revolution. Only when these changes were examined in their historical contexts could one understand their influence on educational and economic structures in society.

The strength of association between an educational system and the policies of the state often depends on the type of government that exists during a particular moment in history, according to Mannheim. Schools cannot perform their essential socialization functions unless they also reproduce the conditions for their own instructional work. Therefore a homogeneous and durable curriculum and selection system is necessary. Schooling's external function of social reproduction will force it to produce children whose way of thinking agrees as much as possible with the state that funds it. This need to assure conformity forces educational systems to move toward a formalized training for both teachers and students. The system uses a standardized curriculum and instructional methods and tests to measure students against one another, providing the state with a measurement to separate successful from unsuccessful learners.[16] The tools of teaching are not only aids in the performance of pedagogic action, but also ways of limiting the goals, perspectives, and content of classroom work. State-certified textbooks, syllabi, and manuals all have the effect of unifying what is taught in different classrooms by different teachers. The need to codify and systematize the instructional communication and culture is conditioned by the demands for harmony and compliance in increasingly strained mass societies. All learning in educational systems occurs within the framework of a relationship that is essentially one of apprenticeship. In this setting, students are socialized out of their ignorant condition over a period of many years. This binds teachers and students to the educational, economic, and social systems in which they live.

Consequently, the state is involved in the political and moral education of its citizens, transmitting certain values, norms, and attitudes to them through years of educational training. In traditional societies of the past, this often meant conveying changeless religious and cultural traditions to each new age group. In more recent times, we have seen schools used to indoctrinate children with political ideas as diverse as communism, fascism, and democracy. In Nazi Germany, for example, the schools were given the task of training the future soldiers of labor in a totalitarian state.[17] Education was required if the minds and bodies of youth were to be harnessed to the nation's military aspirations. In the prefascist period, German business and industry had suffered from inflation and depression, losing ground in national and international markets. This was blamed on the trade union movement and the socialistic ideas of the republican government, which shortened working hours, raised wages, and forced business to implement costly improvements in the working conditions of trade unionists. In the eyes of the fascist regime that came to power in 1933, German workers had become too materialistic. They were too concerned with matters of work hours, wages, and living standards to contribute to the well-being of the German nation. Employers were also censurable in this collapse of German industry and commerce, because they were so absorbed with reducing costs and rationalizing every aspect of the work process that they lost the inventiveness of leadership. The new German schools were to teach values that were non-commercial in character and stressed the greater good of the German nation. They were to indoctrinate children with a sense of duty to the nation and to their work. They were teach young people to respond to the discipline of school life in a cheerful way and place the welfare of group above their own. The fascist schools stressed values that had long been associated with the German home and community. Children, the church, and the kitchen were central concepts, along with a belief in the afterlife, fear of God, and blind loyalty to the Fatherland and its political and social structures.

These values pointed to the state institutions that were important in the new order.[18] German children were to be taught a new respect for the idea of the home, the army, and religion. They were to gain a sense of loyalty to, and respect for, the demands of their superiors, giving them unquestioned obedience. Religious training was to add an other-worldly value to their education, giving them a faith in higher laws and the rewards of the afterlife. To counteract the material rewards of the commercial world, German schools emphasized the intangible and spiritual values that had deep roots in German history and culture. They established stern routines, preparing student-laborers for their work in the labor battles of the future. But these conflicts were with the problems and conditions of their work and not with their employers. In the last analysis, German students were to be prepared for their lives as soldiers and their training must begin when they are still in the cradle.

There are major differences, of course, in the degree to which various governments use schools openly for this type of **indoctrination**. But the political and moral socialization of youth is one of education's primary responsibilities and of great importance to every state and local government. Katznelson suggested that the common school movement in the United States, for example, sought to train students for their citizenship responsibilities in a democratic society.[19] The curriculum was to be fashioned to assure these important values and outcomes. After the Civil War, public schools began to change according to the needs of the new technological and scientific knowledge and innovations. The United States was in the middle of a great period of expansion and development, and new immigrants and urban poor wanted to shape schools that to meet their emerging needs and concerns in an increasingly complex society.[20]

ASSIMILATION AND SOCIAL CONTROL

Urban schools in the United States responded to the new conditions of industrial culture by adopting instructional and disciplinary methods that were inflexible and severe.[21] Debates between progressive and more traditional educators continued to play a role in educational development, although the state's increasing problem of schooling large numbers of immigrant students ultimately proved decisive. One thing seemed undeniable after 1890: some public schools were doing an effective job, but many others were not.[22] Students were required to attend classes for longer periods of time, yet the self-confessed failure rates of the urban schools serving immigrant children was astounding. In 1898, Chicago schools reported that only 60 percent of students were at "normal age" grade level, meaning that 40 percent were failing. The means and materials of education seemed to be in place, but the task of educating and acculturating children from different cultural and linguistic heritages proved to be daunting. In the same year in Pittsburgh, 51 percent of the students in urban schools were failing, or below "normal age" grade level; in Minneapolis, 65 percent of children were failing. Between 1898 and 1917, urban schools continued to release these yearly reports, showing that more immigrant children were failing in schools than were succeeding there.[23] The state had provided buildings, classrooms, teachers, and supplies. Yet the numbers of failing children remained unacceptably high.

The response of educators was to ask for stronger compulsory attendance laws and seek to raise the age at which students could legally leave school. Students were kept in schools even longer so they would not burden an already depressed labor market. As late as 1931, educators were acknowledging that extremely high failure rates were "still characteristic" of the majority of public schools in the United States.[24] Many urban schools produced large numbers of failures because of the linguistic and cultural problems they encountered. Their methods were similar to those used in schools that were more successful, but they made little allowance for the social, economic, and psychological problems youngsters were encountering as they lived in a culture of poverty and despair. Students received a training that emphasized rote learning and a memorization of facts that seemed to have little to do with their life outside school. The schools were given the task of Americanizing youth and providing them with a training that would prepare them for their lives in a democratic society.[25] Nevertheless, the linguistic and cultural backgrounds of immigrant and poor students as well as the overly-corrective instructional methods of teachers caused many to fall behind in their studies and leave school at an early age.

Politicians and educational reformers continued to insist on longer periods of compulsory attendance, hoping to achieve their goals of Americanization. Failure rates in these urban schools, however, continued to rise. Chicago reported a 65 percent increase in the number of failures among immigrant and underprivileged students in secondary schools as late as 1931. At the elementary level retardation was reported at 61 percent of the total student population of survivors, or those who did not drop out; and 41 percent of all students entering the ninth grade were seriously below grade level, too. The figure for tenth-grade students was 32 percent, but the number of drop-outs was high and remained uncounted. Feeblemindedness, overcrowding, and immigrant and poor family backgrounds were given as reasons for these high rates of student failure. They were duplicated in Boston, New York, Philadelphia, Detroit, and Washington, D.C. Thirteen thousand students studied in schools that were on half-day sessions; 60 percent were inadequately housed in urban schools as late as 1925.[26] Who were the students who failed in these crowded urban schools? In the first two decades of the twentieth century, they were the children and grandchildren of East European and Asian immigrants and the urban poor. Later, newer immigrants from every part of the world were joined by Afro-Americans who migrated northward from the South. The Census of 1900 showed 1.25 million of New York City's 3.5 million inhabitants were foreign-born. Of the state's school enrollment, 85 percent were children from foreign cultural and linguistic backgrounds.

State politicians and educators agreed that schooling must return to its fundamental principles if these newcomers were to be effectively assimilated into schools and society. Educators were expected to be strict but fair in their work with immigrant children, while encouraging them to accept the values and beliefs of their adopted country. Moral imperatives were emphasized along with a strict discipline that controlled the movement and speech of children in classrooms across the country. Ideas about what was right and wrong, good and bad, American and un-American were routinely taught in the standardized curriculum. In the classroom the needs, concerns, and opinions of students were discouraged in favor of schooling's primary task: the Americanization of the foreign-born and their integration into the industrial labor force. Schools were to be the great equalizer of the conditions of people, the agencies where the language and culture of the United States provided for all students. A standard curriculum was applied to all students and included the history and workings of American government and the use and appreciation of the English language. The economic system was considered a given in these schools, and, indeed, many of the immigrants had come to participate in its bountifulness. The reward for good conduct and proficiency was the diploma, a document that certified success and opened up employment opportunities to the graduate. Drill was a fundamental method because it taught language through repetition while transforming students into compliant members of the class. Drill and rote recitation of facts trained youngsters in the proper use of their time and effort. These methods prepared students to attend to the instructions of their superiors and do routine work with diligence and care. Children had to be punctual and memorize and practice their lessons. Idleness was discouraged and routinely punished. The principle of continuous activity and work was rigidly followed, mimicking workplaces in the adult society.

Unfortunately, even after many reforms, the educational system from 1890 on was only partially successful in transforming the children of first-generation families into literate and productive workers and citizens. One reason for the failure to educate immigrant children may have been linked to schooling's inability to utilize the cultural and linguistic backgrounds of its students once they began formal classroom instruction. The children of immigrants had the advantage of language and acculturation and have fared somewhat better. More significant, perhaps, are the attitudes of some educators who believe that children should not be educated out of their station or standing in modern society. They suggest that schools attempt to instruct students in the attitudes, beliefs, and knowledge they will need to maintain their station in society and the labor market without viewing these two as ever-changing institutions. This line of thought seems to go against the American credo of equality of opportunity even though it may appear to be functional for the **stratified labor market**.

⑥ *Summary*

Education was supposed to socialize the children of immigrants and the urban poor so they could take their places as workers and citizens. Observers sought to explain the movement toward compulsory education by alluding to functionalist theories that related to the needs of other sectors of modern society. In these theories, schools were reproductive agencies because they reproduced the social relations that existed first in schools and later in society. They prepared youth to work in the ever-expanding factories and mills that developed once industrialism began to prevail over the craft industries of an earlier period. Schools were used to teach children the language and culture of the political and economic systems of their country. These were the givens within which the education of youth occurred. In the United States, they involved the assimilation and acculturation of immigrant children over many generations.

⑥ *Projects*

1. Study schooling as it was in your parents' day. How was it different from your own experiences? How did the values and beliefs of those times differ from what you were taught? How were they the same?

2. What function did your family play in your education? How did they influence you and your schooling experiences? How did your neighborhood school prepare you for your adult life? Were they part of a tracking system? If so, which schools were the better ones, and why?

3. Study the code of morals teachers and students were expected to follow during the pre-industrial period. How were they different from your own experiences? How were they the same? What role did religious ideas and beliefs play in these experiences?

4. Study the ways in which schools reproduce themselves. Do the relationships between teachers and students affect the process? How do these relationships affect the quality of instruction in your community?

⑥ *Endnotes*

1. Durkheim, Emile, *Education and Sociology*, trans. Sherwood D. Fox (Glencoe, Ill.: Free Press, 1956), 78–81. See also Durkheim, Emile, *Moral Education: A Study in the Theory and Application of the Sociology of Education*, trans. Everett K. Wilson and Herman Schnurer (New York: Free Press of Glencoe, 1961).

2. Durkheim, *Education and Sociology*, 28–29, 70–72. See also Durkheim, Emile, *The Division of Labor in Society*, trans. George Simpson (New York: Free Press, 1964), 174–182.

3. Durkheim, *Education and Sociology*, 127–128, 107–110.

4. Durkheim, Emile, "On Anomie," in *Images of Man: The Classical Tradition in Sociological Thinking*, ed. C. Wright Mills (New York: George Braziller, 1960), 449–485.

5. Durkheim, *Education and Sociology*, 78–81.

6. Benton, Ted, *The Rise and Fall of Structural Marxism* (New York: St. Martin's Press, 1984), 151–152.

7. Rothstein, Stanley W., *Identity and Ideology: Sociocultural Theories of Schooling* (Westport, Conn.: Greenwood Press, 1991); Bourdieu, Pierre, and Jean-Claude Passeron, *Education, Society and Culture*, trans. Richard Nice (Beverly Hills: Sage, 1972); Levi-Strauss, Claude, *The Elementary Structures of Kinship* (New York: Beacon Press, 1969); Waller, Willard, *The Sociology of Teaching* (New York: Russell & Russell, 1960).

8. Banks, Olive, *The Sociology of Education* (New York: Schocken Books, 1976), 179–180.

9. Clarke, S. et al., *One-Dimensional Marxism: Althusser and the Politics of Culture* (London and New York: Allison & Busby, 1980), 103–23; Bourdieu, Pierre, *Outline of a Theory of Practice*, trans. Richard Nice (Cambridge: Cambridge University Press, 1977), 21–2; Althusser, Louis, *For Marx* (New York: Vintage Books, Random House, 1970), 71–6.

10. Smith, Steven, *Reading Althusser: An Essay on Structural Marxism* (Ithaca: Cornell University Press, 1984), 176–178.

11. Bourdieu, Pierre and Jean-Claude Passeron, *Reproduction in Education, Society and Culture* (Beverly Hills: Sage, 1977), 54–67.

12. Bowles, Samuel and Herbert Gintis, *Schooling in Capitalist America: Educational Reform and the Contradictions of Economic Life* (New York: Basic Books, Inc., 1976), 125–150; Rothstein, *Identity and Ideology*, 45–66.

13. Rothstein, Stanley W., *Schooling the Poor* (Westport, Conn.: Bergin & Garvey, 1994), chap. 1; Katz, Michael B., *A History of Compulsory Education Laws* (Bloomington, Ind.: Phi Delta Kappa Educational Foundation, 1976), 17–18.

14. Mannheim, Karl, and W. A. C. Stewart, *An Introduction to the Sociology of Education* (London: Routledge & Kegan Paul, 1962), 33–46.

15. Katznelson, Ira, and Margaret Weir, *Schooling for All: Class, Race, and the Decline of the Democratic Ideal* (New York: Basic Books, 1985), 150–177. See also Lazerson, Marvin, and W. Norton Grubb, *American Education and Vocationalism: A Documentary History, 1870–1970* (New York: Teachers College Press, 1974), 17–28.

16. Brady, Robert A., *The Spirit and Structure of German Fascism* (London: Victor Gollancz, 1937), 78–87.

17. Ibid., 103–118.

18. Cremin, Lawrence A., *The Transformation of the School: Progressivism in American Education 1876–1957* (New York: Alfred A. Knopf, 1961), 54–55; Katznelson and Weir, *Schooling for All*, chap. 2.

19. Cubberley, Ellwood P., *Public Education in the United States* (Cambridge, Mass.: Houghton-Mifflin, 1934), 12–136; Edwards, Nathan, and Harold G. Richey, *The School in the American Social Order* (Boston: Houghton-Mifflin, 1963), 237–238.

20. Greer, Colin, *The Great School Legend* (New York: Basic Books, 1972), 13–22, 130–145; Rice, Joseph M., *The Public School System of the United States* (New York: Century, 1893), 30–39.

21. Graham, Patricia A., *Community and Class in American Education, 1865–1918* (New York: John Wiley & Sons, 1974), 78–81; Braverman, Harry, *Labor and Monopoly Capital: The Degradation of Work in the Twentieth Century* (New York: Monthly Review Press, 1974), 296–299.

22. Greer, Colin, *The Great School Legend* (New York: Basic Books, 1972), reports these figures in startling detail.

23. Abbot, Edith, *Truancy and Non-Attendance in Chicago's Schools* (Chicago: University of Chicago Press, 1917), 82–86. See also Katznelson and Weir, *Schooling for All*, chap. 3.

24. Greer, *The Great School Legend*, 146–152.

25. Litwack, Leon, "Education: Separate and Unequal," in *Education in American History: Readings on the Social Issues*, ed. Michael B. Katz (New York: Praeger, 1973), 253–266; Ravitch, Dianne, *The Troubled Crusade: American Education 1945–1980* (New York: Basic Books, 1983), chap. 4.

26. Tyack, David, *Turning Points in American Educational History* (New York: John Wiley, 1967), 314–317, 324–332, 355–357; Callahan, Raymond E., *An Introduction to Education in American Society* (New York: Alfred A. Knopf, 1960), 203–207; Jackson, Peter W., "The Student's World," in *The Experience of Schooling*, ed. M. Silberman (New York: Holt, Rinehart & Winston, 1971).

3

Knowledge and Ideology

ⓑ ⓑ ⓑ ⓑ ⓑ ⓑ ⓑ ⓑ ⓑ ⓑ ⓑ ⓑ

OBJECTIVES

In this chapter you will learn the answers to these questions:

ⓑ *What are ideologies?*

ⓑ *How are ideologies transmitted in schools?*

ⓑ *Why are schools considered as reproductive agencies in mass society?*

ⓑ *What role does pedagogic authority and work play in transmitting educational knowledge to students?*

ⓑ *Why have some writers labelled pedagogic action as a social control mechanism in mass schools?*

Social theorists have shown increasing interest in the ideological dimensions of educational knowledge, and much of their work has focused on the way **ideologies** are transmitted to students.[1] Such ideologies play a significant role in explaining and justifying much of the classwork that takes place in modern schools. Some writers linked ideology to the ability of individuals to understand their position inside the school or society. Some even suggested that individuals do not have the ability to consciously change their behavior or world they live in. Althusser and Bourdieu, for example, saw individuals as being able to recognize themselves only through ideological concepts and language. Any recognition of themselves and their standing in mass schools or society was necessarily limited by their speech and language patterns and the educational knowledge they learned from their parents and schools.[2]

Other writers maintained that ideological understandings were not false or illusionary ideas, of and by themselves. The effects of an ideology, no matter how flawed its logic, were real enough for people who used it to explain their world. These writers viewed educational knowledge as immersed in language and ideological thought, with its foundation in the daily routines and practices of classrooms, workplaces, and homes. They defined educational knowledge as a form of thought transmitted by speech and language, maintaining traditional ideas and values over many centuries. Its content was always determined by the real or imagined experiences of people living and working together in a confusing and troubled world.[3]

The extent to which certain thoughts are or are not ideological has created serious difficulties for reflective thinkers. Many writers have applied the term *ideology* disparagingly to indicate the falsity of a collection of ideas, but more inclusive definitions exist. These definitions view ideologies as the language-based thought of people living and working together in the real world. There is no known instance of a social system that has not accommodated its members. Every estate or class has its own beliefs or subcultures, which are usually founded on ideological understandings of the world. Each ideology has a set of ideas and values that help its members understand who they are and why they live the way they do. Nevertheless, the ideological beliefs of the social and economic groups with the most power usually dominate an era. Althusser argued that a discussion of ideologies cannot be limited in its focus since they exist in many different forms and phases of social life. Ideologies give comfort to some who might otherwise be deeply troubled and confused by the complexities of modern life. From this perspective, ideologies are a necessary and indispensable part of social life, the means through which individuals and groups interpret and understand their life experiences. Moreover, human beings often see themselves as independent and apart from the world they live in. The world appears as though it surrounds them, and they are at its very center. In this way, ideologies help individuals integrate themselves into the physical world, using the language and thought patterns of their parents.[4]

DEFINITIONS OF IDEOLOGY

Geuss[5] provides three definitions of ideology that we will use in our discussions of schooling in mass society. First, in a descriptive application, an ideology includes the beliefs that teachers, parents, and students share about the value of the schooling experience itself. This includes the attitudes of participants and their disposition toward the particular school they attended. According to Geuss, people routinely resort to ideological thinking. They use common sense, or "what everybody knows," to construct meaningful interpretations of what is happening to them in their everyday lives. In this sense, ideology is a type of thought that provides people with a shared store of knowledge and a limited number of explanations for their common experiences and conditions.

Second, Geuss identifies certain ideologies as forms of "false consciousness." In this form, individuals are unable to understand the sources of the ideology and the distortions it creates in their social relations. This definition relates to Marxian ideas of human history and the mastery of subordinate classes by more dominant ones. Even such oppressive relationships, however, can have the mutual support of the dominant and dominated classes, as studies of the Indian caste system have shown.[6]

Third, Geuss describes ideology in a more positive way as an indispensable part of the maintenance of all social systems. In this definition, ideology is the cement of society that helps people understand and accept the beliefs of their cultural groups. For many, however, ideologies are inseparable from the struggles between classes that characterize modern capitalist society. According to Althusser and Bourdieu, ideologies mask the true conditions of life in the classroom and the workplace, substituting beliefs and common sense for logic and rational thought. Even so, ideologies are the instruments people use to make sense of their everyday lives, relying on ideational thought based on faith in the unseen, the supernatural, and so on. These ways of thinking are a natural consequence of membership in families, churches, schools, and society, providing an understanding of the world that is all encompassing. The state and its institutions depend on such thought to carry on day-to-day activities. When situations change, new ideologies come into prominence. When European society moved from **feudalism** to a mercantile, trade-based economy, the new ideology supported the world view and life styles of the new burgher class. These people were becoming dominant in the productive sectors and needed new ideas and beliefs to bolster their growing wealth and power.

In the modern world, the relationship of parents to the workplace appears to shape every aspect of their children's existence. It determines where children live, how good their prenatal experiences are, the amount and quality of time their parents can spend with them, the speech and language they learn, the kind of schools they attend. From this, social theorists have determined that ideologies are formed in the words and thought processes parents first teach their children, making them aware of their social identities and their place in the social hierarchy. Words help children learn about who they are and where they fit into their family and neighborhood structures. Words provide limits, teaching youngsters how they should act and what they can expect in schools and other social situations. Yet words can disguise even as they inform a child, masking the social and economic struggles of the family in the child's formative years at home and in schools.

Even if individuals were to understand why an ideology exists, they might not change it significantly. The conditions of family life have called these ideas into existence and given them strength and power over time. Even if economic conditions were to change radically, new ideological definitions would develop to explain and justify the new circumstances. People in and out of schools need ideologies to lean on and live by in their everyday lives.

IDEOLOGIES IN SCHOOLS

Different ideologies arise when groups of men and women, living and working together, devise explanations for their worldly conditions. People often develop an ideology that relates to their social standing and the particular moment in history in which they live. Through speech and language, they pass on ideas about themselves and their families, providing new members with concepts and memories growing out of past struggles.

Others have pointed to the struggle between equity and elitist ideologies of education in industrial societies to show the conflicting nature of such thinking.[7] Elitist ideologies affect the response of educational systems to the changing needs of democratic governments and their economies at different moments in history. They are found in all industrial nations of the West and cause great controversy and concern. The pace of educational expansion in the United States, for example, has been accelerated partly by the demands of immigrant and poor families for greater opportunities for their children. Adherents to **elitist ideology** have resisted efforts to expand educational services for each generation, preferring to limit education to a small number of people. Their attitudes have stressed the exclusivity of formal schooling, emphasizing the knowledge and ties of the traditionally select few rather than those of the common people. This type of educational philosophy guided the free elementary education that was made available to children of paupers by religious and charitable institutions in England and the United States during the nineteenth century. The aim of these charity schools was to provide poor children with training in the moral and behavioral aspects of good citizenship and labor. They taught children to read from religious texts, including the Bible, and accept the decisions of those in authority without protest or thought. Overeducating the poor would make them unfit for the world they would have to live in, these ideologues supposed. Even as reforms led to widened educational opportunities for most people, the children of the poor continued to receive an education that limited their social mobility.

People's colleges, or high schools, began to appear in the United States at the turn of the twentieth century and quickly became a center of ideological conflict.[8] A high school education had always been limited to students from the upper-middle and upper classes and was thought to be a separate system from the elementary schools that dotted the American landscape. The 1944 Education Act in England, which provided free secondary education for all, has been cited as an earlier instance of this broadening of the opportunities of British children. Nevertheless, selection by ability was retained as a valid way of determining who would go on to higher education and who would not.[9] The ability of some people to pay enormous fees for private schools also separated children from different social classes and the educational knowledge they were taught. Although newer ideologies wished to create an aristocracy of brains, traditionalists sought to maintain tradition and an elite based on birth, social standing, and associations. Some few children were able to break through this rigid classification system, but they simply verified elitist assumptions about basing education on merit.

However, this traditional, elitist idea of education appears to be in conflict with modern society and its ever-widening egalitarian impulses.[10] Modern technology demands citizens and workers with high levels of scientific and mathematical skills, and these needs have transformed European schools since the end of World War II. The number of vocational and academic courses has been greatly increased, and social mobility has become more prevalent than in the pre-World War II period. Secondary schools, in particular, have struggled with the conflict between elitist and democratic ideas, with the demands of the economy remaining as an important outside consideration.

In England, the elitist idea of education has remained dominant, even though there have been challenges to its basic assumptions. In the United States, elitist ideas have persisted and flourished side-by-side with more egalitarian ideas because of the class bias inherent in the neighborhood school concept and persistent housing and racial segregation patterns in many neighborhoods. The demand for equality of access did not end with the high schools that were put in place in the United States from 1890 to 1920. The increasing need for skilled workers and for teachers of the legions of immigrant and poor children crowding into schools made it necessary to establish state institutions of higher learning. It was only after World War II that these two ideological theories sought to compromise their differences. The demands of industrial economies forced the expansion of education on every level, even though within the old framework of an elitist system.[11]

In both England and the United States the elitist ideology was contested by common secondary schools and state colleges, and enrollments rose in both types of institutions. While those seeking greater access have pushed for comprehensive training for their children, recent trends have been less than encouraging. The triumph of the common-school movement in the United States has been cited as evidence of a major victory for those seeking to broaden education opportunity for all children in society.[12] However, more recent developments have shown that traditional, elitist attitudes have persisted in mass schools, and selection processes have continued to limit the social mobility of children from poorer families. Halsey has described universities as ideological bastions favoring "intrinsically inegalitarian" systems of education.[13] University degrees have always carried with them high status and value, providing graduates with a language and culture of distinction and knowledge while opening up many avenues of wealth and power in commercial society.

Industry's need for professional and scientific experimentation and expertise, for example, caused the state of California to develop a three-tiered system of higher education. This system placed students into one of three tracks to prepare for entrance into the University of California, the California State University, or community and junior colleges.[14] There are significant differences in the education and training students receive in each of these institutions, and researchers have found a close correlation between a student's family income and attendance in one or the other of these tracks. Other researchers, studying higher education in Europe, found that differences in attendance could not be explained by the economic development or standing of students alone. Comparing European and American attendance of male students, Anderson found a limited correlation between a country's economic system and its rate of university attendance.[15] He argued that other factors, such as the values, customs, and communal instructional policies of a nation also must be given consideration. Anderson found that differences in attendance among female students in different types of institutions of higher learning could not be explained by economic circumstances but had to be studied on an individual basis. Others have reached similar conclusions: the relationship between graduation rates and economics is not an overwhelming one, but there are unpleasantly conspicuous variances.

Studies comparing the higher educational systems of Europe, the United States, and the former Soviet Union, each of which produced different numbers and types of graduates, showed a surprising similarity in at least one respect.[16] In spite of their varying political and economic ideologies, these systems sought more or less egalitarian educational policies while maintaining elitist concepts and practices in their best universities and graduate schools. In Europe elitist ideologies, which had their origins in the old feudal estate and later in the triumph of industrial culture, strongly influenced recruitment policies. Still, only a small number of people of college age actually attended institutions of higher education during the nineteenth century, and universities at the top of the status pyramid recruited students mostly from upper and upper-middle class families.

Since World War II both Europe and the United States have expanded higher education, and it is no longer correct to describe their educational practices as exclusively elitist. The old class systems of Europe, however, have maintained themselves and flourished. Equal access to the higher reaches of education still does not exist for most youngsters from poor families.

In the United States, the situation is different. Higher education is open to all who would pursue it, but there are still rigid tracking systems that stratify what students can and will learn once they begin their training. Statistical surveys have reported that in 1970 40 percent of college-age students were in attendance, and this number has continued to grow.[17] Schooling in industrial society has become a must for those who wish to work in modern society.[18] Significant differences exist between institutions of higher learning in Europe and the United States, and these have led to different opportunities for graduates. The United States has less formal barriers between institutions of higher learning, but the record of junior college students graduating from four-year institutions has been disappointing. Competition still dominates practices and aspirations in these institutions of higher learning, and this has led to a ranked status scale that businesses use in hiring practices. The apparent embrace of the egalitarian ideology in the United States seems to fit in with populist ideas that have existed from the beginning, but the elitist ideas of education have persisted because competition is a cardinal value of modern commercial systems.

The expansion of higher education after World War II was linked to the rebuilding of Europe, which caused a rapid growth in professional and managerial positions. The Marshall Plan opened up many new economic and educational opportunities, leading state universities to expand hastily in response to these needs. Many individuals who would never have thought of studying in institutions of higher education now did so.[19]

More recently, with the poor economic conditions of the 1990s, these state universities have significantly raised their tuition and maintenance fees, making it more difficult for many students to attend. An elite group of upper- and middle-class students now seems to be emerging, and others who sought greater access to these colleges and universities now seem to be losing ground.

Some writers have produced a great deal of evidence to challenge the extent to which an economy benefits from larger numbers of highly educated citizens. In an increasing number of occupations, better-educated workers have not been shown to be more productive. Again and again, experience has been shown to be the best teacher, and businesses have found that most jobs can be learned in six weeks by workers who earn a great deal less than their better-educated counterparts in First World countries. India, for example, has found that educating people for jobs and economic opportunities that do not exist only creates legions of dissatisfied and unhappy workers and citizens. The ideologies that support democratic reforms in higher education are in constant conflict with the elitist values of the economic sectors of society, where competition rules the day.[20]

The continuing expansion of education in the United States has been a response to the demand of Americans that they be given greater access to the higher reaches of learning and earning. It has been seen as a way of providing better employment opportunities for immigrant and poor students who might otherwise languish in poverty and despair. Nevertheless the economic sector has tended to maintain its elitist ideologies by demanding ever-higher levels and types of educational preparation. This conflict between elitist and egalitarian ideologies must be seen, in the final analysis, as a struggle between classes and ethnic and racial groups over the apportionment of economic opportunity. While educational policy has responded to the demands of people from all classes of society in the United States, in England and the former Soviet Union this has been less so and changes have occurred as a consequence of governmental policies.[21]

Until the beginning of the 1980s, educational opportunities were opening up at a rate that seemed irreversible. However, the process has slowed dramatically since then, and elitist ideas have come back into prominence. The affluence of earlier periods now seems to be giving way to a more competitive, less open educational system. The cost of operating institutions of higher learning is enormous, and state governments are beginning to shrink from this economic drain on their resources. It seems likely that stratified systems of education will remain the rule in Europe and the United States for some time, even as reformers attempt to break down the elitist ideologies of educators and leaders in commercial society.

THE NATURE OF EDUCATIONAL PRODUCTION

Insofar as educational institutions are a part of the reproductive sector of mass society, they are inevitably involved in the production and transformation of youth.[22] Over time, they change the minds of students, training them to be right-thinking citizens and members of society. In the pre-industrial period this often meant transmitting traditional cultures and attitudes to homogeneous groups of youngsters living in small communities. In more recent times, however, it has meant urging changes that would suit the new conditions of an ever-changing commerce and industry. In twentieth-century America, for example, schools have been given the responsibility of preparing the young not only for their lives in a democratic system, but also for the values and norms of the workplace. Students are taught to walk in a line with others, move as directed, sit quietly in their seats, listen and obey instructions, and otherwise work and behave in ways considered proper to their student status. Some writers have suggested that educational production and the demands of teachers are merely a reflection of conditions found in the workplace, where punctuality, dependency, and subordination to authority are very important.[23]

Educational production, then, refers to the way schools transform students into compliant students and adults, ensuring the maintenance and survival of the educational system and society. The school's cultural and linguistic requirements are another important feature of its organization, providing teachers with a primary means of transforming students into what they will become once they reach the higher levels of learning and earning. Conflict between students and teachers in classrooms is inevitable, as shown in later chapters, and inequalities in rank and status pose a continuing problem. The establishment of public schools in modern society, however, has involved a great deal of cooperation and common effort. Katznelson and Weir, in a study of American education between 1850 and 1920, cite the solid collaboration between people from different classes that characterized the establishment of common schools. All groups in society seemed to agree that training children for their future role in society was a worthwhile and achievable educational goal.[24]

Nevertheless, debates between different social groups continued to affect the way schools developed in different parts of the country. Ideological understandings, as in the past, helped people from all walks of life to make sense of what was happening to them in schools and the workplace. These explanations were framed in common sense, giving them added strength and legitimacy. These ideologies sometimes clashed, for example, when working-class children were forced to learn the language and values of the business and professional classes and found themselves at a decided disadvantage. Still, the ideologies of mass schooling, enunciated in terms of egalitarian theories and social mobility for all Americans, won the day.

Educational production has also referred to the specific ways children learn to accept the moral understandings and norms of classroom life. An example is a child's acceptance of the teacher's right to decide everything that happens in the classroom and evaluate schoolwork on a continuous basis. The final product of these practices is one that modern society desires: citizens and workers who are compliant and who seldom question things. This educational production differs from other forms of economic production because no raw materials are transformed into finished commodities. The finished product is seldom seen by teachers and requires the constant labor of many instructors.[25] Structuralists have viewed educational production as a process that contains certain invariant parts common to schooling in every known society. Such constructs can be thought of as ideal types and can help observers analyze ongoing interaction more systematically. The parts include: (1) the teacher who does the actual work; (2) the educational process or instructional work wherein the arbitrary language and culture of schools and society are taught to students; and (3) the outcomes of these processes or the ideas, thoughts, understandings, and attitudes of youngsters. Educational production uses buildings, materials, and organizational structures to transmit knowledge to youngsters and perform its functions as a primary selection agency for modern society.[26]

These structural approaches to schooling sometimes appeared to give insufficient weight to the historical elements that shape the policies and practices of educational systems. Many critics have argued that schooling can never be understood until it is placed within the social, economic, and cultural contexts of its time.[27] The needs and demands of economic production, for example, must be considered as a determining variable to explain the way schools organize themselves at different moments in history.

An important effect of educational production is to transform and correct the speech and language of students in their earliest grades. This way of thinking leads teachers to believe they must restrict the language of the streets and introduce more proper ways of speaking and thinking. Rothstein has contended that the rejection of children's speech and language seriously affects their understanding of their own identity and that of their parents. Of utmost importance in classroom interactions is the fact that curriculum is presented to students as valid knowledge and facts that cannot be disputed. It is offered as objective science, even though it may have very little to do with rational thinking or the scientific method. History is taught as fact, for example, ignoring any differences between words and the deeds that may have actually occurred. The language, culture, and social origin of historians are ignored, as are the distortions that regularly occur when unicultural perspectives are used.[28]

The picture of students as children who do not know, who need instruction, and who can only learn in community-supported schools is all too familiar. They must be instructed in the valid culture and political order of the times if the social system is to perpetuate itself. The training required for children in ancient Greece was quite different from what is needed today. Then, education produced **warrior aristocrats**, who were needed for the city-states to survive against the invasions of larger empires and the internal struggles for supremacy on the peninsula. Later, Athens added a second ideal of the bard or cultivated person who showed interest in drama, dance, and music, and educational needs changed accordingly. The Roman ideal derived from these earlier Greek models, teaching youth that perseverance, discretion, temperance, and pride were needed if the empire was to prosper. Mannheim pointed out that the ancient Hebrews valued holiness, while Christianity taught a more egalitarian doctrine to its faithful.

In our own time, organizational and production changes have had much to do with producing a new ideal. The chief characteristic of that ideal is the concept of individuals and their rights and responsibilities in a competitive, commercial society. It assumes that wealth is a scarce commodity and that the democratic method of political organization is best in such circumstances. Serious students of mass schools point to the scientific management movement in early twentieth-century America as an instance of changes that have occurred in work and our approaches to education. The attempt to simplify and rationalize work processes had some obviously favorable consequences. It led to an increase in the productivity of workers, making mass production and mass consumerism possible. Assembly lines provide one example of this trend, but the idea pervaded all levels of productive labor. Employees were asked to do the same task over and over again without becoming bored or disinterested or simply walking off the job.[29]

This simplification of labor debased the process, reducing employees to mere appendages of machines. Work in business, industry, and education became segmented and increasingly meaningless because of its routine nature. Workers, who had always been an expensive cost of production, now found themselves in organizations that saw them as interchangeable parts that could be moved about for the benefit of increased productivity. The meaninglessness of such work was aggravated further by the powerlessness employees experienced in the new bureaucratic environments. Those who controlled the new production systems had only efficiency and cost-accounting in mind when they did these things. A new kind of person was needed, and schooling endeavored to train such individuals for life in industrial culture.

Schools began to deepen their commitment to drill and rote instruction, teaching students to accept them as part of their educational experiences. Schoolwork was broken down into segments, imitating the new conditions that were coming into being in the workplace. Students found themselves powerless to change either the instructional methods or the harsh discipline that was a carryover from the pre-industrial period. The power of the teacher to decide everything in the classroom was justified in ways that were similar to those used by the emergent managerial classes.[30]

This standardization and simplification of work had its echo in public schools, where bureaucratic reforms were seen as an improvement over the militaristic schools of the 1870s and 1880s. Yet the schools were no less crowded than they had ever been, and militaristic, penal, and religious discipline remained unshaken and unchanged from earlier periods in American educational history.[31] An instructional method that was uninteresting, depressing, and distinguished by an emphasis on drill and punishment caused many students to drop out before they finished elementary education. Educational instruction was dissociated from the everyday experiences of immigrant and poor youth. The ideas of individual freedom and worth were repudiated by the constant control of students' movements, and the ridicule and humiliation children received in competitive and impersonal classrooms. Students living in shabby tenements found little connection between the curriculum of their classrooms and life in urban slums. The problems of poverty and crime were seldom discussed, nor was attention paid to other problems immigrant families encountered. Commenting on this, Young and Davies argued that research into educational knowledge ought to center on who controls the management and validation of knowledge in a given educational and social system.[32] In a society that depended on science, technology, and economic efficiency, they asked, which groups possessed the power to control information and its dissemination to the public sector?

PEDAGOGIC AUTHORITY AND WORK

Writers in England and France have been concerned with the structure of **pedagogic authority** and its implications for instructional practice. Within this focus, they distinguish the school's right and responsibility to exert symbolic control (or violence) in ways that preserve their legitimate functions in modern society. The term **legitimate** is used in a Weberian way, emphasizing the traditional and legal-rational authority on which modern educational systems depend. The academic language and culture of the classroom sensitize children to what they must attend to during their earliest experiences. In the modern state, the right to administer and transmit educational knowledge to youngsters is given to state academic institutions. They alone have the authority to compel attendance while socializing youth into a correct understanding of contemporary culture.[33]

In describing instructional practice, the **pedagogic act** is seen as a cluster of habits and routines that reproduce the culture and social relations of schools and society. This culture reflects the ideologies and beliefs of those who are considered as most worthy of reproduction because of their wealth and standing. Their claim is further strengthened because they appear to have delegated to a neutral and autonomous agency (the schools) the right to reproduce the national language and culture. Instructional work in schools can be judged by the degree to which it succeeds in socializing the young to accept the existing cultural and socioeconomic relations in society.[34]

There is also evidence that the methods and length of this pedagogic work are an important source of power for educational systems and the workplace. Educators and politicians define when children have had enough schooling, even for those who have failed in their schoolwork for many years. They decide when students have sufficient competence in the language and culture of the schools, enough training to be considered people worthy of graduation into the reaches of higher learning or work.

When this instructional work is viewed by observers, it raises problems of constant physical control and constraint. It requires, for example, that teachers force children to sit and attend to their lessons and that they bring proper sanctions against children who are unable to control their bodily movements and thoughts. There are, in this pedagogic work, powerful elements of domination and submission.[35] Students are forced to control their bodily movements; they must attend school long after they have dropped out of the competition. The longer they are forced to sit in classrooms, the more complete is the mastery of teachers over students. Every action of the teacher seeks to control the activities that occur in the classroom, excluding as much as possible those forms of language and culture that are different from those of the educational system. Students who find themselves failing in classrooms are subjected to an instructional method that questions their competency and self-worth on a daily basis. Compulsory education forces immigrant and urban poor children to recognize and accept schooling's version of knowledge and know-how, ignoring and demeaning their own language and competencies. The work of teachers produces a curriculum that validates the history and ideas of those who were and are in positions of power and standing. The effectiveness of teaching is determined by the distance between the teacher's language and culture and those of the student's family and community.

PEDAGOGIC ACTION: THE TEACHING PROCESS

Nevertheless, it is in classroom interaction, Bernstein reminds us, that teachers dictate what students will learn and how they will learn it. It is there that they are subjected to symbolic control, or what Bourdieu and Passeron refer to as symbolic violence.[36] The language and culture of educational systems are seen as socially constructed, varying from age to age and nation to nation. Their task is to transmit the authoritative knowledge of the system, helping to legitimize and transmit power and privilege from one generation to the next. Classroom instruction communicates meaning and values to youngsters, often favoring language and cultural values that are alien to less affluent members of society.[37] Teachers manage to impose this curriculum on students as legitimate knowledge that has been sanctioned by the state and school authorities. According to Bourdieu and Passeron, these pedagogic actions conceal the power that is the basis of schooling's authority while adding to that power by dictating and controlling every thought and movement students are allowed in classrooms.[38] Bernstein differs from Bourdieu and Passeron because he has separated curriculum from pedagogy to facilitate analysis of these terms. The first is legitimate knowledge as it has been defined by tradition and authorities acting for the State. The second is the teaching act itself, wherein hierarchy and important information are passed on to youth.[39] Bourdieu unites these two, claiming that together they account for the arbitrary nature of schoolwork. Such work is, in his view, merely the imposition of linguistic and cultural values on an unsuspecting public.[40] Students are given a logic and rationale for their submissive status that will serve them well in the roles they will be asked to play in schools and the labor market.[41]

Both Bernstein and Bourdieu were interested in the ways that educational knowledge was used to reproduce the social relations that existed in schools and the larger social system. In *Reproduction in Education, Society and Culture*,[42] Bourdieu and Passeron offered a theory of symbolic violence that covered pedagogic action, authority, and work. Logical propositions were deduced about the educational system and its role in mid-twentieth-century Europe. Referring to the interaction that takes place between teachers and students, the authors provide a seminal proposition and focal point: the difference between the language and culture presented by teachers and those of students' families is the most significant reason for one's success or failure in schools. It is in such interaction that students learn the preferred language and culture of authorities. But the schools seem unable to provide children from the poorer classes with sufficient competency in these areas, thus confirming the students' lower ranking and status in schools and society. Apparently, such competencies and understandings can only be provided by a student's family, and are achieved over time in a learning process best described as cultural osmosis. Schooling gives an unstated and unfair advantage to those who already have substantial advantages. It does this by placing a high value on the culture and language of the more affluent, seeking to reproduce their beliefs, values, and ways of doing things. In this way, schooling rewards those who have inherited from their parents the language usage and cultural system of the school, and education becomes an overwhelmingly conservative force in modern life. Teachers teach this language and culture because they have learned to imitate and admire it during their own schooling experiences. In fact, as Bourdieu argues, the language and culture of students is capable of explaining, in a systematic way, the relations that are established between teachers and students in mass schools.[43] Furthermore, given the demand of schooling that students meet minimum levels of proficiency in language and deportment, those from the lower social classes who reach higher educational institutions have undergone a more oppressive and uncompromising selection process than their upper-class counterparts. In short, Bourdieu and his associates affirmed what anthropologists and Freudians had discovered decades earlier: the influence of language and culture shows itself in the earliest years of a child's life and is later used by teachers to measure competency and worth once schoolwork begins.[44] These linguistic competencies never cease to be felt, as authors as diverse as George Bernard Shaw and Paolo Freire have shown.

Still, language is more than a mere communication of words in the classroom. Even in its most benign forms, pedagogic action demands acts of resignation and submission from students. It provides teachers with guidelines to compare and evaluate students against one another. Richer or poorer vocabularies transmitted by parents determine whether students will be able to decipher complex ideas and reading materials. The cultural boundaries of students have already been set by the beliefs, values, and understandings of their earliest relationships with parents and family members. So we can expect to see more failure in students from social classes that are more distant from the arbitrary language and culture of mass schools.

As we will see in a later chapter, Bourdieu was also concerned with the disparity in achievement levels between men and women in French institutions of higher learning.[45] His data observed a constant superiority of men over women, relating these findings to a systematic socialization wherein men were urged to study medicine, science, and law while women were selected into lower status careers. He argues that women, principally through initial processes of selection, are victimized by their social origin and sex. Shakeshaft has provided empirical research to support these assertions, describing the different educational experiences young girls encounter in public school classrooms. Rothstein further argues that children are forced to experience these sexual socialization processes during the first years of life, when they learn the language and culture of their parents.[46] This has a profound influence on children, and the schools often reaffirm such ideas by their classroom practices.

Emphasizing the importance of language and culture, Bourdieu and Bernstein point out that the structure and criteria for selecting survivors in mass schools changes constantly as new criteria are developed by school authorities.[47] This seems to weaken their theories about the relationship between social origin and cultural and linguistic competence in classrooms. Nevertheless, the sons from the highest status occupational groups were extremely well-represented at the best universities, studying the highest status scientific and social disciplines. But social origin and sex, alone, could not explain every attitude and behavior in a student's life. The constraints of selection systems in educational institutions needed to be understood by examining their development at different times in history.[48]

Bourdieu, in trying to describe the social characteristics and associations that defined the student's first schooling experiences, described the social class differences embedded in modern educational systems. He was chiefly concerned with the probable outcomes of different educational training for students from diverse social origins. For manual workers and laborers, it was highly improbable that their children would study Latin and Greek in schools. It was more likely that these children would have to work to help support themselves if they decided to stay in school and pursue a career in higher education.[49]

Bourdieu's work has important implications for those studying educational systems today. Most researchers agree that the schools present an arbitrary language and culture that affects the way children from different social origins and sexes see themselves, their families, and their educational and occupational possibilities. Bourdieu and Passeron related these ideas to empirical data, showing that a social and economic selection process was at work in families and schools. Dominant and subordinate groups were identified and discussed within an examination of the elitist ideologies in present-day France.[50] The words and ideas of the educational system were transmitted to children in ways that maximized class differences. Schools made available to children from diverse social classes offered differing amounts and types of knowledge, mirroring relationships that exist in the world of adults.

Though educational systems perpetuate the myth that all children start their schooling on an equal plane, research seems to indicate that this is not so.[51] The mastery of language and skills in solving everyday problems are developed in kinship relationships, as are the ability to think logically. One's cultural beliefs, attitudes, values, and self-concepts are learned in language, binding the individual to a particular family and social class and deeply influencing the ability to understand and master schoolwork.

⑥ *Summary*

Ideologies are the way human beings make sense of their lives. They combine common-sense understandings of the world with ideas that have been transmitted from parents to children for many centuries. They are used to bind individuals to their families and groups and to interpret everyday events. Ideologies are transmitted in schools through the speech and language of teachers and textbooks. The economic and social values of a nation are encapsulated in these communications and in the pedagogic acts themselves. Schools reproduce the conditions of the labor market, for example, by teaching children the values and preferred behavior patterns of the workplace: punctuality, obedience, deference, and diligence. Pedagogic authority is important in these processes because it is used to force students to attend to curricula and language patterns that are often alien to them. It is an important element of schooling because it often forces youngsters from poor and immigrant families to assume the role of the ignorant and incompetent person in the classroom setting.

⑥ *Projects*

1. Observe a classroom for an hour or more. How does the teacher interact with the students? Who talks to whom and with what effect? How do children and the teacher play out their role? What methods of social control are used?

2. Make a list of ideas about public education that seem to be ideologies. Which definition of ideology do they represent? Why are they used by teachers or students? How do teachers and students explain what is happening to them in classrooms and schools?

3. Schools have been called selection agencies that reproduce the social and educational world they live in. How do schools select and track children in your neighborhood? How do teachers reproduce older teacher-student relationships?

4. How have elitist ideas influenced the way students are taught in your neighborhood or school district? What programs have been implemented to increase equity opportunities for children from poorer family backgrounds? Which high schools in your area are the good ones? What makes them good, and how do they compare to other schools that are not as good?

⑥ *Endnotes*

1. Seidler, Victor J., "Trusting Ourselves: Marxism, Human Needs and Sexual Politics," in *One-Dimensional Marxism*, ed. S. Clarke et al. (London and New

York: Allison & Busby, 1980), 103–156; Bernstein, Basil, *The Structuring of Ped-agogic Discourse* (London and New York: Routledge, 1990), 13–14, 140, 153, 157; Smith, Steven, *Reading Althusser* (Ithaca: Cornell University Press, 1984), 176–178.

2. Rothstein, Stanley W., "Symbolic Violence: The Disappearance of the Individ-ual in Marxist Thought," *Interchange: A Quarterly Review of Education* 22, no. 3 (1991): 28–42.

3. Lacan, Jacques, *The Seminar of Jacques Lacan Book II*, trans. Sylvana Tomaselli (New York: W. W. Norton, 1991) 260–263.

4. Bernstein, Basil, "Class, Codes and Control," vol. 1 of *Theoretical Studies Towards a Sociology of Language* (London: Routledge & Kegan Paul, 1975), 121–122; Gintis, Herbert, and Samuel Bowles, *Schooling in Capitalist America*, (New York: Basic Books, 1976), 53–55; Smith, David, "Codes, Paradigms and Folk Norms," *Sociology* X (1976); Weber, Max, *Essays in Sociology*, trans. C. W. Gerth and C. W. Mills (London: Routledge & Kegan Paul, 1952); Bourdieu, Pierre, *Outline of a Theory of Practice*, trans. Richard Nice, (Cambridge: Cambridge Uni-versity Press, 1977), 21, 33, 37, 62–64, 188.

5. Geuss, Raymond, *The Idea of Critical Thinking* (Cambridge: Cambridge Univer-sity Press, 1981).

6. Cox, Oliver Cromwell, *Caste, Class and Race: A Study in Social Dynamics* (New York: Modern Reader Paperbacks, 1970).

7. Banks, Olive, *The Sociology of Education* (New York: Schocken Books, 1976), 16–21, 117–118.

8. Tyack, David, *Turning Points in American Educational History* (New York: John Wiley, 1967), 355–357; Callahan, Raymond E., *An Introduction to Education in American Society* (New York: Alfred A. Knopf, 1960) 203–207.

9. Banks, *The Sociology of Education*, 77–78, 184–185.

10. Cubberley, Ellwood P., *The History of Education* (Cambridge, Mass.: Houghton-Mifflin, 1920), 670–672; Katz, Michael B., "The New Departure in Quincy, 1873–1881," in *Education in American History*, ed. Michael B. Katz (New York: Praeger, 1973), 68–71; Cremin, Lawrence A., *The Transformation of the School: Progressivism in American Education: 1867–1957* (New York: Random House, Vintage Books, 1964), 3–8.

11. Nasaw, David, *Schooled to Order: A Social History of Public Schooling in the United States* (New York: Oxford University Press, 1979), 30–39; Banks, *The Sociology of Education*, 115–119.

12. Halsey, A. H., J. Floud, and C. A. Anderson, eds., *Education, Economy and Soci-ety* (Glencoe, Ill.: Free Press, 1961), 23–25.

13. Nasaw, *Schooled to Order*, 207, 209, 214, 220; Karabel, Jerome, "Community Colleges and Social Stratification," *Harvard Educational Review* 42, no. 4 (November, 1972): 541–542.

14. Anderson, C. Arnold, "Successes and Frustration in the Sociological Study of Education," *Social Science Quarterly* 55 (1974): 286–287.

15. Banks, *The Sociology of Education*, 35–40.

16. Banks, *The Sociology of Education*, 44–45, 95–96, 159–161.

17. Altenbaugh, Richard J., "Families, Children, Schools, and the Workplace," in *Handbook of Schooling in Urban America*, ed. Stanley W. Rothstein (Westport, Conn.: Greenwood Press, 1993) 19–42.

18. Nasaw, *Schooled to Order*, 173–182.

19. Touraine, Alain, *The Academic System in American Society* (New York: McGraw-Hill, 1974), 43–45; Machlup, Fritz, *The Production and Distribution of Knowledge in the United States* (Princeton, N. J.: Princeton University Press, 1962), 155–156; Hodgkinson, Harold, *Institutions in Transitions: A Profile of Change in Higher Education* (New York: McGraw-Hill, 1971), 16–18.

20. Banks, *The Sociology of Education*, 119–124.

21. Bourdieu, Pierre, and Jean-Claude Passeron, *The Inheritors: French Students and Their Relation to Culture*, (Chicago: University of Chicago Press, 1979), 119–144.

22. Gintis, Herbert, and Samuel Bowles, *Schooling in Capitalist America* (New York: Basic Books, 1976); Rothstein, Stanley W., *Schooling the Poor* (Westport, Conn.: Bergin & Garvey, 1994), chap. 3.

23. Katznelson, Ira, and Margaret Weir, *Schooling for All: Class, Race, and the Decline of the Democratic Ideal*, (New York: Basic Books, 1985), 224–225.

24. Rothstein, Stanley W., *Identity and Ideology: Sociocultural Theories of Schooling* (Westport, Conn.: Greenwood Press, 1991), 9–11, 109–110.

25. Clarke, S., et al., *One Dimensional Marxism: Althusser and the Politics of Culture* (London: Allison & Busby, 1980), 204–207.

26. Rothstein, *Identity and Ideology*, 144–146.

27. Rothstein, Stanley W., "Theory and Schooling," *Urban Education* 23, no. 3 (October 1988): 294–315; Wilson, John, "Power, Paranoia, and Education," *Interchange: A Quarterly Review of Education* 22, no. 3 (1991): 43–54.

28. Braverman, Harry, *Labor and Monopoly Capitalism: The Degradation of Work in the Twentieth Century* (New York: Monthly Review Press, 1974), 284–289.

29. Lortie, D. C., *Schoolteacher: A Sociological Study* (Chicago: University of Chicago Press, 1975); Boyer, E. L., *High School: A Report on Secondary Education in America* (New York: Harper & Row, 1983); Callahan, R. D., *Education and the Cult of Efficiency: A Study of the Social Forces That Have Shaped the Administration of the Public Schools* (Chicago: University of Chicago Press, 1962); Elsbree, W. S., *The American Teacher: Evolution of a Profession in a Democracy* (New York: American Book, 1939).

30. Rothstein, *Schooling the Poor*, 21–24.

31. Young, M. F. D., ed., *Knowledge and Control: New Directions for the Sociology of Knowledge* (London: Collier-Macmillan, 1971); Banks, *The Sociology of Education*, 184–185.

32. Katz, Michael B., *A History of Compulsory Education Laws* (Bloomington, Ind.: Phi Delta Kappa Educational Foundation, 1976), 17–18; Cubberley, Ellwood

P., *The History of Education* (Cambridge, Mass.: Houghton-Mifflin, 1920); Tyack, David, *Turning Points in American Educational History* (Waltham, Mass.: Blaisdell Publishing Company, 1967), 14–17; Katz, Michael B., *The Irony of Early School Reform: Educational Innovation in Mid-Nineteenth Century Massachusetts* (Boston: Beacon, 1968), 185–194.

33. Bourdieu, Pierre, "Cultural Reproduction and Social Reproduction," in *Knowledge, Education, and Cultural Change,* ed. Richard Brown (London: Tavistock, 1973); Eggleston, John, "Decision-Making on the School Curriculum: A Conflict Model," *Sociology* VII (1973).

34. Simmel, Georg, *The Sociology of Georg Simmel,* trans. Kurt H. Wolff (New York: Free Press, 1950), 181–298; Rothstein, Stanley W., "The Sociology of Schooling," *Urban Education* 21, no. 3 (October 1986): 295–315.

35. Bourdieu, Pierre and Jean-Claude Passeron, *Reproduction in Education, Society and Culture* (London and Beverly Hills: Sage, 1977), 13–14, 24–25, 31–32.

36. Young, M. F. D., "On the Politics of Educational Knowledge," *Economy and Society, Vol. I,* (London: Collier-Macmillan, 1971), chap. 1; Holly, David, *Beyond Curriculum* (London: Hart-Davis McGibbon, 1973).

37. Bourdieu and Passeron, *Reproduction in Education, Society and Culture,* 4–5, 9–11.

38. Bernstein, Basil, "On the Classification and Framing of Educational Knowledge" in *Knowledge and Control,* ed. Young.

39. Bourdieu, Pierre, *Outline of a Theory of Practice,* trans. Richard Nice (Cambridge: Cambridge University Press, 1977), 172–173, 183–184.

40. Katznelson and Weir, *Schooling for All,* 121–130.

41. Bourdieu and Passeron, *Reproduction in Education, Society and Culture,* 1–68.

42. Banks, *The Sociology of Education,* 120–131.

43. Freud, Sigmund, *Civilization and Its Discontents,* trans. James Strachey (New York: W. W. Norton, 1961), 46–50; Radin, Paul, *The World of Primitive Man* (New York: Henry Schuman, 1953), 106, 126, 130; Lacan, Jacques, *Speech and Language in Psychoanalysis,* trans. Anthony Wilden (Baltimore and London: Johns Hopkins University Press, 1989), 249–251.

44. Bourdieu and Passeron, *The Inheritors,* 101–110.

45. Shakeshaft, Charol, "Meeting the Needs of Girls in Urban Schools," in *Handbook of Schooling in Urban America,* ed. Stanley W. Rothstein (Westport, Conn.: Greenwood Press, 1993), 175–188; Rothstein, Stanley W., *The Voice of the Other: Language as Illusion in the Formation of the Self* (Westport, Conn.: Praeger, 1993), chap. 1.

46. Bourdieu and Passeron, *The Inheritors,* 1–8; Bernstein, *The Structuring of Pedagogic Discourse,* 65–67.

47. Rothstein, Stanley W., "Schooling in Mass Society," *Urban Education* 22, no. 3 (October 1987): 267–285.

48. Bourdieu and Passeron, *The Inheritors,* 67–74.

49. Ibid., 119–144.

50. Shipman, Martin, "Curriculum for Inequality," in *The Curriculum: Context, Design and Development*, ed. R. Hooper (Edinburgh: Oliver & Boyd, 1971), 104–106; Bourdieu, Pierre, "Intellectual Field and Creative Project," in *Knowledge and Control*, ed. Young, 180–185; Ben David, J., "Professions in the Class System of Present-Day Societies," *Current Sociology* XII (1963–4): 294–295; Banks, Olive, *Parity and Prestige in English Secondary Education* (London: Routledge & Kegan Paul, 1955).

4

The Sociology of School Curriculum

◎   ◎   ◎   ◎   ◎   ◎   ◎   ◎   ◎   ◎   ◎

OBJECTIVES

In this chapter you will learn the answers to these questions:

◎ *What are the central issues in the study of school **curriculum**?*

◎ *What is meant by a **collection-type of curriculum**?*

◎ *What is the social function of school curricula?*

◎ *What role do interaction systems play in classroom life?*

◎ *How do class and cultural backgrounds of students influence their daily experiences in classrooms?*

◎ *What forms of curriculum instruction are needed in modern society?*

T he sociology of education studies the official and unofficial curricula of schools, seeking to learn what happens to children when they begin to interact with others in classroom situations.[1] It explores the relationship between the workplace, commercial interests, and the requirements of an increasingly complex, technological society. Curriculum is seen as a socially constructed knowledge organized into formal educational systems to achieve the social functions of schooling. Certain issues have become central preoccupations: Who decides what official curriculum policy will be? What happens to these policies once they are implemented? What role does social control play in the education of students? Why are there such differences in the curricula taught to children from different classes, races, and sexual backgrounds? Finally, why do some children fail in schools while others succeed? The fact that schools are selection agencies cannot be ignored, but recent focus has been on precisely how information is transmitted to students. At the same time, cultural considerations have come to the fore, and certain writers have studied education as a means for the transmission of thought and value systems. To answer such questions, investigators scrutinized how the attitudes and beliefs of teachers influenced their presentation of the official curriculum.[2]

Bernstein has identified three components of curriculum. The first is the knowledge that educational systems consider valid and worthy of transmission. Set apart from this knowledge are the instructional methods of teachers, or the way in which they convey such information to students. A third element in his schema is the assessment of such educational efforts by administrative functionaries. These three components of educational training are part of what Bernstein calls *message systems*, which transmit the academic educational knowledge that has been identified as valid by schools and society. He distinguishes between old-fashioned, fact-stuffing types of curriculum that seek to cram information, values, and skills into the minds of students and newer models that seek to take into account the ever-changing knowledge base of modern society.[3] The old practices were grounded in the assumption that society and knowledge changed slowly over time and that facts taught to children in the primary grades would still be valid when they reached adulthood. Contemporary thinking has moved away from this assumption, and the emphasis in curriculum studies has shifted to the idea of the learner as a knowledge developer and user rather than a repository of information. Nevertheless, this idea has often failed to influence classroom life because it was formulated without concern for working conditions in mass schools and without the input of teachers.

Following up on these ideas, Bernstein constructed a model of two curriculum types: the collection-oriented model, represented by the fact-stuffing methods of traditional classrooms, and an integrated curriculum model, which was more student- and inquiry-centered.[4] The collection type was characterized by a separation of information from its contexts and a competitive ethos that pitted students against one another in the classroom.[5] The integrated curriculum model was marked by a more unifying approach, presenting information as part of a social entity and not as discrete data separated from its origins. The collection model attempted to classify everything, creating and teaching facts that students were supposed to remember for tests and recitations. It was test-oriented, urging students to learn only what they would need to pass examinations.[6] By contrast, the newer integrated models of curriculum began with different premises but were seldom used by classroom teachers.

Collection-oriented practices appeared most often in the lower grades, where differences between academic disciplines were less important or where one teacher was asked to teach many subjects. Schools were not seen as selection agencies in the worst sense of that term, even though most parents knew the schools were segregated along socioeconomic lines. Where classification was strong in the curriculum, specialized teacher training and the development of subject loyalties were often common, and knowledge was considered the private property of individuals. Students at all levels were cautioned to cover their work, protecting it from others who might copy or steal it.[7]

Competitive values and teacher autonomy and isolation were widespread in these more traditional settings.[8] In schools where educational leaders urged teachers to use more integrative and innovative methods, however, teachers became more collegial and less isolated. In such schools, an emphasis on instructional methods and a more personal educational experience for students replaced the emphasis on factual knowledge that dominated the collection type of curriculum. Following Durkheim, Bernstein studied the patterns of authority and identity that developed in English classrooms and the ways in which different areas of knowledge were separated from one another. He wished to discover the effects of these instructional practices on the self-concepts of children from diverse social backgrounds.[9]

Bernstein argued that integrated forms of curriculum and instruction challenged present-day notions of knowledge and property and were therefore out of kilter with the needs of commercial society.[10] Also, Bernstein found that teachers were very resistant to change when it came to adopting new methods of instruction, especially ones that made it more difficult to control overcrowded classrooms.[11] Supporting this position, other writers cited historical data showing that the new integrated practices had come into general acceptance among specialists but not among teachers.[12] Changes in the structure of curriculum would involve people in new forms of schoolwork and create a crisis in the structure of power relationships now controlling educational systems. Still, Bernstein believed that a moral crisis of unprecedented proportions was moving these types of changes forward and that education, in spite of its change-resistant nature, would find it difficult to accommodate these new democratic social forces. Education would keep its rigid selection system and disciplinary procedures so long as they remained functional for mass schools and commercial society.[13]

Curriculum was still viewed as the principal player in the verification and maintenance of authority in schools and society. But now old questions were placed within a new focus: How does curriculum select, classify, and evaluate the knowledge it transmits? Can it really move from its traditional position of knowledge as a fixed and unchanging reality to a new one that sees knowledge in more fluid terms? Much that passes for school curricula contains ideologies that further strengthen the social standing of teachers and students in schools and classrooms. Bourdieu referred to these messages as a **habitus**, or culture, that helped educators pass on to students the social relationships that were required by schools and society.[14] They were determined by the traditions of schools and by other social forces outside the educational system.[15] To some degree, this was because, like many other organizations in modern life, schools have their own history and tradition. The state has a great deal of power, of course, but the educational bureaucracy, operating with surprising autonomy and freedom, has also had its effect. A recent study shed some light on this phenomenon by showing that schoolteachers were teaching pretty much as they had in the late nineteenth century, in spite of the innovations and reforms since that time.[16] Universities, too, were able to influence the curriculum of public schools by insisting on certain course requirements and grade levels, but this was always done within the collection-oriented curriculum model and did little to change instructional methods.

Researchers in the United States studied the ways in which students responded to mass schools once they were forced to play out the institutional role of the unknowing and incompetent person.[17] How were public schools able to force students to accept such identities? Some writers analyzed their data by dividing student responses into behavioral identities, paralleling the work of Erving Goffman. Goffman[18] had developed a model by observing inmates in mental institutions to determine how inmates coped with their new institutional identities and conditions of servitude. These investigators discovered that, while students came from diverse backgrounds and possessed many different points of view, they could be placed on a continuum of behavior to analyze their responses to the schooling experience. At one end of the continuum were the committed students, who were striving to achieve and conduct themselves in preferred ways. These were youngsters who could understand the language and culture of the curriculum, who were not selected out because of their family background, conduct, or lack of attendance. Second, there were the detached students, who were involved in striving for academic success but were less able to express themselves appropriately. These students were sometimes labelled *difficult* because they seemed beyond the reach of teachers. They were able to turn the acceptable way of learning and behaving on and off while still being able to distance themselves from the more onerous aspects of the student role.[19] Third, there were students who seemed ambivalent about their schoolwork, feeling a sharp conflict between their outside personal identities and those foisted upon them in classrooms.[20] Fourth, there were students who seem to be estranged from their classroom experiences and find it difficult or impossible to meet the demands of teachers. They may participate in non-academic activities, but because of their academic limitations, find themselves placed in tracks that carry the stigma of academic failure. This often has a trau-matic effect, causing them to experience schooling as a series of humiliating and debasing experiences. At the opposite end of the continuum from the committed students were children who appear to be alienated from others and from their own learning experiences. These are the students who seem most opposed to the routine, discipline, and curriculum of classroom life. Perhaps they were influenced by family members or experiences in earlier grades. Or perhaps their alienation was caused by their inability to understand the lan-guage or cultural requirements of their schools.[21] Such students sometimes join negative, antischool gangs that reinforce their attitudes while providing them with the social approval and support they cannot attain in the classroom. They are apt to reject the formal curriculum, pedagogy, and evaluation methods of teachers and schools and drop out at the earliest opportunity.

KNOWLEDGE AND CULTURE

Although the schools' instructional methods play an important role in socializ-ing students, insufficient attention has been paid to the speech and language of the teacher and how these factors affect the success or failure of students in mass schools. To some extent, this is because speech and language are uncon-scious processes, conveying attitudes and emotions that are not always appar-ent.[22] The way individuals treat others is one feature of this cultural communi-cation, especially when those others are from different ethnic, religious, or socioeconomic groups. Classroom discourses also influence the way individu-als see the economic system of society, conveying a preferred cultural heritage and orientation to students at a very young age. Althusser has called these dis-courses cultural communication, in the sense of representing the store of com-mon-sense knowledge that people use to decide things in their everyday lives.[23] Anthropological studies have defined culture as the stored, shared, and legitimate knowledge that provides guidelines for people living and working together in society.[24] Durkheim described such cultural constructs as the means by which social beings were constructed, and other writers have agreed that the learning and internalization of culture is essential to every social sys-tem.[25]

Eggleston[26] has taken these ideas further, suggesting that cultural orienta-tions and the interaction patterns that develop from them profoundly influence the ways in which students from different social origins are taught and evalu-ated in classrooms. He argued that interaction systems which lay beneath the surface of curriculum and pedagogic actions were particularly significant for understanding the ways in which curriculum shapes the thinking of teachers and students. While Bernstein, Durkheim, and others had seen curriculum as valid knowledge, Eggleston challenged these ideas by focusing on the interac-tion systems that embraced not only the content of learning but also its organization. The educational system was concerned not only with transmission, but with the division of labor that dominated economic and social conditions in modern life. This hierarchical system determined the conditions under which teachers and students would come together in the classroom and the methods of instruction that would be used. The evaluation system of educational organizations was, above all else, a selection device: the grading and examination practices of schooling had the effect of labelling and tracking children from the poorer classes. These practices were the cause of the unequal outcomes observed by investigators who studied the experiences of children from diverse socioeconomic and racial backgrounds. Eggleston added another variable of the control system that established behavioral norms for teachers and students. This system included ritualistic behavior, establishing the rights of teachers to make decisions and to stop and question any student anywhere in the school building. A final power system, that of administration, dealt with problems of attendance, health, welfare, guidance, and the daily organization of classes. Naturally, in the everyday world, these systems overlapped and interfaced in ways that often made them indistinguishable from one another. Taken as an entity, however, they provided the necessary conditions for the recreation of existing relationships and conditions in schools and society.[27]

These interaction systems oriented teachers and students inside the school building. Their purpose was to define which forms of behavior were acceptable or unacceptable and which types of student responses would be rewarded or punished. These systems also included ideas about the way in which pupils from diverse backgrounds and with different abilities would be taught and promoted through the grade system, as well as assumptions about the knowledge and skills that would be offered or withheld from such students. We can gain further insight into these power systems by looking at how decisions are made in schools and in the classroom. It is in these value and power systems that investigators have found their most important understandings about school curriculum. It would be difficult to envision classrooms staffed by teachers who did not believe they were teaching children what was right for them and for the society in which they lived. It is precisely these kinds of cultural assumptions that support these power systems in schools legitimating and validating the teacher's role as a dispenser of knowledge and a disciplinarian.[28]

POWER SYSTEMS IN SCHOOLS

Eggleston pointed out inequalities that developed because of these power systems.[29] Citing the findings of the Plowden Report, he showed that inequality and social conflict were widespread in the English schools of the post-World War II period.[30] More complete descriptions of the value and power systems in schools were needed, he suggested, if educators were to learn how schools socialized and stratified children in the classroom every day.

Eggleston argued further that an important aspect of value and power systems was the way they arranged themselves in the daily life of schools so that the distinctive, class-bound practices of English society were preserved and strengthened. The unity and cohesion Durkheim saw in French education and society at the end of the nineteenth century was missing from English history, and social conflict seemed to be much more prevalent. Even when students from diverse backgrounds were taught the same subjects, the outcomes differed according to their social origins. The development of **organic solidarity**, which Durkheim[31] emphasized in his studies of nineteenth-century France, were not readily apparent in the modern English experience.

One of the important aspects educators studied during this post-World War II period focused on the problems that developed when curriculum was presented to students from different socioeconomic and cultural origins.[32] They pointed to various learning and disciplinary experiences, both instrumental and expressive, that were designed to enable students to accept their subservient condition in classrooms and schools.[33] The pattern of teaching, grounded in the conventional view of knowledge as a reasonably permanent reality, provided for a mass schooling experience that was increasingly irrelevant to the rapidly changing world outside the school. Other research coupled access to knowledge with the distribution of resources in educational systems and the workplace.[34] Irvine and Byrne, studying children in the United States and England, showed that resources were appropriated according to assumptions about the type of education needed by students from different socioeconomic, racial, and cultural backgrounds, constantly benefitting more affluent children.[35] Educators believed the better students deserved more schooling, superior teachers, and supplies than those who were less able. The curricula were also significantly different, with children from the poorer classes receiving less challenging materials and instruction.

Byrne provided evidence that discrimination among students extended to gender by showing that the appropriation of resources and curricular selections was severely limited.[36] Even in the United States, recent research has shown that girls are subjected to inferior educational opportunities because of teachers' assumptions and attributions.[37] Other writers argued that curriculum is a normal outgrowth of the normative and interaction systems in society. The aims and contents of curriculum are different in each country, as are their transmissions, timing and ordering sequences of knowledge, and evaluation methods.[38]

One of the main characteristics of curriculum today is its speech and language. These are expressions of class and cultural difference in the adult world and are chiefly concerned with the ethical, moral, and civic responsibilities of students in schools and later in society. Bourdieu has pointed out that certain outcomes must be achieved by educators if individuals are to learn to live and function in modern culture and that these are transmitted through appropriate forms of speech and language. Schools require linguistic and cultural competency that they cannot provide for students from diverse socioeconomic origins. Such learning is accomplished in the home through a form of social osmosis and cannot be easily duplicated in classrooms.[39] Rothstein has linked speech and language to unconscious processes that give children from affluent families advantages that cannot be replicated for students in mass schools.[40] Both authors agree on a correspondence between linguistic competencies and socioeconomic resources, with the possession of one often implying the other.

Moreover, Bernstein, in a recent compilation of his work, has indicated that the interaction systems of schools convey a hidden curriculum to students that profoundly influences their educational success or failure in classrooms.[41] These deal with the structural and relational features of the instructional situation and refer to the physical givens and interactional patterns that arise from the normal interaction between teachers and students.[42] Other writers have pointed out that these hidden lessons often conflict with the formal ones that teachers are supposed to convey to students.[43] Most school systems operate within an economic and cultural system that discriminates against some students because they speak foreign languages or are from different racial and cultural backgrounds.

The hidden curriculum flourished because it seemed to make sense in mass schools, where the official curriculum became increasingly irrelevant. As long as teachers were asked to teach materials that students could not assimilate, such informal structures were sure to persist. Once established, this hidden curriculum helped educators reconcile their frustrations and poor performances in classrooms. A client-culpability syndrome blamed youngsters alone for their classroom failures: teachers could not achieve educational goals because of their students' poor abilities and family backgrounds.

Most curriculum writers agree that the speech and language of teachers and students establish the normative and cultural environment governing much of what happens in schools and classrooms.[44] At the same time, attempts at curricular reform face persistent evidences of discrimination and systemic inequality, no matter where they occur in the commercial world. Bernstein has drawn attention to the school's message system, which constructs the classroom situation in words and memories and governs initial and subsequent teacher-student interaction.[45] He argues that curriculum is merely the designated and validated knowledge of educational authorities, informing teachers and students what they must do on the job and when they must do it. Considering the link of the message system with the establishment of a dominant culture, some of his arguments seem to echo the arbitrary cultural transmissions Bourdieu discussed in his examination of French schools.[46] The emphasis on the message system adds a sociological dimension to curriculum studies, showing how it helps schools and society reproduce the conditions of their own existence. Many children are forced to attend to scholastic language and culture that are foreign to them and devalue their family backgrounds. Curriculum, both formal and informal, is used to teach children what to think about, how to think about the past and present, how to think about themselves and their families, how to think about their future places in the occupational matrix. It becomes an important instrument in the indoctrination of future workers and citizens, stratifying them and the knowledge they are permitted to acquire. Instructional methods, the other side of this inculcation, determine how curriculum will be transmitted to students and what kinds of relationships will be allowed to develop in classrooms. The act of instruction in mass schools creates a conflict, causing young people to assume a subordinate and incompetent role in the schooling situation.[47]

This is similar to Rothstein's[48] argument that an ideology of students continues to challenge their worthiness and capabilities. In describing this ideology, he points to an overly corrective pedagogy that makes it more difficult for children to learn their lessons. This ideology views students as generally inattentive, easily distracted, and unwilling to apply themselves with diligence to the hard work of the classroom. They are resistant to all forms of discipline and authority and lack the inner discipline needed for sustained academic work. They accept the ideas of others without thinking and read as little as possible. Their lives in and out of school are filled with confusion and emotionalism. They do not and cannot initiate independent schoolwork. They show little talent for self-discipline, seeking to avoid schooling altogether when they can. They are prone to idleness and doing as they please while seeking entertainment and excitement from commercial media.

Further, this ideology extends backward in history. It constantly asserts that students cannot be trusted to do their work and are easily distracted from it.[49] Youngsters will move toward whatever is easily understood, whatever is stimulating for the moment, whatever is exotic and out of the range of their everyday experiences. In this view, students are idlers who must be forced to work and discipline themselves in classrooms. They do not and cannot understand the relationship between their present behavior and their later lives in schools and the workplace. They will react poorly to criticism even if it is fair and accurate. Nor can students tell the difference between mere appearance and the essence in their home environment. They easily accept one for the other and can be led about by slogans that mirror their emotions of the moment. They are generally self-centered and unwilling to sacrifice anything for the common good of classrooms or for their own good later in life.

Such ideologies exist for schoolteachers, too. Sergiovanni,[50] for example, describes the supervisory assumptions of McGregor's Theory X as a set of conventional beliefs that school administrators can use in dealing with teachers. According to the ideological suppositions of this set of beliefs, teachers are average people who are by their very nature lazy—they try to work as little as possible when left to their own devices. They lack a sense of ambition, disliking responsibility. They are followers by nature and inherently self-centered in their interests and concerns. They are indifferent to what is happening to the school organization outside their enclosed classrooms. Teachers are by nature resistant to all types of reform and change in their routine, preferring to do what they have always done before without much thought or concern. As a group they are very naive and gullible, not very intelligent, and open to every kind of charlatan and demagogue. Sergiovanni goes on to assert that "one can find many instances in schools when the assumptions of Theory X do indeed seem to be true." Teachers, he goes on to say, appear to work as few hours as they can and then only under supervisory surveillance. They show little initiative or imagination in their work and are very defensive when presented with constructive feedback. McGregor believed that when such conditions existed in an organization, the problem was less with employees than with the assumptions of their supervisors. When teachers sense that administrators have negative ideas and expectations about them, they often respond to them in angry and unproductive ways. The relationship between teacher and administrator seem to mimic that of worker and boss in industrial society, as Bowles and Gintis recognized in their studies of American education.[51]

CURRICULUM DEVELOPMENT AND REFORM

In summary, European and American researchers have been able to furnish us with social descriptions of curriculum's role in socializing and controlling youth in modern society. Following the work of Weber and Durkheim[52], they found that educational knowledge and its dissemination in schools were closely related to the needs of the industrial system they served. Curriculum development was seen as a slow and gradual process that reconciled the interests of important client groups. Because of this, the essential features of mass schooling were signified in ways that emphasized its ideological characteristic. Bernstein's message systems provided two opposed communications to teachers and students. The first, a **received perspective**, was strongly moral and normative in its orientations and mirrored the thought and attitudes of traditionalists. The second, a **reflexive perspective**, was new, insisting that the new technologies of modern society demanded a more flexible and inquiry-based method of instruction.

Eggleston, seeking to develop a reform or restructuring of modern schooling, encouraged schools to feature both the received and reflexive perspectives in their classwork. This would make teachers more aware of their students as people with needs and concerns that demanded their attention. At the same time it would make them more aware of the disciplinary features of school life and the problems those features caused for everyone working there.[53]

Agreeing with Katznelson, European social scientists saw the conflict over curriculum as a permanent feature of mass schooling in modern society.[54] They sought solutions to present-day problems of inequality by asking how a reflexive and integrated curriculum could better respond to the needs of children who are poor, immigrant, racially different, female, or cannot speak the formal language of educational systems. How could such students acquire a more supportive, favorable curriculum experience, one that allowed them to succeed on academic and psychological levels? How could they be given the status, recognition, and opportunity that was now being denied them by the regular curriculum?

In trying to answer these questions Bernstein argued that schools would not and could not make up for the shortcomings indigenous to modern society. He insisted that a reflexive curriculum perspective could allow students a chance to succeed in regular classroom work. Such an opportunity would require smaller classes and more intensive forms of instruction. Students would need the support and counseling of trained and sympathetic personnel, especially well-trained and well-supervised teachers.

This approach viewed poorly prepared students as children who were not performing well in classrooms. They were disadvantaged, or deprived, and in need of help. If they could be helped to succeed, if they could be taught the language, culture, and information they needed, then they would cease to be different and deprived. Eggleston suggested that the extreme competitiveness of present-day schooling be replaced by more cooperative and accepting practices, by systems that gave parity to different curricular studies and performances.

These solutions posed major difficulties for would-be reformers and for modern industrial society, and Eggleston seemed to understand this. They conflicted with long-term trends in educational administration and teaching and ran counter to the social and cultural contexts in which they occurred. The reflexive solution that Eggleston advocated could only be done with a small number of students. The political and social structures of Europe and the United States tended to stress the need for hierarchy in mass society, with schooling acting as one of the institutions that socialized people into accepting traditional successions of power and control from one generation to the next.

Hargreaves pointed out that the opportunities to succeed across class lines were an essential part of the modern educational culture, reflecting the needs of an industrializing society to discover ever-new types of expert knowledge.[55] The selection apparatuses restricted the numbers and types of students who could become successful in mass schools, penalizing some for their speech and language. These were the determining forces in the type of curriculum used in English schools after the feudal period. The reflexive solution to curriculum discrimination would validate the nonstandard English of immigrant and poor children, providing them with a less stressful schooling experience. This solution, however, would also tie them and their identities to a language and culture that differed from the larger, dominant culture and would therefore ensure their exclusion. Although these reforms envisioned freedom and self-realization, they would still not remove most of the disadvantages and inequities that society imposed on poor and immigrant students in mass schools. Bourdieu saw this desire to reform educational systems as illusory and contrary to the weight of historical evidence. Educational systems were to maintain only the ideology of equality and fair and open competition between children. The truth was more difficult to perceive. More and more researchers, however, concluded that schooling in modern society was both repressive and overly ideological in its methods of social control and stratification. They believed the repressive mode used by schools was necessary to physically constrain large numbers of students in confined settings. But it caused teachers to use methods that were more suited to the police and military than to people coming together for educational purposes.

In these views, schools were seen as state ideological institutions that took part in reproducing the social relations and structures of modern society, along with the family, the church, the media, and other agencies. Of these, Althusser believed that schools were the most productive because of their cumulative effects, with their long years of inculcation and forced attendance. Educational systems insured a continuous supply of like-minded individuals who had the minimum skills needed to maintain the bureaucratic structures of mass society, while providing a small cadre of others who could experiment and create more efficient levels of technology and production. They reproduced youngsters who accepted the discipline of schools and the workplace without thought, thus making them perfect workers in an increasingly mechanized and computerized society. The ideologies that supported such efforts were reflected in the curriculum and pedagogy of teachers working in overcrowded, congested schools.

How, then, could there be a restructuring of the educational experience? For many educational researchers, the problems of poor achievement, truancy, and high drop-out rates indicated pervasive problems in modern educational systems rather than a disadvantaged student population.

CAN CHANGES BE MADE?

The problems described by English and French social scientists arise partly from the definition, distribution, and evaluation of knowledge and partly from the change-resistant nature of modern schooling. Still, many observers persisted in asking: How can we make changes to allow students from poorer and culturally diverse families greater access to opportunities and power in schools and in work later in life? Bernstein criticized these reformers for believing that educational systems could make up the deficiencies of society. If children from poorer families experienced inferior prenatal care, if they lived in despair and abject poverty, if they remained untutored in the speech, language, and culture of the educated classes, then there was little formal schooling could do to break their cycle of academic and economic failure.

But Eggleston persisted, believing that youth wanted to count for something in life and that an informal system of leisure and youth services could make a significant difference in their lives. He believed this even though evaluation research in this area showed that such experiences had neither satisfied youth nor changed the conditions of their educational or work lives. While a few students were given the opportunity to participate in self-governance, most had remained in traditional, autocratic schools. The few lucky ones were usually those who had internalized the speech, language, and culture of the educational system and the voluntary organizations that composed the youth services agenda. For most students in these programs, the experience was shadowed by their own low status and inferior prospects in the workplace and society. Later, other reform projects, which gave youth opportunities to experience participatory democracy, had some small success with a few more students. Students were encouraged and allowed to work on equal terms with staff members, deciding much of the agenda. But these projects were oases in an otherwise unrelieved, authoritarian, and overly corrective schooling experience.[56]

Eggleston's studies of the British Youth Services Organizations showed that young people did not wish to change English society in any significant way. Rather, they wanted to gain a more desirable occupation and status in the existing social order. As long as the social system remained so resistant, changing the structural and relational features of schooling seemed impossible. Reformers have consistently urged that the reproduction function of educational systems be moved aside so that new methods of teaching and curriculum could be put in place. These new approaches would force teachers and students to think critically about the aims, motivations, and assumptions of their schoolwork.

Supporting these ideas is the notion that curriculum is best when it is used by those who can answer the following questions: (1) How does activity-based, problem-solving education help students share and understand the human condition today? (2) To what degree does it question or threaten existing knowledge and power relationships in society and schools? and (3) What is knowledge to be used for, and how is it treated as we approach the twenty-first century? A true reform of schooling can only be practiced by those who can answer these questions with understanding and insight. The restructuring perspective is not a call for social revolution or the dismantling of the class system. Rather it is a model of curriculum for a democratic society, one that is concerned about individuals living in an increasingly depersonalized, mass society.

Freire[57] has attempted to refute these ideas by insisting that researchers keep an eye on the unavoidable relations that exist between educational systems and society. He suggests that it is impossible to understand education without discussing its ties to the economic and political power of a particular social system. School curriculum is first and foremost an instrument of social control, transmitting the values and power of particular groups and agencies. It is the key mechanism that mass society uses to control youth and the people who teach in our schools. For this group of researchers, the issues revolve around a concern for the way in which knowledge is organized. Returning to the ideas of Bernstein, these educators ask: Are the present-day specialists to be used in integrated departments, or will they remain essentially separate? What is the actual content of curriculum knowledge? How much will be taught to children from diverse backgrounds? In what order will it be taught and in what relationship to the lives of students? From these questions, others follow: How should the curriculum be taught, and who should teach it? What methods should they use? Who shall judge these efforts, and how?

Researchers have defined curriculum as the knowledge base that is transmitted to students in mass schools. It includes learning experiences that children can understand, and it is a response to society's view of knowledge at a particular time and place in history. Curriculum usually includes the following elements, which spring from the formative power systems of a given society: (1) aims that specify why this body of knowledge is being validated by school authorities; (2) content that delimits what will and will not be included; (3) technique that explains how things will be taught and why; (4) timing that explicates the order in which material will be presented to children progressing through the grade system; and (5) evaluation of the level of success achieved in transmitting knowledge to students.

Curriculum is often presented to teachers as a syllabus or a series of aims and objectives to be achieved by students at certain points in their educational experience. It is also presented as a way of learning materials that the state has decided must be taught in public schools. Goodlad defined several perspectives of curriculum. The first is the *ideal* curriculum, which is steeped in tradition and folklore and expressed in abstractions about patriotism, morality, and its outcomes. Such viewpoints are concerned with what ought to be included in the formal curriculum and how it should be delivered to students. Another perspective, the *formal* curriculum, refers to expectations and is often embodied in state and district guidelines, syllabi, school board policies, and laws. Here, the heavy hand of the state and community are unmistakable, but most American researchers have tended to ignore these areas of concern. Another perspective is the *instructional* curriculum, wherein teachers bring their own attitudes, values, and beliefs into the classroom. These influence what is taught, as do different ability levels of teachers. The results are seen in the ways teachers are able to adapt and conform to the formal curriculum they are supposed to transmit. Goodlad identifies another form of curriculum, the *operational* variant, or what actually happens when teachers and students work together in insulated classrooms. Both groups influence one another over time, thus changing further what is taught in modern schools. A final perspective, the *experiential* curriculum is seldom seen in American schools but has its roots in the work and philosophy of John Dewey. Here the emphasis is on the student's views of the curriculum offered as well as evaluation efforts that learn what actual outcomes occur once these perspectives have had their effect. From this we can say that in the United States, curriculum studies have been more concerned with technical rather than social studies of school curriculum. Even scholarly work has been more concerned with this viewpoint, seeing teachers as technicians who need to provide the correct procedures and materials to students at the proper moment in their development. Reformers have tried to use these studies to synthesize the work of specialists and schoolteachers, but outcomes have been disappointing.[58]

⑥ *Summary*

Schooling in modern society is caught in a conflict between old and new ways of thinking about curriculum. In the old view, schools sought to fill students with facts they could use in their adult lives. The new way of thinking is that education needs to move away from this collection model because the knowledge base of modern society is doubling every two years. In the past, schools have used curriculum to stratify and select students for the higher reaches of learning and earning. However, the new information age requires individuals who can think on their feet and generate new knowledge as they work in an ever-changing workplace. The interaction systems of the past, which regimented students and prepared them for a world of work dominated by Taylorist ideas of management, are no longer functional. New interactional patterns need to be devised to empower teachers and students to work together in more collegial relationships. These needs may be confounded by the historic bias of schools against students from poor and immigrant families.

⑥ *Projects*

1. Ask some teachers you know to talk about their methods of instruction. Ask their opinions about teaching with the goal of preparing students to take tests and the problems this can present for teachers and students. How do they feel about more student-centered methods of instruction? Do they use them?

2. Compare the courses you took in high school and college. Were these more collection-oriented in their presentation of facts, or did they encourage you to be more introspective?

3. Make a case study of a teacher you know who is thought to be effective with students. To what factors can you attribute that teacher's success? How does the teacher interact with students in class?

4. Analyze the role that competition and grading have on students in a nearby school. Are youngsters in slower classes treated differently from more normal groups? In what ways? How do success and failure affect the dispositions of students?

⑥ Endnotes

1. Young, M. F. D., "Knowledge and Control," in *Knowledge and Control: New Directions for the Sociology of Education,* ed. M. F. D. Young (London: Collier-Macmillan, 1971); Bernstein, Basil, *The Structuring of Pedagogic Discourse* (London and New York: Routledge & Kegan Paul, 1990), 161–163.

2. Warwick, David, "Ideologies, Integration and Conflicts of Meaning," in *Educability, Schools and Ideology,* ed. M. Flude and J. Ahier (London: Croom Helm, 1974); Banks, Olive, *The Sociology of Education* (New York: Schocken Books, 1976), 174–178; Becher, Tony, and Stuart Maclure, *The Politics of Curriculum Change* (London: Hutchinson, 1978), 10–12; Eggleston, John, *The Sociology of School Curriculum* (London: Routledge & Kegan Paul, 1977), 15–16, 109–118; Lutz, Frank, and Carol Mertz, *The Politics of School/Community Relations* (New York: Teachers College Press, 1992).

3. Bernstein, *The Structuring of Pedagogic Discourse,* 140–141, 212–214.

4. Banks, *The Sociology of Education,* 179–183.

5. Bernstein, *The Structuring of Pedagogic Discourse,* 60–61; 138–144; Whitty, Geoff, *Sociology and School Knowledge: Curriculum Theory, Research and Politics* (London: Methuen, 1985), 54–56, 121–123.

6. Wirt, Frederick, and Kirst Michael, *Politics of Education: Schools in Conflict* (Berkeley, Calif.: McCutchan, 1989), 5–12; Apple, Michael W., "Regulating the Text: The Socio-Historical Roots of State Control," in *Textbooks in American Society,* ed. Philip G. Atbech (Albany, N. Y.: State University of New York Press, 1991).

7. Rothstein, Stanley W., *Schooling the Poor* (Westport, Conn.: Bergin & Garvey, 1994), chap. 5.

8. Bernstein, Basil, "Code, Modalities, and the Process of Cultural Reproduction: A Model," in *The Structuring of Pedagogic Discourse,* 13–62; Cuban, Larry, *How Teachers Taught: Constancy and Change in American Classrooms 1890–1980* (New York: Longman, 1984), 22–25.

9. Bernstein, Basil, "Education, Symbolic Control, and Social Practices, in *The Structuring of Pedagogic Discourse,* 133–164; Durkheim, Emile, *Education and Sociology,* trans. Sherwood D. Fox (Glencoe, Ill.: Free Press, 1956), 88–90.

10. Bernstein, Basil, "Language and Social Class," *British Journal of Sociology* 11 (1960): 271–276.

11. Cuban, Larry, *How Teachers Taught: Constancy and Change in American Classrooms 1890–1980* (New York: Longman, 1984), chap. 1.

12. Adler, Louise, and Kip Tellez, "Curriculum Politics in Urban Schooling," in *Handbook of Schooling in Urban America,* ed. Stanley W. Rothstein (Westport, Conn.: Greenwood Press, 1993), 91–111.

13. Rothstein, Stanley W., *Identity and Ideology: Sociocultural Theories of Schooling* (Westport, Conn.: Greenwood Press, 1991), 25–32; Bowles, Samuel, and Herbert Gintis, *Schooling in Capitalist America: Educational Reform and the Contradictions of Economic Life* (New York: Basic Books, 1976), 34–35, 110–114; Katznelson, Ira, and Margaret Weir, *Schooling for All: Class, Race, and the Decline of the Democratic Ideal* (New York: Basic Books, 1985), 71–73, 176–177.

14. Bourdieu, Pierre, *Outline of A Theory of Practice*, trans. Richard Nice (Cambridge: Cambridge University Press, 1977), 76–85.

15. Katznelson and Weir, *Schooling for All*, chap. 2–3.

16. Darder, Antonia, *Culture and Power in the Classroom: A Critical Foundation for Bicultural Education* (Westport, Conn.: Bergin & Garvey, 1991), 20, 35, 107–110.

17. Fuchs, Estelle, "How Teachers Learn to Help Children Fail," in *Children and Their Caretakers*, ed. Norman K. Denzin (New Brunswick, N. J.: Transaction Books, 1973), 29–42; Rothstein, Stanley W., "Orientations: First Impressions in an Urban Junior High School," *Urban Education* 14, no. 1 (April, 1979): 91–116.

18. Goffman, Erving, *Asylums: Essays on the Social Situation of Mental Patients and Other Inmates* (New York: Doubleday-Anchor, 1961), 14–28.

19. Rothstein, Stanley W., "The Ethics of Coercion: Social Control Practices in an Urban Junior High School," *Urban Education* 22, no. 1 (April 1987): 53–56.

20. Kozol, Jonathan, *Savage Inequalities: Children in America's Schools* (New York: Harper, 1991), 57–59.

21. Nadal, Antonio, and Milga-Morales Nadal, "Multiculturism in Urban Schools: A Puerto Rican Perspective," in *Handbook of Schooling in Urban America*, 145–160.

22. Irvine, Jacqueline Jordan, and Darlene Eleanor York, "Teacher Perspectives: Why Do African-American, Hispanic, and Vietnamese Students Fail?," in *Handbook of Schooling in Urban America*, 161–174.

23. Smith, Steven, *Reading Althusser: An Essay on Structural Marxism* (Ithaca and London: Cornell University Press, 1984), 176–178.

24. Benedict, Ruth, "Continuities and Discontinuities in Cultural Conditioning," in *A Study of Interpersonal Relations*, ed. Patrick Mullahy (New York: Hermitage Press, 1949), 305–306; Radin, Paul, *The World of Primitive Man* (New York: Henry Schuman, 1953), 106, 126, 130; Rothstein, Stanley W., *The Voice of the Other: Language as Illusion in the Formation of the Self* (Westport, Conn.: Praeger, 1993), chap. 3.

25. Durkheim, *Education and Sociology*, 30–34; Simmel, Georg, *The Sociology of Georg Simmel* (New York: Free Press, 1950), 385–387; Rothstein, *Identity and Ideology*, 67–86.

26. Eggleston, *The Sociology of School Curriculum*, 35–36, 62–64.

27. Waller, Willard, *The Sociology of Teaching* (New York: Russell & Russell, 1961), 19–22.

28. Rothstein, *The Voice of the Other*, chap. 6. See also Altenbaugh, Richard, ed., *The Teachers Voice: A Social History of Teaching in Twentieth Century America*

(London: Falmer Press, 1992); Apple, Michael, "Cultural Form and the Logic of Technical Control," in *Culture and Economic Reproduction in Education*, ed. Michael Apple (London: Routledge & Kegan Paul, 1982), 250–257.

29. Eggleston, *The Sociology of School Curriculum*, 8–11, 140–148.

30. Banks, *The Sociology of Education*, 77–78, 184–185.

31. Ginsburg, Morris, "Durkheim's Ethical Theory," in *Makers of the Modern World: Emile Durkheim*, ed. Robert Nisbet (Englewood Cliffs, N. J.: Prentice-Hall, 1965), 142–155.

32. Ogbu, John, *Minority Education and Caste* (New York: Academic Press, 1978), 220–228. See also Freire, Paulo, *The Pedagogy of the Oppressed* (New York: Seabury Press, 1970).

33. Eggleston, *The Sociology of School Curriculum*, 35–36.

34. Bourdieu, Pierre, and Jean-Claude Passeron, *The Inheritors: French Students and Their Relation to Culture* (Chicago: University of Chicago Press, 1979), 101–118.

35. Byrne, Edwin M., *Planning and Educational Inequality: A Study of the Rationale of Resource Allocation* (Slough: N. F. E. R., 1974), 12–17.

36. Banks, *The Sociology of Education*, 134–135.

37. Shakeshaft, Charol, "Meeting the Needs of Girls in Urban Schools", in *Handbook of Schooling in Urban America*, 175–185. See also AAUW, *How Schools Shortchange Girls* (New York: American Association of University Women Educational Foundation).

38. Eggleston, John, *The Sociology of School Curriculum*, 11–12, 35–42.

39. Rothstein, *The Voice of the Other*, 118–121; Sarason, Seymour B., *Schooling in America: Scapegoat and Salvation* (New York: Free Press, 1983), 109–111.

40. Rothstein, *The Voice of the Other*, 58–84, 108–110. See also Bourdieu, *Outline of a Theory of Practice*, 177–183.

41. Bernstein, *The Structuring of Pedagogic Discourse*, 77–79.

42. Waller, *The Sociology of Teaching*, 19–22; Rothstein, "Orientations: First Impressions in an Urban Junior High School," 91–94.

43. Bowles and Gintis, *Schooling in Capitalist America*, 18–25; Katznelson and Weir, *Schooling for All*, 86–101.

44. Bernstein, *The Structuring of Pedagogic Discourse*, 45–46, 134–135; Bourdieu and Passeron, *The Inheritors*, chap. 1–2; Eggleston, *The Sociology of School Curriculum*, 142–143; Rothstein, *The Voice of the Other*, 93–97, 103–105.

45. Bernstein, *The Restructuring of Pedagogic Discourse*, 33–39.

46. Bourdieu, Pierre, and Jean-Claude Passeron, *Reproduction in Education, Society and Culture* (London and Beverly Hills: Sage, 1976), 71–106.

47. Waller, *The Sociology of Teaching*, 194–195; Rothstein, Stanley W., "Symbolic Violence: The Disappearance of the Individual in Marxist Thought," *Interchange: A Quarterly Review of Education* 22, no. 3 (1991): 28–42.

48. Rothstein, *Identity and Ideology*, 12–13, 109–110, 125–126, 131–132; Darder, *Culture and Power in the Classroom*, 15–17, 17–19.

49. Waller, *The Sociology of Teaching*, 110; Rothstein, *Schooling the Poor*, chap. 1.

50. Sergiovanni, Thomas J., and Robert J. Starratt, *Supervision: Human Perspectives* (New York: McGraw-Hill, 1988), 165–168.

51. Bowles and Gintis, *Schooling in Capitalist America*, 102–124.

52. Weber, Max, *The Protestant Ethic and the Spirit of Capitalism*, trans. Talcott Parsons (New York: Scribner's Sons, 1958), 155–185; Durkheim, *Education and Sociology*, 65–66, 94–99, 144–145.

53. Eggleston, *The Sociology of School Curriculum*, 99–118.

54. Katznelson and Weir, *Schooling for All*, 5–7; Bourdieu and Passeron, *Reproduction in Education, Society and Culture*, 152–162, 218–219; Bernstein, *The Structuring of Pedagogic Discourse*, 135–140.

55. Hargreaves, David H., *Social Relations in a Secondary School* (London: Routledge & Kegan Paul, 1967), 214–215.

56. Eggleston, *The Sociology of School Curriculum*, 144–150.

57. Freire, *The Pedagogy of the Oppressed*, chap. 1.

58. Goodlad, John, *What Schools are For* (Bloomington, Ind.: Phi Delta Kappa, 1979); Goodlad, John, *A Place Called School: Prospects for the Future* (New York: McGraw-Hill, 1984), 33–60, 233–234.

5

Schoolteachers

ⓖ　　ⓖ　　ⓖ　　ⓖ　　ⓖ　　ⓖ　　ⓖ　　ⓖ　　ⓖ　　ⓖ　　ⓖ　　ⓖ

OBJECTIVES

In this chapter you will learn the answers to these questions:

- ⓖ　*How do teachers see themselves?*

- ⓖ　*How do others see them?*

- ⓖ　*What kind of person is likely to become a teacher?*

- ⓖ　*What is the status of teachers in American society?*

- ⓖ　*How do problems of order and control influence the teacher-pupil relationship?*

- ⓖ　*When was teaching feminized, and how did that affect the profession?*

- ⓖ　*What kinds of teachers' organizations developed in the United States?*

- ⓖ　*Why did teachers become more militant in the 1960s?*

TEACHERS' SELF-PERCEPTIONS

Although studies have demonstrated the importance of the teaching profession, the conflict between teachers' self-images and stereotypes of teachers in mass society is largely unexplored. Some perceptions of this occupational type have developed in response to negative ideas that were present in commercial society, while others have resulted from early inclinations and training. Yet the way teachers see themselves, whether in teacher-preparation programs or the context of their work, provides a basis for their behavior in the classroom. Bowlby[1] has suggested that these self-images result from years of student socialization and teacher-training programs and that they provide new teachers with a so-called professional way of viewing schools and classrooms. On the other hand, most self-perceptions are based on empirical experiences in families and schools, and they change very little over time. Studies suggest that image building is particularly important for teachers in inner city schools, where they generally work under very stressful circumstances. Lortie has suggested that new teachers must have strong, positive self-images to survive the tension-filled weeks of their first teaching assignment. What teachers learn in these earliest experiences depends on their relationships with supervisors and veteran teachers. These interactions form the context in which new teachers develop assumptions about students, classroom life, and the use of disciplinary methods.[2] After a time, these suppositions are changed by experiences with students and other members of the schooling community.

The prevalence of overcrowded classrooms in both elementary and secondary school may make it more difficult for new teachers to establish the order and control essential to the learning situation. It is generally conceded that the no-talking rule is needed for meaningful instruction to take place in mass schools. New teachers are advised to be stern in their first communications with students and punish lapses in decorum as fairly as possible.[3]

Undoubtedly some of the appeal of the profession stems from deeply held ideals and values of teachers who see their vocation as a calling. These norms seem to sustain them no matter how bad the working conditions become, and they seem able to urge students to fulfill themselves to do their best in difficult circumstances. Bowlby has suggested that such ideas have their beginnings in the individual's earliest relationships with parents or teachers.[4] As primary school students, children sometimes identify with the powerful adult who is so helpful and knowledgeable about their own best interests. Such identifications can lead to transference later in life and to career choices based on an idealization of the profession. More realistic ideas about their work will develop only after they begin to teach children from diverse or challenged backgrounds.[5] This movement toward realism can begin during student-teaching and in contact with master-teachers and teachers with many years of experience. Undoubtedly, these socialization experiences provide the apprenticeship new teachers need to copy the behavior and teaching styles of experienced teachers.

The more positive self-perceptions of teachers can also be seen as a defensive response to the middling status of the profession in commercial society. These ambiguities in the teacher's image allow teachers to pick and choose how they will identify themselves. Cusick has pointed to the elusive character of the teacher's role in mass society, which leads some to see educators as central persons in the transmission of knowledge from one generation to the next.[6] Others espouse less flattering views, seeing teachers as caretakers and worse, while teachers remain acutely aware of the many extras that go into doing their job well, citing them to all who will listen. Teachers often feel they need to take on roles of the substitute parent, the understanding adult, and the expert and specialist in areas of curriculum and child-development. These roles all contribute to the way teachers see themselves and their profession. Teachers may show frustration and anger at times, but they usually accept these added responsibilities as best they can.

There is, furthermore, a profound difference in the way that elementary and secondary teachers see themselves. Secondary teachers may well see themselves as interpreters and disseminators of knowledge and skills related to their areas of academic expertise. Although the idea of personalized education exists, most teachers on this level seek to provide students with important knowledge and skills in their field of study. This differs from the self-images of elementary teachers, who often see themselves as surrogate parents for children who have severe social and economic problems at home. Insofar as teachers are expected to maintain order and control and teach a formal curriculum, the consequences of their work inevitably lead to directive styles of instruction. In the learning situation teachers do the talking, while students are expected to listen and respond. Children must respect those in authority and look to them for guidance and direction. There are some teachers, of course, who see these organizational roles as barriers to better relations with their students and seek to change them when they can. The humanists in education are attracted to cooperative learning and other approaches that move away from rote learning and busy work, which characterized teaching in the past. They seek to provide students with experiences that allow them to think about what they are doing and why they are doing it. As Tracy[7] points out, experienced teachers often desire to act in more friendly ways but have trouble dealing with the disciplinary demands inherent in the mass school. They find themselves presenting an impersonal image to students because of the demands of bureaucratic structures and the ever-present tracking system. Nevertheless, their style of teaching is also influenced by their personal values and beliefs and those of their students.

The reasons teachers give for choosing the teaching profession vary, but they usually include some idea of helping children and sharing knowledge with them. Many tend to see themselves as well-educated individuals with important expertise in scientific and academic disciplines. Secondary teachers, as noted, often see themselves in these ways, prefacing their remarks by citing their area of disciplinary expertise.[8] There is also some evidence that teaching provides intrinsic rewards that are related to the choice of the profession as a life-long pursuit. Ayers found that watching children grow and develop was one such intrinsic reward.[9] Salzberger-Wittenberg and Osborne have shown that many teachers choose the profession in spite of bad experiences as students in the public schools. They found that such respondents were more likely to see themselves as child advocates, seeking to redress some of the unsound educational practices they saw around them.[10]

In most instances, however, the pervasive image of the teacher is that of surrogate parent and nurturing person. This archetype has a long and rich tradition in Western society, recognizing the central role that teachers play in the care and development of maturing children. According to Sigmund Freud,[11] children have a propensity to identify with powerful adults to assure their own survival and social development. So important are these identifications that it seems virtually impossible for children to learn the language and culture of their group without attaching themselves firmly to their parents and their first teachers in school. Teachers become substitute parents for students because their work mirrors that of other nurturing adults the children have known before entering school. Much like parents, they redirect the thoughts and feelings of pupils, forcing them to re-invent themselves to adapt to new, institutional roles. Some youngsters who were well-thought-of at home may find themselves playing out the role of incompetent student in the classroom. Others who have not had a good home life may gain new status because of skills in reading or other academic pursuits. In every case, teachers and their evaluation methods decide these matters and assign new identities to students.

An important outcome of teacher self-images has been the role of teachers in motivating children and helping them pay attention to ideas and academic subjects the students might otherwise ignore.[12] This role enables teachers to introduce children to the wonders of science, mathematics, and the social world they live in. They encourage students to learn about the history of their country and events taking place in every part of the world.[13] A few teachers go a step further, seeing themselves as friends and companions, even when they must often direct and coerce the students to attend to lessons and homework assignments. Such teachers try to personalize their instruction, getting to know their students as well as possible.

SOCIETY'S PERCEPTIONS OF TEACHERS

Social scientists have seen teachers as the most important people in modern schools. Their right to decide in the classroom has been widely reported, and there have been numerous studies of their authority and power inside the school building. Initially, studies tended to look at schoolteachers as a profession or occupational type. Waller,[14] writing in the United States in the early 1930s, pointed to four factors that require attention when comparing teaching to other occupations in mass society. First, there were elements that determined the composition of the occupational category, focusing attention on the type of people who became schoolteachers. Where did these men and women come from, and why did they choose teaching? Second, there were roles, attitudes, and behaviors that schoolteachers had to display once they were on the job. How did they develop their commanding voices and stern expressions in classrooms? Third, there was the effect of the community's opinion on individual members. What were their reactions to the middling-to-low status and pay that accompanied employment in the public schools? And finally, there was the problem of traumatic, early experiences that were part of the occupational initiation into the everyday occurrences and routines in the workplace.

Waller described the way that other professions had attracted certain types of individuals, using social origins and personality types to reproduce themselves in each decade. Medicine, law, and the ministry tended to attract certain kinds of people.[15] This was not to say that each of these occupations was completely consistent in its members' characteristics, but there was sufficient evidence to justify an assumption that certain personality types were drawn to certain kinds of work.

Studies in Great Britain and France have shown that teaching draws most of its recruits from the lower-middle and working classes.[16] Since most of these individuals did similar work once they began their teaching careers, it was not surprising that they found themselves in typical situations that strengthened their occupational culture and world view. New teachers had to learn how to control and teach their first classes effectively, just as new lawyers had to work as apprentices, and new doctors had to work as interns and then residents for many years. These occupational situations demanded that newcomers respond in ways that were judged professional and appropriate to their new positions by coworkers and clients alike. New teachers, therefore, played the role of newcomer and apprentice, initially not knowing what they should do or say.[17] Once they had assimilated the world view and culture of the mass school, they could react to situations in ways that reinforced the views of coprofessionals who had preceded them; they could play out their new role as schoolteachers. Student teaching was an apprentice experience designed to show prospective teachers how to teach, how to control a discussion, how to control a student's body movements, and so on. In this way, newcomers began to experience classroom life through the eyes of veteran teachers. They learned to accept the understandings and values of their profession and apply them to everyday classroom life.

One of the significant problems facing the teaching profession is its intermediate-to-low status in commercial society. At first this image affected only those who taught in the lower grades or inner-city schools, but more recent studies have indicated that negative stereotypes affect the way all teachers are seen by parents, students, and other members of the communities in which they serve. During the post-World War II era, these stereotypes have been strengthened because of the occupational demands of teaching. Attempts to break away from these negative stereotypes have been seen as simply another confirmation of the community's original assumptions about the type of people who go into the profession.

An important strategy by which the profession maintains its hold on members is the common struggle to improve the working conditions, salary, and status of schoolteachers.[18] Another is the common culture that arises from certain initial experiences, which can be viewed as rites of passage for most new teachers. These experiences enable newcomers to see the need for overly corrective and directive teacher behavior within the context of managing large numbers of students. This need to control the bodily movement of students establishes teachers as the agent of outside social forces that cannot be ignored or pushed aside. One of the main reasons for the drone-like nature of many classroom activities is the need to conform to formal curricula, educational schedules, and timetables. Teachers are now surrogate parents who provide students with the direction they need to navigate life in urban schools. This role leads some teachers into certain types of personality adjustments, which help them rationalize their imposing behavior while confirming the stereotypes of the community.

Research on the occupational types that supposedly move toward the teaching profession has not yet reached a level of sophistication where it can tell us what kinds of people might seek out different occupational categories. The social influences that would drive young men and women to teach seem particularly obscure, even when one allows for the fact that the teaching profession is often chosen as a last resort. The salary and status have been and remain intermediate or low, presenting a deterrent to many who might otherwise seek membership in it. Economic security, career possibilities, and opportunities for advancement are all important indicators of desirability, but all are limited for teachers. The social standing of the profession says something about those who choose to teach. The nature of the work itself is another important consideration. Some naturally seek more routine work, while others desire control over individuals, even if those individuals are children. The obscurity of the position does not seem bothersome to some, but others have a need for more fulfillment and recognition. Some feel that the ability to express themselves is of great importance, outweighing factors such as pay and prestige. The limited amount of educational and professional training is certainly another factor, allowing those who have failed in more promising careers to fall back on education. This is part of the stereotype of teachers, affecting the way that others in the community see them and their work.[19]

These, then, are some considerations young men and women use when they are determining the attractiveness of professional careers. In an ideal scenario, potential members would weigh them against one another and make careful choices. But the choice to teach is rarely rational. It is most often a consequence of early identifications or nurturing parental attitudes. These factors are supported further by the desire to work with and help children and sometimes the need to supplement the salary of a spouse. As noted in Chapter Three, the social class of a family is also likely to be a strong indicator of professional preferences. The social and educational experiences of the individual, too, will have an effect and influence on the selection process.

The status of the teaching profession has been and remains intermediate or low in commercial society, and the more capable have sought careers and satisfaction elsewhere. Looking after the concerns of children can be an overwhelming chore, forcing teachers to develop directive personalities that may be dysfunctional in their relationships with adults. Moreover, the community places many restrictions on the types of personal conduct it considers acceptable for teachers, causing many teachers to leave the profession.[20] The stereotype of schoolteachers is one that includes the idea that they are people who shun the give-and-take of the commercial world and seek refuge in the sanctuaries of the schools.

Lortie[21] and Joyce[22] have provided further information about the kinds of people who choose to teach in the United States. In Waller's time and also today, most schoolteachers are white, native-born, English-speaking, and from lower-middle-class and working-class families. They are young, with more than two-thirds under the age of thirty.

THE TEACHER-PUPIL RELATIONSHIP

Despite the community's view of teachers, the most important relationships for teachers are those with students. It is in the classroom where they undertake to teach children and where the social conflict between teacher and student becomes most apparent. It is around this struggle for dominance that the teacher's personality is formed; teachers learn to press their case until they prevail. The relationship between teachers and students is a special case of dominance and submission,[23] a relationship that rests on acceptance of the teachers' authority and right to decide things in the learning environment.[24] A similar point is made by Cusick in his study of teacher-student relationships. He found that teachers, in spite of any ideological commitments they might have had to democratic ideas, were universally forced to establish norms and social controls to avert anarchy. All teachers learned that they had to enforce their demands. They had to teach students to enter the classroom in an appropriate way, seat themselves quietly, put away their clothing in rows and on numbered hooks, and so on. Teachers believed they must enforce rules of silence while taking attendance, giving assignments, writing on the blackboard, or speaking to the class. They must alert children to what they are studying. When the classroom period is over, they must initiate students into the kind of work they demand and alert them to the fact that the teacher is the sole and final arbiter of their deportment and schoolwork. It is a difficult and unpleasant role to control the bodily movements of students while forcing them to attend to a curriculum that is often unrelated to anything in their personal lives. Constant student submission is possible only because the authority of the teacher is limited to the classroom and school, and youngsters have an outside personal identity they can use to sustain them while playing out the role of the ignorant and often unworthy person in classroom situations. Some students withdraw or conform unthinkingly to the demands of the teacher, while a few resist for a time and then suffer the punishments and consequences for which mass schools are infamous. The necessary aggressiveness of teachers stems from the precariousness of their authority and the students' resistance to the overly corrective curriculum and constant regimentation.

The stereotype of teachers as inflexible and stubborn comes from the demand that they act as agents of the adult community, that they direct the lives of children inside the urban school. Teachers must present students with a personal front that is consistent and unyielding, at least in the beginning. They must not give in to children's demands or desires, even at the risk of alienation. They must impose their own definitions on situations and not compromise on matters of educational content or morality. At all times, they must maintain discipline and order. This is more easily done if teachers make constant demands on the energies and time of students, if they keep them busy.[25]

There are only a few moments in the school day when teachers can relax in front of students, when they can be more friendly and less the drill master. They must change behavior constantly, keeping in mind what they wish students to say and do. They must maintain control and dominance over pupils throughout the long school day. Students must be kept off balance, lest they begin to ask why they are learning certain materials and ignoring others. They must be kept on task, with little time given over to idleness.

All this has predictable and observable effects on the minds of teachers, engulfing them in a mass of routine.[26] Some teachers do not succumb to these bureaucratic demands of classroom life, but they are in the minority. Perhaps these effects have led to the view of teaching as a profession that tends to narrow the scope and world view of its members. Classroom life seems much more rigidly organized than the clinical settings and legal chambers of many other professions, imposing a structure of deportment and learning from one semester to the next that seems resistant to change. Teachers often find themselves teaching basic skills year after year, without ever going beyond the simple understandings these skills require. These routine and unchallenging situations give way to habits of social conduct that teachers use to adapt themselves to life in and out of classrooms.[27] Teachers are often limited in their choices for adapting to or changing the situation in which they work. When they begin to reform or liberalize classroom practices, teachers frequently come face-to-face with the normally hidden power structures that support, operate, and control state schools.[28] They become aware of the contradictions between what they thinks they are doing and the realities that prevail in the classroom. These unseen political and social forces have always imposed definitions on the learning situation as to what should be taught, how it should be taught, who should teach it, how it should be evaluated. Teachers may gain little value by developing an oppositional attitude and culture toward school authorities, as some did in the 1960s. Even if they decided to act, they would still have difficulty helping others recognize the damaging effects of competitiveness, individualism, emphasis on ignorance, and selection-obsessed education on teachers and the children they serve. In the act of trying to reform the overcrowded, urban classrooms, teachers come up against defenders of the status quo, who control the nature and meaning of teaching and learning, and jeopardize their own career and the future of their families.

Moreover, teaching often involves a psychological violation of the personal identities of students. The need to learn under penalty of failure places an enormous burden on students, as well as on their teachers. Many children learn in the early grades that because the language and the culture of the public school are different and difficult to understand, in the classroom they will be seen as the ignorant one, the one who needs constant correction and instruction. Children enter the urban school with presenting personalities that often emphasize their worthiness and abilities. Once in the classroom, however, their competency and self-worth are challenged and judged on the basis of their familiarity with and ability to manipulate scholarly language and curriculum. They are forced to assume the demeanor and world view of the dependent, submissive student. Teachers often maintain this type of relationship even when it obviously hinders learning in particular youngsters or classrooms.

THE FEMINIZATION OF THE TEACHING PROFESSION

The feminization of the teaching profession was first observed in the late 1890s, and educators began to consider it a problem as late as 1911. The phenomenon was most noticeable in the townships of America, where teaching was considered an occupation suitable for women to perform. Women of eighteen, nineteen, and twenty were encouraged to become teachers, especially in the Midwest and the South. Since many young women viewed teaching as a temporary stage before getting married and raising a family, teaching became a revolving-door profession instead of a career. A domestic ideology that supported these practices was used to further exploit them. It put forth the notion that women were less competitive than men and more likely to do things to please others. As potential mothers, they were naturally more nurturing than male teachers and would do a better job with students. By hiring young women, schools ensured that teaching remained a fringe profession, as it had always been. Many educators were fearful because they believed that women were perpetuating and even worsening the anti-intellectual biases of the nation.[29]

Female teachers, too, accepted these ideologies and the regimentation and control townspeople and school boards placed on them in schools and public places. Most were graduates of **normal schools**, and many had even less education than that. They were obedient and compliant young women, often from lower-middle-class families who accepted all conditions foisted upon them. This was a natural consequence of the traditional female roles in their families, where they were expected to be acquiescent and compliant in response to those in authority.[30]

At the turn of the century, teaching was a domestic occupation. Teachers carried a double domestic burden of caring for their students and their own children, yet many found it amenable to their needs. Parents would often bring children to school and ask teachers to keep an eye on them while doing their own work. Teachers seemed to draw this comparison between family life and school life without thinking too much about it, because the skills needed for both seemed so similar to them. They routinely met all the needs of their students, tending to them when they were ill or when they needed babysitting. Their home lives were not separate or apart from their work lives, and those who were unmarried often lived with the school superintendent's family during their first years on the job. School administrators, in turn, adopted paternalistic forms of leadership, seeing the young women as daughters needing guidance and protection. Many of these attitudes have persisted into our own times, but with one significant difference. Teachers are often unwilling to provide such paternalistic leaders with the rewards they expect. They are unwilling to react as dutiful children who owe their father loyalty and unquestioning allegiance.[31]

In the early 1900s, women teachers began an equal-rights campaign in New York that showed a growing political awareness as well as a desire to be treated more professionally. Their central demand was equal pay for equal work, a demand that still has not been met almost a hundred years later. Low status and a lack of respect were eating away at the self-esteem of schoolteachers, and the sex-segregated job market meant that women were being shunted into areas where wages were routinely suppressed. The justification for these practices was embedded in other ideological traditions. Women were thought to be mentally and physically inferior to men and overly emotional in their responses to life. Men used education as a career that allowed them to support their families while women taught in a more temporary way until they could begin families of their own. Also, many who saw the injustices of unequal pay for women were afraid that demands for equality would have the effect of lowering wages for men. Women were seen as a peril to education by many in leadership positions, who believed that women feminized the educational system and emasculated male students. This would lead to a weakening of national resolve and consequently a nation less able to defend itself. No one wondered why, if women were so bad for male students, they should be permitted to socialize their own children, many of whom were boys. Still the stereotypes went on. Women teachers were seen as subverting men's dominant role in the workplace and home. They were considered biologically and intellectually inferior and unsuited to serious careers outside the primary grades.[32]

Robert Reid argued that the need to professionalize teaching in America originated from excesses of urbanism and industrialism in the nineteenth century. The impersonal and ever-expanding modes of production and consumption de-emphasized work, simplifying it so that the skills of artisans and professionals were eliminated. But teachers, seeking security and status, began to identify with those professions that were given a privileged place in the otherwise harsh labor market. Teacher federations were formed in many large cities, seeking to increase revenues for education while improving the salaries of schoolteachers.[33]

These problems were made worse when race relations were introduced into the equation. African-American teachers in Buffalo, for example, had to struggle with significant levels of discrimination and bigotry during the late nineteenth and early twentieth centuries. They sometimes taught in all-white schools while their own children were forced to attend segregated schools elsewhere. This led them to demand an African-American school where their children could learn more about their own heritage and history. African-Americans were caught between the worst of two worlds: segregated schools kept them separate, identifiable, and, therefore, easily exploitable in the labor market, while Black Nationalism separated them further from normal interactions that might have broken down the amoral excesses of a cruel and unyielding segregation system.[34]

Ozga and Lawn, studying the class position of schoolteachers in Great Britain, came to the conclusion that professionalism was an ideology.[35] The struggle among occupations for the exalted status of professionalism lessens and often mutes class conflicts, since energies are directed toward achieving recognition rather than changing occupational relationships. Schoolteachers, as one example, were co-opted by this ideology, identifying themselves with an unchanging system that kept their wages and social status low. They did not see themselves as workers in an industrialized system but rather as people who were apart from it and striving for high-minded educational goals.

TEACHER ORGANIZATIONS

Any complete discussion of the teaching profession must consider the role of teachers' organizations in the struggle for professional status in the United States.[36] The National Education Association (NEA), the largest of these organizations, was founded in 1857 in response to the urging of educational leaders. The NEA was formed to protect the interests of educators and advance their professional status. It included the National Teachers Association, the National Association of School Superintendents, and the American Normal School Association. The newly formed NEA offered membership to all who were actively involved in the field of education. Superintendents, principals, and other educators were all members of the association, leading to a charge by more militant teachers that the organization was dominated by administrators.

Apart from providing its members with information about curriculum, pedagogy, and administrative matters, the NEA sponsored discussions about school reform. In 1922, the Research Division of the NEA was established, providing members with information and consultations. Another important development in the NEA was the formation of the National Commission on Teacher Education and Professional Students. Established in 1946, its declared purpose was the improvement of the caliber of professional students and teacher preparation programs.

The NEA was a large, national organization that was never able to galvanize teachers because its leadership limited its aims and objectives. For many years it insisted that a professional association should not be concerned with teacher salaries and working conditions. The great rival of the NEA was and is the American Federation of Teachers (AFT), which was affiliated from the outset with organized labor. Founded as a trade union, it excluded administrators and other non-teacher members from its ranks. The AFT was affiliated initially with the American Federation of Labor (AFL) and later with the Congress of Industrial Organizations (CIO).

The first teachers' unions were organized in the early 1900s. These fledgling associations were hindered by the general hostility and aversion to trade unionism that characterized the United States at this time. School boards dismissed teachers who joined unions, and membership was relatively low until the beginning of World War II. Since that time, membership in the AFT has risen sharply, although it has never approached the size of the NEA.

The success of the AFT as a teachers' union can be traced to working conditions that developed in large school districts in urban centers in the twentieth century.[37] From its earliest days every effort was made to improve the salaries and working conditions of teachers. Moreover, as early as the 1930s, some attention was paid to professional issues. The AFT was active in protecting the civil and professional rights of teachers, often neglecting professional matters that were important to the NEA. Membership in these organizations tended to mirror their different emphasis and goals. Primary teachers were much less likely to join the AFT than secondary teachers, and women were less likely to join than men. Teachers who were more dissatisfied with their work and status tended to join the union, while those who were more satisfied joined the NEA.

During the 1960s, however, both of these organizations became more militant as teachers began to struggle for higher wages and more professional working conditions. The NEA called a teachers' strike in Florida, and the AFT won a one-day strike in New York City in 1962, which will be discussed in the following section.

By 1968 the AFT was a permanent part of the educational power structure of the city. In a series of strikes that year it resisted attempts of community forces to take over the schools and destroy the tenure rights of teachers.[38]

TEACHER MILITANCY: A CASE HISTORY

The probability that the demands of teaching shape the personality and consciousness of educators was raised in the previous section. It was thought that their powerlessness in the school hierarchy, for example, may explain some of their dissatisfaction with working conditions. The consequences of poor pay and working conditions have also contributed to teacher burn-out and disillusionment, especially in the larger school districts of urban America. Rothstein has argued that the teachers' language and culture can also have a profound influence on the way they define what is happening to them in schools and classrooms. They may appear to be dutiful, obedient employees in the school building because that is what they have been taught is their proper role. It is only recently that attention has been turned to studies of what teachers feel about the meaningfulness of their work and their need to band together in professional associations and unions to protect themselves against the arbitrariness of school administrators.

These changes found a voice in the organization and strike for better working conditions and wages in New York City in 1962.[39] Teachers had been intimidated and overwhelmed by the conditions of their work and salaries that were below those paid to postal clerks. School administrators responded to their growing militancy with threats, warning teachers they would be penalized or fired for honoring picket lines and holding union meetings on school grounds. Teachers were confused and troubled by what was happening to them, many unaware of the history of their profession and the union movement in New York City. After many false starts, they participated in a citywide strike, picketing schools and demanding better conditions for themselves and the children they served. Since striking was against the law in the state of New York, this action became a test case over teachers' rights to organize and withhold their services just as industrial workers had done. Many teachers believed that the problems they were facing were caused by short-sighted politicians and administrators who had a deep disrespect for schoolteachers and their work. Teachers, through their union, were refusing to subsidize public schools by accepting the traditionally low wages paid by city and state officials. Their ideological demands of fairness and equity were coupled with others for smaller class sizes, more educational materials and texts, and special schools for children who were failing in regular classrooms. On the day of the strike, there was mass confusion, with 20,000 teachers showing up for work and an equal number walking picket lines. Some believed that striking was wrong and would hurt students. Others said that it was against the law for teachers to strike in the state and strikers should be fired and thrown in jail. Many strikers, on the other hand, felt things could not continue as they had in the past. They needed and deserved a living wage. Their students deserved smaller classes, more individual attention, new ways of teaching and learning, and new and more relevant materials. Strikers called those who were working *scabs* and felt they were too cowardly to take action on their own behalf and on behalf of their children. These strikers had set themselves in opposition to the state, the city, the Board of Education, and school administrators. They believed that deep changes were needed in the structure and practices of public schools. Their resolve was strengthened by the adamant position taken by school administrators, who threatened them with disciplinary action and dismissals if they joined the union, participated in the strike, or met together to discuss these matters. This represented a struggle between the old and the new over who would ultimately control and operate the schools. It was part of a series of conflicts that had taken place over time, not something that suddenly appeared on the horizon. Only now, teachers were forced into consciousness as younger members, who had benefitted from the G. I. Bill programs after World War II, entered the profession. Many of them were men and women who had to support families on a meager teacher's salary.

The changing relationships between teachers and administrators were a result of the heightened consciousness of teachers who came together to change the social and educational conditions in their schools. They were a consequence of the historical experiences of teachers, who had often faced their employers disunited and uncertain of their economic and educational needs and demands. Many teachers had come to accept a subservient position in schools once they were outside their classrooms, and these relationships and attitudes had a long and dishonorable history.

This strike occurred after World War II, when a large number of atypical college graduates entered the teaching profession. They forced a change of attitude and orientation among teachers, insisting on new approaches to the way schools were organized. Sociocultural theories of schooling will have to make sense of these historical events and the ways they changed teaching and learning. Teachers found that their work no longer gave them a sense of satisfaction and identity they could accept. Many had outside lives that were much more important to them than their school work. It was after school that they could be individuals with worth and value, that they could participate in the new counter-culture which was just beginning to take hold in the United States.

A FINAL NOTE

In this section, we will further discuss some of the implications of the lower-middle-class and working-class origins of the teaching profession. First among them is the inherent conservatism of the public schools and of the people who are hired to staff and operate them. Socialization, as Durkheim called it, or indoctrination as modern theorists refer to it, is the essential task of every educational system. We can no longer take seriously the notion of this task being carried out by families and urban schools that appear to be independent of one another and of economic and social institutions. We must specify the relations between educational and other systems in society, and we can do this by examining the structure of the socioeconomic relations that exist in the adult world.

Durkheim noted almost a century ago that urban schools represented one of the most conservative institutions in society.[40] So we can expect that teachers will subscribe to an ideology of conservatism that is functional for their work in the urban schools. Yet Durkheim misread the conservatism of these urban schools. He saw it as a mechanism for preserving the valued culture of the past and not as the place where conflict between the classes occurred. Perhaps this was because traditional society had just given way to industrialism, and the social movement still seemed more benign than it was to become in our time.

The stratification function of schooling, then, has led to a pedagogic conservatism that causes teachers to place the survival of their jobs and schools as their primary goal or mission. This leads them to become a mainstay in preserving the status quo. But it is not a contemporary status quo they seek to preserve. Rather it is one that existed thirty, forty, and more years ago, when they were young and students themselves. In this sense, schooling is a reactionary institution that finds itself unable to respond to the present or the future, no matter how evident the need may become.

To implement the conservative goals of the public school system, an ideology of merit has persisted from the pre-industrial past. The apprentice system has attempted to meet the demands of the institution so that its services will be performed by individuals who are interchangeable, who provide students with the same basic educational experiences. This assures the perpetuation of the profession, the urban schools, and the society. The tradition of competitiveness, which also has roots in antiquity, causes students to emulate their masters slavishly, learning to see and do things as they do. No wonder then that so little ever seems to change. No wonder, also, that examinations are so important and that status hierarchies are developed around these evaluation instruments. Such hierarchies have obvious importance in a bureaucratically organized society, one in which the legitimacy of power and authority is less clear than in tradition-based social systems.[41]

Of course, such tendencies are best understood in their historical contexts and in the functions they perform for the school system in mass society. The medieval university perpetuated itself through the use of the examination system, and that system has continued to function into the present. Teachers are educated, licensed, and inducted into the profession with rituals and ceremonies that incorporate them into the ranks and culture of their peers. And always they are examined and separated from those who have not taken the necessary tests. Academia has a tradition of hierarchy and authoritarianism that dates back to the Jesuits in France, and then into prehistory. Always, the need for self-perpetuation remained a central tendency for urban schools and social systems. The examination system was a central feature of the merit system and the ideology that supported that system. It sought to do away with the favoritism, nepotism, and biases that were part of tradition-based societies.

A second outcome of this merit system was the establishment of rigid class systems based on ability as well as social position. The abilities that were examined by these tests were in the language of the privileged. These tests demanded a knowledge of the culture and everyday life experiences of the privileged. Children born to lower-class families had to learn in classrooms what this language and world view was; those from more affluent families gained this knowledge in daily interaction with their parents. Everyone lived within this ethos of merit, and teachers who succeeded found themselves wedded to a system that allowed them to emerge from the lower groups in society into a status that was better than what their parents had known before them. They were predisposed to serve this ethical and social order without questioning it, since they themselves were recent beneficiaries. Objectively, teachers were condemned to serve in the lower and middle ranks of the educational order. But in reality many saw their new status as a step up the ladder.

These, then, were some of the consequences of the lower-middle-class and working-class origins of most teachers. They fit perfectly into the logic of the bureaucracy that operated the urban schools. Crozier,[42] writing in 1964, has provided us with a description and analysis of urban schools, emphasizing ritualistic practices and their usefulness in maintaining bureaucratic structures. Pedagogic practices that have not changed substantially for centuries allow teachers to keep their distance from students. The classroom tendencies toward routine and ritualistic beginnings are supported by the schools' curricula, manuals, and so forth, and have been part of urban schools in pre-industrial Asia and Europe. The distance between teachers and students has an important function. It reproduces the stratification of the bureaucratic system of organization, which in modern times is society-wide. It also reinforces the teacher as the person who knows, the person who is in authority. Teachers are also the ones who evaluate children, who tell them whether they can go on to better urban schools and occupational categories or whether they must learn to be satisfied with less. Teachers do not like to look at this role or at the physical and symbolic coercion they enforce in the urban schools. But the position of the teacher has within it elements of the soldier, the judge, the policeman, and the boss.

From this standpoint, the possibility for change seems indeterminate at best. The social origins of teachers have changed little over the years and are unlikely to change in the foreseeable future. This is simply another way of saying that bureaucracies, once they are established, seem to perpetuate themselves long after the reasons for their establishment have vanished.

⑥ Summary

There is a disparity between how teachers see themselves and the way in which the profession is perceived by much of American society. Teachers feel they belong to a profession and that they have responded to some calling that is different from and superior to that of the rest of commercial society. Commercial society tends to see teachers in a less flattering light. Teachers are most likely to come from the working and lower middle classes, to be white women who have graduated from a four-year college or university. Nevertheless, their status in American society is an indeterminate one, and the professional status of teaching has not brought with it the respect and monetary rewards associated with other professions. Perhaps this is because, since the end of the nineteenth century, teaching has been predominantly a feminized profession. This has kept the wages and status of the profession from equalling those of other professions such as medicine and law. The early teacher organizations included school administrators and focused mostly on the problems of teaching and learning in classrooms. However, in more recent times, such organizations have had to address the demands for better wages and working conditions. Teacher organizations have found themselves behaving in more militant and unionist ways, and teacher strikes have become more common.

⑥ Endnotes

1. Bowlby, J., *A Secure Base* (New York: Basic Books, 1988), chap. 1.

2. Ayers, W., "Teaching and the Web of Life: Professional Options and Folk Alternatives," *Holistic Education Review* 3, (1990): 19–21. See also Lortie, D. C., *Schoolteacher: A Sociological Study* (Chicago: University of Chicago Press, 1975).

3. Joseph, Pamela Bolotin, and Gail E. Burnaford, ed., *Images of Schoolteachers in Twentieth Century America: Paragons, Polarities, Complexities* (New York: St. Martin's Press, 1994), 40–44.

4. Bowlby, *A Secure Base*, 23–24.

5. Cusick, Philip A., *The Educational System: Its Nature and Logic* (New York: McGraw-Hill, 1992), 41–59.

6. Ibid., 211–212.

7. Tracy, D., *Plurality and Ambiguity: Hermeneutics, Religion and Hope* (New York: Harper & Row, 1987), 43–46.

8. Cusick, *The Educational System: Its Nature and Logic*, 45.

9. Ayers, "Teaching and the Web of Life," 46.

10. Salzberger-Wittenberg, Henry I., and X. Osborne, *The Emotional Experience of Learning and Teaching* (London: Routledge & Kegan, 1983), 57–59.

11. Gay, Peter, *Freud: A Life for Our Time* (New York: Anchor Books, Doubleday, 1989), 415.

12. Goodlad, John, *What Schools Are For* (Bloomington, Ind.: Phi Delta Kappa, 1979).

13. Dewey, John, "My Pedagogic Creed 9," in *Dewey on Education: Selections*, ed. M. S. Dworkin (New York: Teachers College Press, 1897), 19–42.

14. Waller, Willard, *The Sociology of Teaching* (New York: Russell & Russell, 1961), 375–409; Tropp, Andrew, *The School Teachers* (London: Heineman, 1957), 6–9; Banks, Olive, *The Sociology of Education* (New York: Schocken Books, 1976), 145–154. See also Cuban, Larry, *How Teachers Taught: Constancy and Change in American Classrooms 1890–1980*, (New York: Longman, 1984).

15. Waller, *The Sociology of Teaching*, 375–379.

16. Bamford, Theodore W., *The Rise of the Public Schools* (London: Nelson, 1967), 118–121; Thabault, Rene, "The Professional Training of Teachers in France," in *Year Book of Education*, (London: Evans Brothers, 1963), 242–245; Webb, Rodman B., and Robert R. Sherman, *Schooling and Society* (New York: Macmillan, 1989), 229–235.

17. Rothstein, Stanley W., "Orientations: First Impressions in an Urban Junior High School," in *Urban Education* 14, no. 1 (April 1979): 91–116; Gilligan, Carol, *In a Different Voice* (Cambridge: Harvard University Press, 1982), 151–174.

18. Cubberley, Ellwood P., *Public Education in the United States* (Cambridge: Houghton-Mifflin, 1934), 120–136; Edwards, Nathan, and Harold G. Richey, *The School in the American Social Order* (Boston: Houghton-Mifflin, 1963), 237–238.

19. Gallup, Alec M., and David L. Clark, "The 19th Annual Gallup Poll of the Public's Attitudes Toward Public Schools," in *Phi Delta Kappan* 69 (September, 1987): 26–27; Sergiovanni, Thomas J., and Robert J. Starratt, *Supervision: Human Perspectives* (New York: McGraw-Hill), 1988, 164–168, 306, 357.

20. Carter, Patricia, "The Social Status of Women Teachers in the Early Twentieth Century," in *The Teachers Voice: A Social History of Teaching in Twentieth Century America*, ed. Richard Altenbaugh (London: Falmer Press, 1992), 127–138.

21. Lortie, *Schoolteacher: A Sociological Study*, 81–87. See also Fuchs, Estelle, *Teachers Talk* (Garden City, N. Y.: Doubleday, 1969) for an excellent anthropological study of the first few months of life for new inner-city schoolteachers.

22. Joyce, Bruce, Richard H. Hersh, and Michael McKibbin, *The Structure of School Improvement* (New York: Longman, 1983), 23–35.

23. Simmel, Georg, *The Sociology of Georg Simmel*, trans. Kurt H. Wolff (New York: Free Press, 1950), 181–192.

24. Waller, *The Sociology of Teaching*, 9, 10, 196, 198–199; Darder, Antonia, *Culture and Power in the Classroom: A Critical Foundation for Bicultural Education* (Westport, Conn.: Bergin & Garvey, 1991), 70, 107–110.

25. Waller, *The Sociology of Teaching*, 12, 93–94, 251.

26. Ibid., 391–392. See also Altenbaugh, *The Teachers Voice*, for more on this subject.

27. Waller, *The Sociology of Teaching*, 203–205, 279–291; Becker, Howard S., "Social Class Variations in the Teacher-Pupil Relationship," *Journal of Educational Sociology* 25 (April, 1952): 451–465; Dreeben, Robert, *The Nature of Teaching* (Glenview, Ill.: Scott, Foresman, 1970), 40–81.

28. Nelson, Margaret K., "The Intersection of Home and Work: Rural Vermont Schoolteachers, 1915–1950," in *The Teachers Voice*, ed. Altenbaugh, 13–26. See also Boneparth, Ellen, ed., *Women, Power and Policy* (New York: Pergamon, 1982), 55–62.

29. Vaughn-Roberson, Courtney Ann, "Having a Purpose in Life: Western Women Teachers in the Twentieth Century," in *The Teachers Voice*, ed. Altenbaugh, 7–12.

30. Quantz, Richard A., "The Complex Vision of Female Teachers and the Failure of Unionization in the 1930s: An Oral History," in *The Teachers Voice*, ed. Altenbaugh, 127–138.

31. Carter, Patricia, "Becoming the 'New Women': The Equal Rights Campaigns of New York City Schoolteachers, 1900–1920," in *The Teachers Voice*, ed. Altenbaugh, 40–58.

32. Altenbaugh, *The Teachers Voice*, 122–124.

33. Chase, Phyllis McGruder, "African-American Teachers in Buffalo: The First One Hundred Years," in *The Teachers Voice*, ed. Altenbaugh, 65–77.

34. Altenbaugh, *The Teachers Voice*, 123, 159.

35. Banks, *The Sociology of Education*, 166–171. See also Herrick, Mary J., *The Chicago Schools: A Social and Political History* (Beverly Hills, Calif.: Sage).

36. Banks, *The Sociology of Education*, 171–172.

37. Nasaw, David, *Schooled to Order: A Social History of Public Schooling in the United States* (New York: Oxford University Press, 1979), 173–182; Becker, Howard S., "Schools and Systems of Social Status," in *Sociological Work*, ed. Howard S. Becker (Chicago: Aldine Publishing, 1970), 213–225; Newman, Laurence, "Teacher Competency in New York City Schools: Administrator and Supervisory Perceptions," in *Handbook of Schooling in Urban America* (Westport, Conn.: Greenwood Press, 1993), 131–144.

38. From my field notes.

39. From my field notes.

40. Durkheim, Emile, *Education and Sociology* (New York: Free Press, 1956), 28–29, 70–72, 121–122.

41. Ibid.

42. Crozier, M., *The Bureaucratic Phenomenon*, (Chicago: University of Chicago Press, 1964), chap. 7.

6

The School as a Bureaucracy

ⓖ   ⓖ   ⓖ   ⓖ   ⓖ   ⓖ   ⓖ   ⓖ   ⓖ   ⓖ   ⓖ   ⓖ

OBJECTIVES
In this chapter you will learn the answers to these questions:

ⓖ   *What are the general characteristics of bureaucracies?*

ⓖ   *Why have bureaucracies become the dominant form of organization*

ⓖ   *in mass society?*

ⓖ   *Why are the schools considered bureaucracies?*

ⓖ   *How is policy determined in educational bureaucracies?*

ⓖ   *What are the good and bad features of bureaucratic educational systems?*

ⓖ   *How does the bureaucratic organization of schools affect the people who work there?*

B
ureaucracy has prevailed in mass society because of the huge numbers of people that state and commercial organizations must serve. It is necessary, therefore, to have some understanding of bureaucracy's development in Western society and its role in present-day mass schools. All discussions of bureaucracy are related to Max Weber's treatment of the subject and the ideal type he used to define it. His typology assumed that bureaucracies would be distinguished by a graded system of authority; precise rules and regulations that defined what each person in the organization was to do and how to do it; the use of an objective attitude in the performance of official business; fairness in the management of lesser functionaries and clients; hiring of experts; the existence of career paths for employees; and a high degree of specialization.[1]

CAPITALISM AND THE RULE OF LAW

Weber emphasized the importance of legal domination as a distinguishing feature of modern capitalist systems. Within this new form of legal domination the state played a decisive role that was quite different from previous civilizations. In the feudal period, power and authority had been centered in the clergy and the nobility, the two estates that possessed landed wealth and the power to make war. Traditional forms of domination prevailed; the eldest sons of landowners, for example, inherited all the wealth and position of their fathers because "that was how things were always done".[2] Weber stressed the importance of religion during this period in European history yet he also described the ways in which the rite of baptism eroded the extended family structure of Christian communities. Every baptized person became the equal of every other in the eyes of God. When the transition from feudal to capitalist society began, the emerging bourgeoisie used these ideas of equality to establish their own centers of wealth and power. The modern state emerged from these new conditions and from the need of commercial communities to codify into written laws the basis of their power and authority.

For Weber, a **modern state** possessed the following characteristics: (1) administrative apparatuses that were formed by legislated laws; (2) a set of organizations that performed the official acts demanded by such legislative acts; (3) actual power and authority over all citizens and over most happenings that occurred within a certain bounded area; and (4) the right to use police and military action to force people to behave in accordance with legal prescriptions and statutes. From these powers came organizational structures that are now commonplace: bureaucracy, rules, regulations, and laws that provide government with the power to use coercion to achieve their aims and objectives, the same type of power given to corporations today. These governments that rule by the force of law represent legal order and authority as opposed to the tradition-based, authoritarian forms that typified the precapitalist period.[3]

Such legally based **authority** naturally required the consent of the governed. It differed from traditional and charismatic authority in significant ways. Traditional authority was based on the notion that things were done in a particular way because of religious beliefs or simply because they had always been done a certain way. It was passed on from one generation to the next without much thought or resistance. Charismatic authority was based on the people's belief in the message or character of an individual. This type of authority disappeared when people no longer believed in that individual. Legal-rational authority, on the other hand, exists once laws have been passed and citizens have accepted the right of government officials to govern according to those laws. Since laws can be altered or replaced with new laws, the system supposedly has a self-correcting mechanism. Weber also wrote of the "rightness of laws" and of the "natural law" that revolutionists had invoked in France and the United States. Natural law referred to those ideas and beliefs that were above and beyond the laws of the state, grounded in norms that owed their power to faith and religious convictions.

Weber identified this rule of law with democracy and representative government. Its application and most of its institutional structures were established as modern bureaucracies that based their power and authority on the legally constituted laws of the state.

BUREAUCRACY

Weber's discussion of bureaucracy indicates that he saw it as a rational response to the needs of an emerging commercial and scientific society. The ascendancy of the rule of law was reflected in the rules and regulations that governed how things would be done in modern organizations. The power of functionaries was determined by them as were the authority gradations that were developed in a pyramidal structure. Official business was to be conducted on a continuous basis rather than on the whim of a nobleman, as in the feudal period. It was to be conducted according to the rules within an administrative structure containing officials who (a) did certain types of work using impersonal methods and criteria; (b) had the authority to carry out their assigned functions; and (c) had sufficient means of compulsion even as such powers were strictly limited and defined by typical situations.

Every official's responsibility and authority was part of a pyramid of authority, with higher bureaucrats supervising lower ones. Weber pointed out that this new managerial class did not own the resources they used to carry out their functions, but they were accountable for how they used them.[4] Weber used the following criteria to characterize the position of typical **bureaucrats**: (1) They were personally free of all servitude to others and appointed to their position on the basis of a contract; (2) they exercised their authority in accordance with the impersonal rules, and their loyalty was enlisted on behalf of their faithful execution of official duties; (3) their appointment and placement in the organization depended on their technical qualifications; (4) administrative work was their full-time occupation; and (5) their work was rewarded by a regular salary and the prospects of advancement in a lifetime career.

Weber believed that bureaucracy was a big improvement over what had preceded it. It had the virtue of being uniformly reliable and predictable in the performance of duties. Individuals who needed funding or supplies knew where to turn for assistance, since the administration of such supplies was concentrated in particular offices. Full-time administration by men and women who were professionals did away with plutocracy while rejecting case-by-case decision-making that had characterized previous methods of management. The requirements and benefits of the system were now the same for all **functionaries** and clients.[5]

Weber saw bureaucracy as part of the triumph of rationalism and more scientific modes of thought and administration in Western society. It was established with the support of democratic movements that demanded equality before the law and guarantees against legal and administrative arbitrariness. These groups favored an impartial, impersonal exercise of administrative authority and control. They wished to see a government of laws and the recruitment of its officials from every stratum of society. Bureaucratic organizations thus had a levelling effect, subjecting people to the law and to officials who exercised authority under the law.

However, this increase in formal equality had unintended results, subverting democratic values in unforeseen ways. Policy, as we shall see in a later section of this chapter, was often made outside the bureaucratic structure for political reasons, and some people were able to skirt the rules and regulations because of their wealth and power. The recruitment of officials based on educational qualifications led to a privileged class, which was chosen on the basis of the ability to take and pass tests and accumulate diplomas. Bendix[6] points out that the expansion of individual freedom that initially accompanied the rise of bureaucracy is no longer part of the public consciousness. More recently, bureaucracies have come to be identified more with a diminution of individual freedom and with administrative practices that are unimaginative and **dysfunctional**. Research in this area has tended to follow the popular denunciations of bureaucracy, and topics such as judicial review, separation of powers, and administrative discretion have received much attention. Scholars[7] have emphasized the problems modern bureaucracy have posed, using Weber's ideal typology to guide their research. Bureaucracy has tended to act like a giant machine with officials performing their duty in routine, impersonal ways. As a result, procedures and policies are determined at the top of the organizational matrix and ideally outside the executive branch itself. These policies are relayed throughout the bureaucratic system and, at each step in the hierarchy, carried out in accordance with the intent of the original decisions of top functionaries. Consequently, the administrative power of bureaucratic agencies is their life-blood, but that power often lies outside their immediate awareness or jurisdiction.

Obviously, no organization conforms completely to Weber's ideal type. But most correspond to Weber's characterizations in at least two ways. First, bureaucracy in modern society is characterized by an increasing administrative autonomy that is based on the importance of technical skills. When a bureaucracy provides higher functionaries with knowledge, skills, and insights that make them irreplaceable, a managerial class that holds an administrative monopoly may be said to exist. Second, reform of modern governmental bureaucracies—schools, for instance—has become more and more difficult. A complete overhauling of such systems is very difficult, since it would involve the interruption of public services, such as education, that are considered essential to the community and nation. Modern governmental bureaucracy therefore holds a monopoly of power.

These specific traits, and the concentration of administrative power they point to, have led to denunciations of modern bureaucracies of all kinds. Leftists have often seen bureaucracy as an administrative apparatus that does the bidding of the ruling classes in commercial society. Rightists have seen it as the enemy of those who would like to return to more traditional forms of administration and education. Both groups agree that the recruitment system is part of the problem and that lifetime tenure is another, since it completely ties the functionary to the organization.

Restating the problem, we can say that bureaucracy has become increasingly more specialized and distant from the clients it serves. Administrative skills have become so important that no bureaucracy could function without a professionally trained staff. Weber was aware of this professionalization of modern bureaucracy. More and more functionaries were subjected to a code of professional ethics that prescribed when and how they would perform their assigned tasks. It emphasized how they were to execute their duties, with no concern for their personal sentiments or disagreements with the policies they were carrying out. As a consequence, the governmental bureaucracies of modern states are ever ready to serve whichever political party comes to power. Commercial interests depend on their professional neutrality and the reliability of the civil service.[8]

THE SCHOOL AS A BUREAUCRACY

Modern educational systems possess many characteristics of bureaucracies, as do other state and commercial enterprises. Schools have hired more expert and specialized personnel to serve the increasingly complex needs of its expanding organizational structures and varied student population.[9] A graded system, or hierarchy, of authority exists in schools, with the chain of command clearly laid out for teachers, administrators and board members. Standardized texts and examinations, developmental lesson plans, schedules, timetables, salary schedules, and lifelong careers indicate that there is a good deal of standardization, even though teachers still have some latitude in their classroom work with students. Nevertheless, teachers are expected to apply the rules and regulations of the organization without favoritism and use objective criteria to grade and promote students.

Some reasons for the development of bureaucracy in education deal with social forces outside the system. The sheer increase in the number of people living on the planet is one significant factor. Also, the spread of commerce and industry has brought inevitable urbanization and population mobility. The United States, for example, continues to assimilate millions of immigrants from other countries and cultures, much as it did in the eighteenth and early nineteenth centuries. Moreover, the communication explosion has created new forms of knowledge and technology and a need for a more educated, competitive work force. The emergence of the educational equality movement has given birth to new demands for standardization of the educational curricula and programs.[10]

Schools have strengthened their bureaucratic tendencies by professionalizing teaching and administration requirements. Educational policymakers have tied hiring and promotion policies to examinations, academic requirements, and state licensing procedures. At the same time, schools offer teachers and administrators lifetime security through the tenure system as well as career opportunities for those ambitious enough to embark on further graduate work. Experts have come to control business administration, academic administration, special education, teacher mentoring, attendance, discipline, and counseling, developing a separate language known only to insiders.

These attempts to rationalize and standardize the educational process create a conflict with the instructional activities of teachers in classrooms. Teachers see themselves as professional mentors and guides for the children in their classroom. These students are often quite different, however, from those children who are used as the norm to develop the school's mandated goals and curriculum. For example, the reading requirements of the educational bureaucracy sometimes conflict with the empirical realities of classrooms in which students are woefully unprepared to do grade level work. Teachers seek to provide such youngsters with individual attention in conformance with their professional training in universities. However, the bureaucratic standards of school organizations consider such children as failures and track them accordingly. Another conflict exists between the administrative structure of bureaucratic schools and the values of the teaching profession, which desires more control over what happens in classrooms and schools. Consequently, the pressures on educational systems exist inside and outside their organizations. These pressures often create conflicts between teachers and administrators, leading them to work against one another as well as against outside critics. It is necessary, therefore, to examine the school as a bureaucracy to uncover the effects of these conflicts on educators and students.

Studies have long argued that the clashes between bureaucratic and professional perspectives and values are inevitable in mass institutions. Bureaucrats find justification in their work by referring to an individual's standing in the organizational pyramid and deferring to that person accordingly.[11] They believe they should obey those in higher positions and make decisions on the basis of written rules and regulations. Professionals, on the other hand, value competence and expert knowledge, and they make decisions on a case-by-case basis. As a result, bureaucrats are loyal to superiors and to the organization itself, while professionals are loyal to their professional standards. Functionaries heed the commands of their superiors in the hierarchy and work according to their directions, while professionals do their work in accordance with their training and insights in particular situations. Role conflict, then, is one consequence of the professionalization of the teaching staff and their employment in huge bureaucracies. Some have questioned whether these conflicts exist in actual practice.[12] They suggest that the two systems are complementary in nature and that the actions of teachers often reflect both points of view. Others have found that teachers have little influence in the decision-making processes of educational systems. Decisions are actually made by higher administrators in the district or state and by boards of education.[13] When teachers are asked to participate, their input is usually limited to making comments on existing policies, giving advice, or discussing how an existing policy can best be carried out.

A number of studies have also explored the extent to which schools can be thought of as **total institutions**, in Goffman's sense of the term. Webb and Sherman[14], seeking to apply the characteristics of total institutions to schools, found that educational systems provided a place where adults and youngsters worked together in enclosed, formally administered institutional settings. Schoolwork occurred under the direction of a managerial group, and activities were scheduled and carried out in uniform ways. Schools, like total institutions, had severe rules and regulations that governed the everyday life inside the building. Students, like inmates, had few rights and privileges there. Other characteristics of total institutions are that membership in these type of institutions was forced and the staff had little choice in admitting persons into the institution. Roles were defined by agencies outside the institution itself, which was supported by taxes. Such organizations were united in their desire to correct deviant behavior and alter the character and behavior of clients. Webb and Sherman admitted that the fit is not exact when schools are described as total institutions. First, not all the activities of a student's life happen within the school building. Students are in school for part of the day and are free to assume their personal lives once the school day is over. Schools use cumulative files to monitor the progress of students while they are in school, but students spend less time in school than elsewhere. Second, total institutions usually serve adults, while most schools educate the young. Webb and Sherman wrote that these two groups may react differently to humiliating experiences, but they presented no evidence to support this presumption.

Undoubtedly there are similarities between total institutions and educational systems. Both have their own rules and regulations, which differ from those governing life in general society. As with inmates in total institutions, students do lose many of their rights to determine when they will move, when they will talk, what they will do, when they will do it, and so on. As in total institutions, teachers often find themselves enforcing coercive rule structures. Students must attend school because the law says they must, and they often cannot choose the school they attend. They are almost always assigned to teachers on an arbitrary basis. Similarly, teachers have little to say about who will be in their classes.

Another aspect of bureaucracy in education is that the functions of schools are often decided by people who are not professional educators. Policies are determined by boards of education and state legislatures and may often reflect the attitudes of their members about the job that schools are doing. State agencies often determine accountability measurements, justifying their activities by noting their role in funding the school system. They insist on introducing new programs and expanding the role of schools as new social problems arise. Mass schools are involved in the moral persuasion or education of children, as Durkheim observed more than a century ago.[15] In more stable societies, this has meant inculcating children with a common language and culture steeped in traditional custom and lore. In more diverse or changing social systems, however, we have seen schools given the task of indoctrinating youth so that new political ideas could triumph over older ones. Lutz and Iannaccone[16] described the local control of schools as giving more power to parents and community groups and less to the professional bureaucracy. School boards controlled jobs and resources and what would and would not be taught in classrooms. They distributed these resources in accordance with their own values to those who were their friends and commercial associates. Adler[17] studied the ways in which members of the religious right movement in California tried to take over the educational bureaucracy to get curricular changes they believed in. Their strategies included getting elected to school boards and working with other administrators, politicians, and business people "to assure a more sensitive presentation by teachers" of certain materials and ideas. In a second example, Adler argued that local school boards had a great deal of freedom to implement state policies in ways that suited their own interests. The Oakland school board, for example, chose textbooks that presented a "more transformational view of history."

A more extreme case of using educational systems for political purposes can be found in Nazi Germany. German schools were given the assignment of preparing youth for militarism and war with the state's enemies while imbuing them with extreme sentiments of patriotism. Education was used to regiment and militarize the youth in the earliest grades to lessen dissent when the government acted in dictatorial ways. Nazi Germany openly indoctrinated its youth in the values and moral understandings of the warrior nation. Extreme levels of social integration were achieved at the expense of those outside the nationalistic group, and this was done in a society that was thoroughly bureaucratized from top to bottom. Brady has suggested that this was necessary for the total integration of the Nazi party.[18] Adolf Hitler incited youth under the banner of "Sword and Plough for Freedom and Honour." In his personal journal, the *Nationalsozialistische Monatschefte*, he called the youth of the nation to arms: "The National Socialist people's youth affirms battle and submits to the carrying of arms as the obvious foundations of all people's labour. They hope for the day in which the weapons will be placed in their hands which are associated with the full consciousness of manhood."[19] Manuals were prepared for all teachers and passed down through the bureaucratic chain of command. Physical exercises, games, and calisthenics were highly valued, and performance standards were rigidly enforced. Another important part of these teacher guides was directed toward military activities. Sports was to provide the transition. The German word **Wettkampf** was used repeatedly. It called upon the youth to struggle, fight, and prepare for the inevitable military combat that would give meaning to their lives. All sports led finally to Wettkampf, and military training began with guns or shooting at an early age. The discipline imposed by sports was to provide youngsters with the physical strength and stamina they would need to face the demands of war. According to one entry of a teacher's manual, "Shooting sport demands the greatest concentration and control of all physical and spiritual powers."[20] Such training provided youth with the cold-bloodedness and calm they would need to shoot other people, giving them added confidence in themselves and a spirit of comradeship with other youngsters. All instructions were passed down from the elaborate Ministry of Education, the bureaucracy that administered education throughout the nation.

BUREAUCRATIC STRUCTURES AND PERSONAL NEEDS

Fuchs[21] has described the clashes that often occur when teachers begin to teach for the first time. Faced with the need to maintain order and control in overcrowded classrooms, they find themselves repressing certain ideas and attitudes they have carried with them since childhood. They must revise or reject certain prebureaucratic views as they assume the role of responsible adult in the classroom. Personal roles from the past that clash with the new position and responsibilities will have to be set aside or abandoned entirely as they strive to take a place on the professional staff of the school.

New teachers often find themselves swamped by the demands of classroom life, with administrators and longtime teachers forcing them to see the school through different eyes. They feel forced to act in ways that differ significantly from the way they acted before assuming their new job. When these things happen, the bureaucratic structure of the school may be seen as changing the personalities of staff members. Teachers are now seen as state employees who direct and manage the daily affairs of children. Their chances of succeeding depend on their ability to maintain control in the classroom and develop good relations with school administrators.

New teachers must be sure to hide certain parts of their personality that might conflict with a desire to succeed in the new endeavor. To gain the confidence and support of supervisors, they must sometimes hide their real attitudes and preferences, their true likes and dislikes. Bureaucrats place a high value on surface harmony and teamwork, urging employees "to go along to get along." New teachers often develop a personality aimed at pleasing other teachers, parents, and administrators, or they may fail to retain their position. In a bureaucratic world, where most Americans become employees in large corporations or government institutions, teachers must learn to sell themselves and their amicability just like other workers in less sheltered occupations. This pressures teachers to make themselves amiable and bland toward those who are above them while remaining impositional and overbearing toward the students they serve. Repressing their real likes and dislikes forces teachers to fractionate their personalities, causing them to feel a certain sense of powerlessness in their work.[22]

Another basis for a feeling of powerlessness in teachers emanates from the increasingly segmented and specialized nature of educational work. As teachers, resource specialists, program specialists, psychologists, and administrators try to develop effective individualized programs for special education students, for example, teachers begin to lose sight of the tasks they are trying to perform in their classrooms. They may feel that students are being dumped into their classrooms, having a negative effect on other children's progress and development. They may not understand the reasons behind these practices partly because they are isolated for most of the day in enclosed classrooms. Many teachers are unaware of the purposes of the new full inclusion programs that are being put into practice in many states, and they are frustrated by the lack of communication with their administrators.

One response to these feelings of meaninglessness and powerlessness on the job is increased authoritarianism. Feeling little or no power to influence the decisions of their superiors, teachers may redirect their resentment toward those below them in the hierarchy. As a result, they may punish students when they perform in an inadequate way in the classroom. They may humiliate students who need their help, forgetting that, in the classroom world, they are the ones who possess considerable power. Some teachers who regard themselves as an unimportant part of the school organization may become rigid and overbearing when they meet with parents or other members of the community. Because they feel so powerless to influence things outside their classrooms, they may remind these outsiders that they are the professionals who know what is best for the children.

Many teachers who rule their classrooms with an iron hand behave in a timid and fawning way to those who outrank them in the school's organization. Such behavior is typically bureaucratic, because it assumes that all people in authority should be respected and that the respect should stem from their position in the organization. In the presence of administrators, for example, teachers are often eager to conform to their suggestions and to please.[23]

Several studies indicate that communication patterns in schools are often one-sided. In a steady flow of messages from above, memos, reports, orders, instructions, and data are placed in teachers' mailboxes, while very little information flows the other way. Such communication is often stifled by the submissiveness of teachers behaving as bureaucrats, thus depriving administrators of information they need to do their work effectively. Teachers are supposed to be the agent of the state and school administration, reporting problems that demand attention. They are supposed to keep their superiors up-to-date to prevent errors based on misinformation or ignorance of changing situations. In an ideal setting, dedicated teaching professionals would openly differ with superiors, explaining why they disagree with certain policies. In reality, teachers are often too afraid or too alienated from school administrators to provide this kind of helpful feedback. Many teachers simply remain quiet when supervisors reveal their plans, saving their most telling criticisms for the teachers' lounge.

School administrators are unable to perform their tasks when they are denied accurate information from classroom teachers. They are deprived of the knowledge they need to make intelligent decisions. For this reason, enlightened administrators may try to avoid sycophantic teachers, knowing such teachers may try to isolate them from what is happening in their schools. Some schools have initiated ongoing feedback sessions to eliminate attitudes and behaviors that stifle two-way communications between teachers and administrators.

The effect of the school's bureaucratic structure on students is even more dramatic than its effect on teachers and administrators. It usually conflicts with their previous definitions of themselves. In particular, there is a separation between what students do as individuals and how they must act once they begin to play out the role of the incompetent student. Goffman has referred to the **looping effect** in describing how individuals are deprived of their ability to defend themselves against assaults on their self-concepts.[24] Students are unable to defend themselves by making themselves absent because of strong truancy laws. Although the situations they must respond to in the schooling situation vary greatly, deference is a constant factor in all of them. In other situations, children are allowed certain face-saving devices when they are confronted with unpleasant circumstances. In school, these same devices—acting sullen, failing to be properly deferential, cursing under one's breath, making faces—are all punishable offenses. When children use these devices in the classroom, teachers often penalize them without taking into account the humiliating experiences that engendered their actions. Outside the school, the roles that youngsters play are kept reasonably separate from one another. In schools, teachers often presume students are guilty because of their reputation rather than their actions.

Other assaults on the self of students occur in the constant regimentation and control that typifies some classrooms. Students must exhibit the proper and preferred behavior at every moment of the school day while being forced to work and learn at the pace set by the teacher. Children's daily life in school is subjected to a constant scrutiny by staff members. Students must show evidence of their right to be present in certain parts of the building whenever teachers require it. Any member of the teaching staff has the right to challenge any student anywhere in the school building. In the classroom, teachers constantly monitor the dress, behavior, manners, and work habits of students while providing them with an overly corrective instructional experience. Students are required to perform the same tasks as others in their ability grouping and to do it in the assigned manner. As we will show in Chapter 10, students must be willing to regress to infantile behavior if they wish to stay out of trouble. They must not talk. They must not move without permission. They must move only when told to do so. They may not leave the room without permission. They must enter the room in a prescribed way, sitting in their seats and waiting to hang up their coats in an orderly manner. They must sit quietly in their seats.

Another dramatic effect of the system is known as *tracking,* in which students are labelled and forced into course work leading to different levels of learning. In recent years there has been some disagreement over ability grouping that is routinely used by traditional schools. On the whole, teachers have preferred this method because it allowed them to teach children of like ability, and brighter students were not held back by slower ones. This grouping system has been part of an early identification effort and is a form of social selection. As a result, these practices have tended to stigmatize students in the slower groups since they often find it very difficult to get out of such groups. Rothstein found that making children repeat kindergarten was a common practice in southern California and in New York, and that teachers often complained about children from lower-class families who "did not know their colors, their numbers, or that they had a last name!"[25] One reason for these practices was the anxiety of parents and of schools competing with other schools for academic excellence. Teachers have long favored programs for gifted children, saying that abler students should not be penalized by learning in comprehensive schools and classrooms.

Mass schools have often been found to be impersonal, unfriendly places where teachers and students struggle to perform their educational tasks. Some evidence of this is provided in ethnographic studies of schools in St. Louis and

New York in the 1970s and 1980s.[26] In these studies of schools in inner-city districts over several years, the results indicated that children of minority and poor families were not receiving an effective education. For example, pupils entering junior high school in the South Bronx were more likely to be severely retarded in reading even though their official records showed they were reading on grade level. The reasons for this are complex and varied, but there appears to be a link to the privations of poverty and the language and culture children learn from their parents and friends.

On the other hand, a study of a reading clinic in southern California found that the reading ability of students could be improved when significant educational support systems were put in place.[27] Not only did test scores improve, but teachers began to act more authoritatively in the search for new ways of teaching their students. The study also found a clear correlation between the improved relationships between teachers and students and their ability to perform academic tasks more efficiently. Teachers were given time to discuss their problems with the center's director once a week and then meet in group sessions to help one another. In one such session, the lead teacher admitted she did not know how to teach individualized reading even though the center had been funded to do just that. She was still teaching reading in groups. After some discussion, this teacher decided to embark on a staff-development program of her own. She was joined in this effort by other teachers and within a matter of months the staff was using the methods of individualized reading to improve their instructional services. Although the number of children the reading center had to accommodate was very large, this proved to be no barrier to the staff's determined effort to personalize their relationships with their students.

Nevertheless, there have been continuing problems of low student achievement on standardized test scores, and teachers have cited class size as one reason for the students' poor showing. There is little doubt that teachers prefer small classes and that large classes are one of their most constant complaints. But studies in England[28] in the post-World War II period showed that there was little relationship between class size and the long-term achievements of students. Taking into account the size of the schools studied, the length of schooling, the class size, and parental concern, the studies found no indication of higher student academic achievement in smaller as opposed to larger classes. Banks argued that these results may be the consequence of the way teachers teach and their unwillingness or inability to do their work differently, even when class sizes are reduced.[29]

The funding of schools can be considered part of its organizational structure, because it affects the conditions under which administrators, teachers, and students do their work. Research in the United States raised some questions about this several decades ago, citing a lack of improved educational performance in schools where funding had been increased. Coleman's study[30] sought to learn whether equal educational opportunity was available to all in

American schools. He found that the academic achievement of students in one school district did not show much variation from achievement in other school districts that were spending less money per pupil or had better library and other facilities. Educators and reformers were outraged. They pointed to the large number of subjects who failed to respond to the study's queries. They also complained that the calculation of per-student outlay of money was done on a district-wide basis rather than for individual schools in each district. Other studies have come to different conclusions.[31] Banks cites several studies that show a strong relationship between per-pupil expenditures and high scores on achievement tests. In still another study, the establishment of extra school services was shown to increase the distinction between students. Two examples were special education placement and programs for gifted children. Such studies seem to support another of Coleman's findings that there was more difference in academic accomplishment inside individual schools than between them.

⑥ Summary

In this chapter we described a bureaucracy as a large organization in which face-to-face engagements between employees are often impossible. It has its roots in the legal-rational authority that developed with the triumph of industrialism and the commercial age. It has become the dominant form of organization because it allows business and citizenry of modern states to conduct commerce and trade on more reliable and equitable lines. Schools have many of the characteristics of bureaucracies. Policy is decided from the top down, and teachers and students seldom have much to say about where they will teach and learn or under what conditions they will work together. By using a historical perspective, we have shown that bureaucracy, with all its faults, is an effective and fair way to administer corporate and governmental agencies. Unfortunately, bureaucracy in education often has adverse, though sometimes unintended, effects on relationships between teachers and students.

⑥ Projects

1. Make diagrams of your school and school district organization to show hierarchy, division of labor, organizational roles, and career paths of educators. How do they compare to Weber's typology of bureaucracy?

2. Write a short paper showing how state bureaucracies work together to fund the public schools in your area.

3. Write a short paper giving examples of how your school acts like a bureaucracy and how it does not.

4. How does bureaucracy affect the way you work with children or teachers in your school?

⑥ *Endnotes*

1. Banks, Olive, *The Sociology of Education* (New York: Schocken Books, 1976), 191.

2. Bendix, Reinhard, *Max Weber: An Intellectual Portrait* (New York: Anchor Books, Doubleday, 1962), 294–295; Weber, Max, *Theory of Social and Economic Organization*, trans. A. M. Henderson and Talcott Parsons (New York: Oxford, 1947), 332–335.

3. Bendix, *Max Weber: An Intellectual Portrait*, 424; Weber, Max, "Bureaucracy," in *From Max Weber*, ed. Hans Gerth and C. Wright Mills (New York: Oxford, 1946), 212–213.

4. Bensman, Joseph, and Bernard Rosenberg, "The Meaning of Work in Bureaucratic Society," in *Identity and Anxiety: Survival of the Person in Mass Society* (Glencoe, Ill.: The Free Press, 1962), 181–197; Bendix, Reinhard, "Bureaucracy and the Problem of Power," in *Reader in Bureaucracy*, ed. Robert Merton, Asa Gray, B. Hockey, and H. Selvin, (New York: Free Press, 1967).

5. Bendix, *Max Weber: An Intellectual Portrait*, 427–428.

6. Bendix, *Reader in Bureaucracy*, 114–115.

7. Ibid., 117–118.

8. Ibid., 128–130.

9. Sergiovanni, Thomas J., and Robert J. Starratt, *Supervision: Human Perspectives* (New York: McGraw Hill, 1988), 57–60.

10. Clignet, Robert, *Liberty and Equality in the Educational Process* (New York: Wiley, 1974), 183.

11. Corwin, Ronald, *A Sociology of Education* (New York: Appleton-Century-Crofts, 1965), 275; Boyer, Ernest, *High School: A Report on Secondary Education in America* (New York: Harper & Row, 1983).

12. Banks, *The Sociology of Education*, 193–194.

13. Cusick, Philip, *The Educational System: Its Nature and Logic* (New York: McGraw-Hill, 1992), 70–92.

14. Webb, Rodman B., and Robert R. Sherman, *Schooling and Society* (New York: Macmillan, 1989), 299–306.

15. Durkheim, Emile, *Education and Sociology* (Glencoe, Ill.: Free Press, 1956), 71–72.

16. Lutz, Frank W., and Laurence Iannaccone, "Policymakers and Politics in Urban Education," in *Handbook of Schooling in Urban America*, ed. Stanley W. Rothstein, (Westport, Conn.: Greenwood Press, 1993), 75–76.

17. Adler, Louise, and Kip Tellez, "Curriculum Politics in Urban Schooling," in *Handbook of Schooling in Urban America*, ed. Rothstein, 105–107.

18. Brady, Robert A., *The Spirit and Structure of German Fascism* (London: Victor Gollancz, 1937), 177–178.

19. Ibid., 178.

20. Ibid., 178–179.

21. Fuchs, Estelle, *Teachers Talk* (Garden City, N. Y.: Doubleday, 1969).

22. Rothstein, Stanley W., *The Voice of the Other: Language as Illusion in the Formation of the Self* (Westport, Conn.: Praeger, 1993), chap. 6.

23. Abbott, Max G., "Hierarchical Impediments to Innovation in Educational Organizations," in *Change Perspectives in Educational Administration*, ed. Max G. Abbott and John Lovell (Auburn, Ala.: Auburn University School of Education, 1965), 43–45.

24. Goffman, Erving, *Asylums* (New York: Doubleday, 1961), 35–37.

25. From my notebook of teacher interviews in Irvine, California, 1980.

26. Rist, Ray C., *The Urban School: A Factory for Failure* (Cambridge, Mass.: The MIT Press, 1973), 189–190, 237–238; Rothstein, Stanley W., "Orientations: First Impressions in an Urban Junior High School," *Urban Education* 14, no. 1 (April, 1979), 91–116.

27. Rothstein, Stanley W., "High Trust Climates: Training the New Administrator in Feeling Expression and Inquiry Skills," *Education and Urban Society* IX, no. 1 (November, 1976), 81–102.

28. Hodgson, George, "Inequality: Do Schools Make a Difference?" in *Equal Opportunity in Education*, ed. H. Silver (London: Methuen, 1973).

29. Banks, *The Sociology of Education*, 208–209.

30. Coleman, James S., et. al., *Equality of Educational Opportunity* (Washington, D.C.: Department of Health, Education and Welfare, U.S. Office of Education OE 38001, 1966).

31. Banks, *The Sociology of Education*, 218–219.

7

The Social Relations of Classroom Life

ⓖ   ⓖ   ⓖ   ⓖ   ⓖ   ⓖ   ⓖ   ⓖ   ⓖ   ⓖ   ⓖ   ⓖ

OBJECTIVES

In this chapter you will learn the answers to these questions:

ⓖ   *Why is the teacher the most important person in the classroom situation?*

ⓖ   *How do students get their first impressions about their school?*

ⓖ   *What are the basic functions of classroom life?*

ⓖ   *Why is there a separation between students and their teachers?*

ⓖ   *How do the physical conditions of classrooms influence teaching practices?*

ⓖ   *What are classrooms like in many inner-city schools?*

ⓖ   *What are the unchanging elements of classroom life?*

ⓖ   *How do teacher attitudes affect the success or failure of students?*

Many writers have studied the idea that teacher attitudes influence the educational achievements of students. One point of view argues that the cultural backgrounds of teachers sometimes clash with those of students, especially when the students come from diverse and lower-income families.[1] The nature and consequences of tracking have also been explored and related to the expectations teachers have for students of varying abilities.[2] Some writers have found that beliefs about innate differences in intelligence between the races and sexes deeply influence the way students are taught.[3] These findings confirmed earlier studies that found the relationship between teachers and students to be the most important one in the learning situation.[4] Nevertheless, it is only in the last few decades that ethnographic studies have tried to describe the actual conditions that govern classroom life once the school day begins. Their findings agree on one point: the teacher is the person who is the most important person once the classwork begins, the person without whom the schooling situation cannot begin.[5] The teacher directs the children in their classwork, deriving authority from the laws and customs of the educational system and community. Teachers usually have their desk in the front of the room, and they demand that all eyes must be focused on them once they begin to speak. Their words inform students about what they will be doing and why their work together is important. They orient the students to proper forms of behavior and work, choosing language they will understand.[6]

In the years before they attend school, children are influenced by what their parents and friends tell them about school life. They use such information to guide them during their first moments in the classroom.[7] Echoing in their ears are the words of parents, older siblings, and friends, who gave them their first impressions about what school life would be like. Once they enter school and meet the teacher, these ideas move from an imaginary state to a more concrete one. The teacher now appears as the important person and authority in the classroom, the adult who is in charge of their educational well-being.

The social world of the classroom exists only in the mind of the student at first. Once students enter the classroom, however, they quickly learn what they are to do and when they must do it.[8] They learn that they are students, with a role that has significance for them as long as they are in school. Through a common speech and culture, teachers and students are able to construct a world that is supported by the customs and traditions of their community. Each has certain rights and privileges in the classroom; each has certain responsibilities they must meet. Teachers are expected to present a curriculum that has been certified by educational authorities and other important persons in the larger culture. Teachers have some degree of freedom in teaching such materials, but they cannot teach anything that happens to suit their fancy. They are products of their educational training and subculture and usually perform their work within an approved range of theory and practice.

A second function that teachers must fulfill is to encourage students to adopt certain attitudes and behaviors that will make them more cooperative in schools and later in society. This includes preparing youngsters for their later experiences in institutions of higher learning and the workplace. Indirectly, they must prepare students during their early and adolescent years for adult life while keeping them in a subordinate and economically dependent condition and denying them entrance to an already overcrowded labor market. Their authority to decide things in the classroom is seen as reasonable by most parents and students, who believe that the teachers' efforts will help students grow and develop into upright citizens and workers.

Another idea that teachers must put forward is the notion that education should be the sole function of public schools. This supports the teaching profession's contentions that experts and professionals are needed and that appropriate training is imperative for schooling to accomplish its social and educational goals. Some writers have focused on the types of leadership teachers use in classroom situations and the patterns of dominance and submission that develop there.[9] They expect students to listen and respond to their words, since they are the ones who can help children learn effectively. Teachers, in turn, are expected to set limits for students and provide an orderly and safe learning environment. These features of classroom life are nearly universal and seldom vary. Many teachers, for example, demand a silence rule, which can best be understood in terms of the school's need to protect its members from disorder and provide them with continuous direction. Teachers approve of the silence rule because it makes it easier for them to do their work in over-crowded schools and classrooms. Their words may seem overly corrective to some but are necessary if schoolwork is to be carried out in the mass school. Students must be taught to accept these social relations of classroom life without question or debate and to see their work with teachers as serious work that they must not neglect. Certain qualities are valued in classroom life and in commercial society. Obedience, punctuality, and compliance are important attitudes and behaviors that are considered necessary in both settings.

The fact that teachers enjoy complete autonomy within the classroom affects the way they interact with students. Since control can easily be lost, teachers often seem anxious and attentive to any breach in discipline once they begin their work with students.[10] This leads to a separation between teachers and pupils that is not easily bridged. Teachers may project their own disappointments or triumphs of the past on their students, making assumptions about how children are responding to their demands of the moment. Nevertheless, at times they will have to talk constantly to make themselves understood as they urge students to attend to the work they must accomplish in the classroom. They will sometimes find themselves saying the same things over again, wondering whether students are as tired of the words as they are or whether they are simply obtuse. They may even come to see that all their words serve their need to define and control everything that happens during the school day. Much of the need to control comes from overcrowded conditions. Many elementary classrooms have thirty-five or more children, and secondary teachers often interact with five or more classes in one day. Classes are organized according to grade levels that reflect the ages of their students, intensifying the peculiarities and deficiencies of each age group. Students are expected to sit quietly at desks that are not bolted down yet usually face toward the blackboard, the place where the constantly talking teacher stands or sits.

THE FRAMEWORK OF CLASSROOM LIFE

In the mass school, teachers are almost always adults with professional training and certification. They have little or no choice in the classes they are given to teach, and students do not usually select them as mentors. During their first encounters, students and teachers are strangers and come together for what Tonnies would call "use-relationships." Students soon learn the idiosyncracies of individual teachers and adapt as best they can. They sit quietly in their seats and speak only when told to do so. In most instances, only the teacher has the freedom to move about and speak, help pupils who are having trouble with their lessons, and correct and supervise what is happening in the classroom.

Hence the physical characteristics of classroom life provide a basic framework for understanding relationships that develop there. These are supported by certain assumptions and attitudes that are grounded in the culture of the school and community. Students are graded according to their ability to do the work, allowing schools to perform their selective functions. This process must be done in a competitive ethos where all children are given an equal opportunity to perform the schoolwork. Grading in these circumstances indicates levels of student success or failure and is usually accepted by parents and children alike as a valid measure of achievement.

In secondary schools, timetables and schedules are a more important part of the organization of the school day. These structures alert teachers and students to outside control elements they cannot ignore. School attendance is compulsory in most modern states, and pupils learn even in preschool to arrive at and leave school on time. On every level of schooling, schedules and timetables decide when teachers and students will begin their classwork, when they will take a break for recess or lunch, when they will play, and so on. Classroom work is usually split into formal or informal periods, and students are expected to turn their attention from one subject to the next when asked to do so. Students find themselves organized into groups according to ability so they can be more easily instructed in the formal curriculum. Teachers spend a great deal of time working with these groups, checking and correcting the work of individuals to see if they have actually learned their lessons. Behind these obvious functions of instruction are other, less obvious ones. Students learn the routines associated with regular attendance, punctuality, submission to authority, the silence rule, and so on without much thought. The formal curriculum instructs them in the active learning of ideas and information, while the informal curriculum provides them with passive learning experiences, habits, and attitudes that will serve them well in classrooms and the workplace.

To summarize, students sit at their desks and interact with their teachers, who are located in the front of the room. Teachers are typically adults who have been trained and certified in a university. Teachers choose the materials and methods for the students' work in class, assuming their need for instruction in these areas. Teachers are more mature physically and have greater experience, competency, and status than their students. Nevertheless, their authority is derived from their appointment to a teaching position in the school bureaucracy. They lead as a consequence of this organizational role, following behavior patterns that have been developed over many years. Teachers are the institutional leaders of the class, and their status and charisma are attached to their rank as teacher and not to any particular qualities they may possess. They are the mentors in the teacher-student relationship and their authority rests on traditions and legal mandates only. Of course, when the job is done well, teachers combine these organizational elements with personal forms of leadership that win the recognition and affection of students.

During their first meetings, teachers and students are engaged in a struggle for control. Until teachers feel certain that their dominant status has been accepted by students, they cannot relax. More friendly attitudes and behaviors will have to wait until this acceptance is assured and students submit to their unquestioned authority. Only then can teachers and students begin to deal with the educational experiences that are required by the school organization. Of course, teachers bring other attitudes into the classroom: they have certain feelings about the profession and other predispositions that will influence how they do their work. They will see their students as individuals with different social, cultural, sexual, and racial backgrounds and differing abilities to learn. How will they interact with students? In most instances, teachers will insist on their own terms, although there are exceptions. They will insist on their right and duty to decide things in the classroom and discipline children as the need arises. If they find they cannot do these things, classroom life will become more stressful and the learning situation will come apart. Of course, they will not be able to command everything that happens in the classroom, but they will insist on their right to decide things whenever possible.[11]

Examining these conditions of classroom life, some writers have pointed to certain characteristics that teachers seem to prefer in their students. Among these are good speech habits, proper dress, punctuality, and proper deference.[12] For many teachers the job of controlling and moving about large batches of children in confined spaces and classrooms has become an overriding concern. When teachers begin their training in apprentice situations, they learn the world view and methods older teachers have used in the past. They learn to see students as immature individuals who may, under certain circumstances, behave in ways that threaten the order and decorum of the school. Teachers who fail to develop such attitudes find themselves contradicting the wisdom of others who have gone before them and risking the disapproval of veteran teachers and administrators. Mostly, however, teachers are unquestioning in their responses to this type of training since they can see quite clearly what might happen to them if their authority were subverted by rowdy students.

THE INSTRUCTIONAL ACT

Another problem researchers have studied is the way teachers actually do their work. Even though schoolteachers come from many walks of life, they have assumptions about schools that are based on their own experiences as students. Most have the best of intentions when they begin to teach in mass schools. Some beginning teachers have said they want to work with children, that they want to help children learn what they will need to know when they are adults. These attitudes reflect those of the profession while strengthening the idea that the teacher is the source of all knowledge in the classroom. Many teachers find it difficult to reconcile their desire to help children with their role as agents of cultural diffusion. Their responses to actual contact with students can leave them deeply troubled and confused, especially at first. Some will find themselves ill-prepared to control and discipline certain students, and this will limit their ability to teach the other children effectively. After a few months, however, many new teachers will learn the control techniques of the mass institution, using their personality to assert authority over the classroom situation. Talking to other teachers, they will take their places in the subculture of the profession, sometimes putting greater distance between themselves and the students they must order about and control.[13] The following ethnographic report, describing the orientation of new teachers at an inner-city junior high school, provides a glimpse of some of the worst excesses that can occur.

> Today we met a new bunch of teachers, and they were mostly kids without any experience. Just kids! For the most part they sat around at long conference tables and waited. A few read the materials we had passed out and talked about. Others just sat by themselves and smoked. An assistant principal passed out more materials and explained them. We leaned forward in our seats when the principal began his welcoming speech. The next week, these young people would be in the middle of a ghetto school.
> "At first," the principal was saying, "you won't know what to do. You'll flounder. Don't worry. Everyone does. . . . You'll make mistakes. After all, what do you know about teaching? You've been in the learner's seat all your life!"

Several newcomers moved about uneasily in their seats.

"What should you do?"

Hands shot up in the audience.

"No, no. Don't raise your hands! Don't think! Just listen! I'll tell you what to do. . . . Pick out someone on our staff who looks like he knows what he's doing. A veteran teacher. . . . Then, do what he does. Walk like him. Talk like him. And soon, you'll be like him! Watch the way he gets out of his car each morning, and then you do it the same way. Watch how he reacts under stress, and then, you do it the same way. Watch the way he controls his classes, and then, you do it the same way. Before you know it, the words and actions will become your words and actions, and you'll be an effective teacher too!"[14]

Ethnographic research has tried to describe the essential features of classroom life, focusing on its unchanging elements. In every instance, the teacher is described as the formal leader of the class, the legal representative of adult society. Rituals have a significant place in the teacher's efforts, and students are expected to obey the silence rule and to sit attentively in their seats. Again and again, students are shown waiting for the teacher to begin the lesson, move them about, or give them permission to speak. The teacher sits or stands at the front of the room, watching to see which of the students are doing the work they have been given. The following example, taken from a study of an inner-city junior high school, provides an instance of such surveillance methods.

This morning I made my first observation of a reading teacher. At the front of the room sat Mrs. Harris, the principal's prime target of the moment. Her powdery face was partly concealed by tinted spectacles. She seemed nervous. Every boy and girl sat silently in their seats. (She must be doing something right, I thought.) A monitor walked up the aisles distributing some reading materials. To one side, another checked attendance. A very well run class! Very attentive!

Mrs. Harris gave her directions in a flat, metallic voice.

"Turn to page 74 in your reader, and read pages 74 through to page 83. Then complete the questions on page 83 in your notebooks. . . . Are there any questions? Begin!"

At her command, books were opened, and eyes became absorbed in the assigned reading. I was surprised that no attempt had been made to motivate the lesson or review difficult vocabulary, but I assumed this might have been done earlier. They hadn't speculated on the title of the story or what it might be about. Still, everyone seemed to be working! Mrs. Harris was working, too. She sat at the front of the room doing clerical chores! I felt very ill-at-ease. After a few moments, I began to move about the room. Several students didn't have any idea about what the story was about. Others didn't know key words and concepts. They scribbled and drew pictures in their notebooks or just stared out the window. After 25 minutes, everyone was asked to turn back to page 74. Then each child read a paragraph aloud while the others followed along by pointing to the words as they were read. At that point, I left the room. If this was the way one of our more experienced teachers was teaching, what could we expect from our raw recruits?[15]

While this lesson showed very poor pedagogical skills, another example, taken from an inner-city school three thousand miles away, provides an instance of more enlightened instructional methods:

Today I visited an eighth grade classroom in a ghetto community. Mr. Sands stood at the front of his class and spoke animatedly to his students. They listened with an intensity that surprised me and, as he asked a question, they raised their hands to answer it.

They spoke in the language of the streets, but no one seemed to think they should be corrected. They talked the way they did in their community, and Mr. Sands, their teacher, understood what they were saying. In this classroom, teacher and students were trying to communicate with one another.

There were thirty or more youngsters in the class, and many of them did not participate in this discussion.

"Being able to talk depends upon your confidence and how long you have been in the country. If you can get them to talk in English or Spanish," this teacher said, "you can gain their confidence and interest."

I watch as he discusses some problem students are having with another class. Parliamentary rules are observed, and a committee is formed to study the matter further. Some students suggest that they write about this matter, and Sands suggests that they prepare an edition of their class newspaper. After much talk, they decide on what they will write about, and the class grows silent as each student works on the article. Sands walks up and down the aisles, stopping now and then to help students who seem to be having problems. I do the same and find that several of the students are writing about their recent visit to the planetarium. Others have completed their written work and are illustrating it. After twenty minutes or so, Sands collects the articles and redistributes them to students. Then everyone is given time to read the work of other students and to correct their papers as best they can. Some of the papers are read aloud by volunteers, and all of the articles are finally given to an editorial committee that does the final editing. Sands showed me some older copies of *The Planet*, and they were printed up very much like a real newspaper.

"The students like to see their names in print," Sands told me afterward.[16]

As noted, teachers are almost always at the front of the room. From that position they can look out at the overcrowded classroom, command the attention of their students, and watch what they are doing during the school day. Some lessons are poorly prepared, as in Mrs. Harris' classroom, while others show teachers who care deeply about the children they teach. Sometimes teachers do not seem to know how to reach their students, while others bend the rules of the system and make contact with children from the inner cities of America. Many teachers fail to provide students with individual attention, either because they have not been properly trained or because of the stressful conditions of their work. Some fail to motivate their pupils, while others take students on trips, print class newspapers, and otherwise make the classroom experience an exciting one. All too often, teachers seem insufficiently aware of the effects of their behavior on the educational and psychological well-being of students. Many children in inner-city schools seem bewildered and defeated, going through the motions of learning or sitting quietly in the back of the room. Some teachers ask students if they have any questions but seldom encourage them to speak. Once students have been told what to do they are expected to stay on task. Many teachers do move about their rooms to clarify any problems that may arise. However, in almost every instance, teachers use a surveillance method to determine whether the thirty-five or more students sitting in rows of desks are doing their work.

Teachers express themselves in their speech, in the words themselves as well as in the attitudes and postures they assume as they speak to students. Their task is to teach, to educate students in the folklore and realities of mass society. Few like to think about indoctrination, even though they may be aware that such things occur in other societies. Many are aware of the problems associated with racial and socioeconomic segregation, but they are confused and deeply troubled by their inability to reach such children. Still they do what they think is best for their students, even when their overly corrective methods do not seem to work well. In this they are doing what teachers have always done: they are passing on the values and beliefs of American schooling and society. These beliefs are supported by another assumption. Teachers must, in the end, force students to learn. Otherwise, youngsters will simply idle their time away, becoming malcontents, malingerers, and worse.[17]

THE LANGUAGE OF DEVALUATION

Recent research has drawn attention to the consequences of these educational practices for students.[18] It suggests that such practices force youngsters to regress to earlier stages in their mental and physical development. Once students leave the school building, they revert back to their personal identity and more mature behavioral patterns of interaction. Nevertheless, the psychological cost to students is significant. After learning to talk and move about during their preschool years, they are now required to behave in passive, inert, and silent ways that are reminiscent of early infancy. They must now wait until the adult authority commands them to move or speak, much as many employees do in the modern workplace.

Some teachers ignore these psychological realities, while others seem all too aware of them and eager to develop better relationships with their students. Open communication is restrained, however, by the bureaucratic nature of school organizations and the roles both teachers and students must play in mass schools. The training that teachers receive instructs them to accept the educator's view of schooling, sometimes sharpening their differences with the parents and students they serve. Cuban, for example, points out that teaching is not much different from a century ago.[19] This may be one reason why many inner-city students make so little progress in their schoolwork, becoming less interested in reading and academic work as they grow older. Parents and official study groups complain that students do not study much at home and that the drop-out rate, although difficult to count, still seems unacceptably high. Students resist and accept institutional definitions of themselves that are unflattering, as do their teachers. Yet when students act out some of their resentments, teachers often respond the only way they know. They seek to control the behavior of such students as best they can so they can continue to instruct the other members of their crowded classrooms.

Other writers have criticized teachers for not personalizing their instructional efforts. Classwork is usually group- or class-oriented, and students are expected to keep up with the work of other members in their ability groups. This tracking of students stigmatizes children at an early age, as the following example shows.

> Today I talked to the kindergarten teacher in our neighborhood school. She sat on my couch and complained about the many problems she was having with her classes. Since she was a teacher in an affluent district in southern California, I was surprised at her complaints and asked her to explain herself.
>
> Apparently, a number of children were being bussed into her class from a military base nearby, and these children were from families with poorer educational backgrounds.
>
> "Mr. Rothstein," she was saying, "these children don't know their colors, they don't know their numbers, and they don't know how to behave in school. Why, you know," she continued, "they don't even know they have a last name!"
>
> I wanted to say something to this teacher but decided against it. Later, I asked my daughter about what was happening in her kindergarten class. She told me she had been placed in the green group. When I asked what that was, she replied, "That's the smart kids' group."
>
> "Was there another group?" I asked.
>
> "Yes," she answered. "The orange group. That's for the dummies in our class."[20]

Many teachers are concerned with the psychological and educational effects of such practices, but these practices have persisted in spite of their best efforts. In many instances, teachers believe that grouping youngsters according to ability makes it easier for them to teach in their classrooms of thirty-five and more. Many believe that children can, with hard work, have themselves moved to more advanced groups. Many other teachers are concerned with the psychological effects these practices have on children and on their relationships with these students.

When questions are asked in classrooms, students are usually the ones who respond to them. They seek to avoid, whenever possible, the corrections that inevitably follow incorrect responses. Their own needs for recognition and respect are sometimes ignored during these traditional lessons, forcing them to play out the student role no matter how unpleasant it may be at any given moment. Many teachers are aware of the devaluation of their students' personal heritages that occurs in classrooms with diverse students. Still, they feel overburdened by the large numbers of students they must serve during any given school day, convinced of the need to maintain order and control inside the school building.

RESISTANCES AND FAILURES

Studies of classroom conflict are considerably less developed than other areas of educational research.[21] If directive leadership and instruction are the cause of resistance in classrooms, why have they continued to persist throughout the educational history of schooling? Perhaps it is because schooling merely reinforces the socioeconomic and status difficulties of children from diverse and impoverished families. Teachers assess the speech, language, and educational attainments of children and record them in cumulative files. These records make it possible for the school bureaucracy to further evaluate and place individual students throughout their schooling experiences. Words take on a life of their own in these files, providing teachers with a set of givens before they actually begin to work with students in their classes. Through these cumulative files and the words of other teachers, new teachers learn what to expect from new students at the start of each semester. Many track students once they open their mouths and speak, noting that they appear to be members of subcultures that have not done well in schools in the past. Those who are from less affluent families often have poor vocabularies and find it difficult to master the academic curriculum of the school. Such students often learn to see themselves as incompetent individuals who are personally responsible for their school failures. Their failures take place in front of other classmates, subjecting them to the humiliating experience of failing in front of peers. The cumulative record, then, plays an important role of the life of students, even though they are often unaware of such a document. It catalogs their successes and failures, their indiscretions and behavioral lapses so that new teachers will be aware of them even before meeting the students.

Instructional work is, above all else, concerned with words and the social relations that develop from them.[22] Students are exposed to ideological communications that make them more willing to accept the ideas their parents and others have given them during their preschool years. Words place youngsters in their families and later in classrooms, forcing them to accept a destiny they are often unable to influence or understand. When they become students, the teacher's words come to describe them as more or less advantaged, depending on their ethnic, racial, and socioeconomic circumstances. These students find themselves adrift in a competitive, impersonal educational system, deeply troubled and confused by their failures.

The relationship between these words of remembered successes and failures confound the behavior of teachers and students alike. Teachers believe they know something about a child when they read the cumulative file or after a few days of interacting with the student in class. But their views of these circumstances are only what is real for them. Sometimes they omit the courage and bravery of children who attend mass schools with surprising grace and dignity. Even the overly corrective instructional practices of many schoolteachers are ignored by parents and students, since these are always justified by their supposedly helpful orientations. There is evidence, however, that many teachers may actually understand some of these problems and the way they affect the relationships that exist in classrooms. But their speech and language tend to separate them from students because of the problems they encounter when they try to manage large batches of students in confined spatial areas. This is because the speech and language that structures classroom communications were developed to solve such pressing problems and concerns many years ago and still are relevant to present-day classroom life.

This relationship between the language and social structures of classrooms further justifies educational practices that may appear outdated to some. Noting that instructional methods had changed little in the past century, Waller and Cuban pointed out that these methods provided students with a world of words that made their existence seem more rational and orderly than it really was.[23] Entering schools for the first time, students often found themselves committed to an institutional identity and training from which there was no recourse. They had to play out the student role of unknowing individual at all times during the school day. This requirement was supported by state law and social traditions that commanded students to attend to the teacher no matter what their personal preferences or concerns. They were to accept their need for instruction, discipline, and guidance from the professional person who was responsible for molding their character and intellect. They were to accept the institutional view of themselves as undisciplined individuals who needed constant supervision, the childish ones who needed to be forced to work. All this happened in a social and educational world in which the student identity was constituted and reproduced so that teachers could prepare youth for the world of work and citizenship.

THE INSTRUCTIONAL SITUATION

How do teachers use speech and language to accomplish their instructional tasks? Recent research has been concerned with the subcultures of the teacher or student, studying their effects on the interaction that takes place in classrooms. Meanwhile, there is some evidence that teachers and students know what classroom life will be like even before it actually begins. These suppositions allow the learning situation to begin even when teachers and students have not yet introduced themselves to one another. They form a set of givens or a structure within which individuals can orient themselves before the actual classroom interaction begins. Youngsters entering an inner-city school often know whether their school is a good one or not, whether students succeed or fail there, whether it is a safe place to be, and so on.[24] Even the youngest of children often have knowledge of what things will be like once they enter the school building. Their first actions are influenced by the ideas and language of others, who pass on to them the cultural understandings of their group. Once they actually start to play out the role of students, newcomers adjust their behavior to the realities of classroom life. The teacher's speech helps students to reaffirm their own ideas about their educational experiences: the classroom is to be seen as a serious situation requiring their best efforts and attention. It is a place where teachers can and do reprimand and correct students so they can receive the coveted education that American society values so much. Both teachers and students use their ideological understanding of their work together to justify certain types of behavioral responses. Teachers are often given the benefit of the doubt when they act in unpredictable or overly directive manners because it is assumed that they are acting in the best interests of the children they serve. Nevertheless, teachers and students never really know what to expect until they actually enter classrooms and begin to work together. Even then, their ability to understand what is happening to them will often be influenced by their cultural heritage and the speech and language they use with one another.

Studies of communication systems in classrooms have shown extreme one-sidedness in many traditional classrooms.[25] Students are the central concern, of course, but their right to speak is often limited by traditional silence rules and the need for order and control in overly large classes. Teachers address their students, directing their attention to what they will be doing in the classroom and checking to see if they are doing the work. But the work itself is not individualized, and students find themselves competing with one another throughout their schooling careers. In classrooms, children are students who by definition are required to listen and respond to the directives of their teacher. In their dependent role, they must listen carefully to the teacher's meanings to properly define the preferred behavioral and learning patterns in classroom life.

Clearly, then, classroom life is structured by words and ideas that make its mores and moral understandings seem like reasonable and legitimate activities for teachers and students. Students come to accept the idea that teachers should have the right to stop and question children anywhere in the school building. It is in such encounters, when students must prove to teachers that they have the right to be in a particular location inside the school building, that the separation between these two groups becomes more pronounced, as in the following example.

"You! Yes you! Come here!"
 "Yeah?"
 "Let me see your pass."
 "Pass?"
 "Come on. Come on. Your pass."
 "Here."
 "This thing isn't any good!"
 "Huh?"
 "It isn't signed."
 "No?"
 "Let me see your program card."
 "I'm in Mr. Brown's class."
 "I don't remember seeing you around. You better come with me."
 "But why?"
 "Because! Because you don't have a pass. YOU DON'T HAVE A PASS!"[26]

I heard this exchange of words in an urban junior high school and recorded them soon afterward because it seemed so typical of teacher-student encounters in inner-city secondary schools. In describing this incident, it was necessary for me to identify who was speaking. No student would think of beginning a conversation with a teacher by calling out, "You! Yes you! Come here!" The right to stop and question individuals in hallways resided in the role of the teacher. Teachers were responsible for order and control in the school building, and they had to determine whether youngsters were legitimate members of the school organization or intruders.

The meeting began ritualistically, with the teacher exercising the power to stop and search students. It could occur whenever a teacher encountered a student in the hallways during class time. The primary feature of such meetings was the questioning process wherein teachers determined whether students had a legitimate right to be present in a particular school location. These initial elements of the situation were followed by others in which the youngsters were either detained or sent on their way. Again, the teacher was the important person in the situation, the only individual who could initiate it. The teacher's mode of speech was usually that of the coercive inquirer, and student responses were generally deferential in nature, helping to reestablish the relevant membership categories in the school.

Such encounters were also governed by the norms of social intercourse in hallway situations. These norms, which seldom varied, also demanded of students that they behave in ways that were nonthreatening in nature. When youngsters failed to meet this requirement or to produce a valid pass, they broke the norms governing such encounters. Students seemed aware of their subordinate position and the right of teachers to question them to assure the order and control that were needed for effective learning. The correction-invitation form of questioning was similar to that of a police officer interrogating a suspected law violator, and students were expected to respond in ways that justified their presence in the hallways. The teachers controlled the talk by the way they chose to understand the situation and the student's faltering responses. They were the ones who had the right to stop and question individuals. They were the ones who decided whether a youngster had the right to be present or not.

⑤ *Summary*

Teachers are seen as the important person in the classroom because they have decisional rights in the situation. They decide what will happen and when it will happen. They derive these rights from the legal-rational authority that supports schooling in modern society and from the traditions of American society. Students come to schools with suppositions about what it will be like, suppositions often transmitted to them from older siblings and friends. Classroom life teaches children to subordinate their own feelings and needs to those of the classroom group. In this way, it prepares youth for their lives as citizens and workers in modern society. Observers have noted a separation between teachers and students that mirrors those of other agencies in which managers and managed populations work together in close quarters. These groups tend to develop subcultures and ways of seeing their common situation. Classrooms in urban schools are often characterized by problems of order and control, which cause some teachers to become more stern in their relationships with students. Still, the classroom remains change-resistant because schooling is mired in ideas that were first used to cope with the rise of industrial culture in the nineteenth century. The large numbers of immigrant and poor children crowding urban schools today is reminiscent of earlier times. Still, teacher attitudes are an important element in the academic success or failure of students.

⑤ *Projects*

1. Observe and analyze the roles students play in elementary and secondary classrooms. Describe the ways that these roles have influenced the behavior and psychological well-being of these youngsters.

2. Select a teacher in your school who is popular with the students, and try to learn why. What does she or he do that students like?

3. Sit in a classroom with a teacher who uses teaching methods that are not overly directive. Make a list of the things the teacher does to get children to talk to one another. Talk to some of these students after class, and ask them how they feel about the class.

4. Make a case study of a boy or girl who is having difficulty in a class-room. Carefully analyze and record everything the teacher does to help this child.

5. Observe and analyze the roles and experiences young girls have in ele-mentary classrooms in your school. Do your observations support the idea that their teachers are discriminating against them? Talk to some of the girls. What role do their previous socialization experiences at home play in the type of education they receive?

Endnotes

1. Darder, Antonia, *Culture and Power in the Classroom: A Critical Foundation for Bicultural Education* (Westport, Conn.: Bergin & Garvey, 1991), 1–24; Irvine, Jacqueline Jordan, *Black Students and School Failure: Policies, Practices, and Pre-scriptions* (Westport, Conn.: Greenwood Press, 1990); Drew, David, "Mathe-matics, Science, and Urban Education," in *Handbook of Schooling in Urban Amer-ica,* ed. Stanley W. Rothstein (Westport, Conn.: Greenwood Press, 1993), 297–315; Goodlad, John, *A Place Called School* (New York: McGraw-Hill, 1983), 111–113.

2. Shakeshaft, Charol, "Meeting the Needs of Girls in Urban Schools," in *Hand-book of Schooling in Urban America,* ed. Rothstein, 175–187; Chase, Phyllis M., "African-American Teachers in Buffalo: The First One Hundred Years," in *The Teacher's Voice: A Social History of Teaching in Twentieth Century America,* ed. Richard J. Altenbaugh (London: Falmer Press, 1992), 65–77; Bowles, Samuel, and Herbert Gintis, *Schooling in Capitalist America,* (New York: Basic Books, 1976), 190–195; Fuchs, Estelle, "How Teachers Learn to Help Children Fail" in *Children and Their Caretakers,* ed. Norman K. Denzin (New Brunswick, N. J.: E. P. Dutton, 1973), 29–42; Ogbu, John, and Signithia Fordham, "Black Students' School Success: Coping With the 'Burden' of 'Acting White'," *The Urban Review* 18, no. 3 (1986), 176–206.

3. Rist, Ray, *The Urban School: A Factory for Failure* (Cambridge, Mass.: The MIT Press, 1973), 216–219; Sergiovanni, Thomas J., and Robert J. Starratt, *Supervi-sion: Human Perspectives* (New York: McGraw-Hill, 1988), 150–153; Freire, Paulo, *The Pedagogy of the Oppressed* (New York: Seabury Press, 1970).

4. Rist, Ray, *The Urban School: A Factory for Failure* (Cambridge, Mass.: The MIT Press, 1973), 216–219; Sergiovanni and Starratt, *Supervision: Human Perspec-tives,* 150–153; Freire, Paulo, *The Pedagogy of the Oppressed;* Waller, Willard, "What Teaching Does to Teachers," in *Identity and Anxiety: Survival of the Per-son in Mass Society,* ed. Maurice Stein, Arthur Vidich, and David Manning White (Glencoe, Ill.: The Free Press, 1962), 329–350.

5. Waller, "What Teaching Does to Teachers," *Identity and Anxiety,* ed. Stein, Vid-ich, and White, 329–350; Quantz, Richard A., "Interpretive Method in Histori-cal Research: Ethnohistory Reconsidered," in *The Teacher's Voice,* ed. Alten-baugh, 164–165.

6. Rothstein, Stanley W., *The Voice of the Other: Language as Illusion in the Formation of the Self* (Westport, Conn.: Praeger Publishers, 1993), 93–116.

7. Lacan, Jacques, *Speech and Language in Psychoanalysis*, trans. Anthony Wilden (Baltimore and London: Johns Hopkins University Press, 1989), 263–268.

8. Bernstein, Basil, *The Structuring of Pedagogic Discourse: Class, Codes, and Control*, (London and New York: Routledge, 1990), 52–54, 89–90; Rothstein, *The Voice of the Other*, 117–122.

9. Mannheim, Karl, and W. A. C. Stewart, *An Introduction to the Sociology of Education* (London: Routledge & Kegan Paul, 1962), 138-142; Sergiovanni and Starratt, *Supervision: Human Perspectives*, 129–133; Webb, Rodman B., and Robert R. Sherman, *Schooling and Society*, 2nd ed. (New York: Macmillan, 1989), 281–282, 291–292.

10. Waller, Willard, *The Sociology of Teaching*, (New York: Russell & Russell, 1961), 9–10, 401–402.

11. Mannheim and Stewart, *An Introduction to the Sociology of Education*, 134–142; Smith, Joan K., and L. Glenn Smith, *Education Today: The Foundations of a Profession* (New York: St. Martin's Press, 1993), 128–129; Joseph, Pamela Bolotin, and Gail E. Burnaford, *Images of Schoolteachers in Twentieth Century America* (New York: St. Martin's Press, 1994), 11–12, 55–59, 74–76, 202–205.

12. Rothstein, Stanley W., *Schooling the Poor* (Westport, Conn.: Bergin & Garvey, 1994), chap. 1; Banks, Olive, *The Sociology of Education*, (New York: Schocken Books, 1976), 234–235.

13. Bernstein, *The Structuring of Pedagogic Discourse*, 56–59; Banks, *The Sociology of Education*, 227–232.

14. From my notebook.

15. Rothstein, Stanley W., "The Ethics of Coercion" in *Urban Education* 22, no. 1, (April, 1987), 53–72.

16. From my field notes.

17. Lightfoot, Sara Lawrence, *The Good High School: Portraits of Character and Culture* (New York: Basic Books, 1983), 335–337; Brophy, James E., and T. L. Good, *Teacher-Student Relationships* (New York: Holt, Rinehart & Winston, 1974), 246–252; Davidson, Harold, and George Lang, "Children's Perceptions of Their Teachers," *Journal of Experimental Education* (1960–1961).

18. Rothstein, *Schooling the Poor*, chap. 1.

19. Cuban Larry, *How Teachers Taught: Constancy and Change in American Classrooms 1890–1980* (New York: Longman, 1984), 22–27.

20. From my notebook.

21. Hawley, William, "The Importance of Minority Teachers to the Racial and Ethnic Integration of American Society," *Equity and Choice* 5, no. 1 (1989): 31–36; Irvine, *Black Students and School Failure*, 172–173; Rist, Ray, "Sorting Out the Issues and Trends in School Desegregation," in *Schools and Society*, ed. J. H. Ballantine (Palo Alto, Calif.: Mayfield, 1985), 330–337.

22. Rothstein, *The Voice of the Other*, chap. 5.

23. Waller, "What Teaching Does to Teachers," *Identity and Anxiety*, ed. Stein, Vidich, and White, 329–350; Cuban, *How Teachers Taught*, 18–25.

24. Rist, Ray, *The Invisible Children: School Integration in American Society* (Cambridge, Mass.: Harvard University Press, 1978), 242–246; Sudnow, David, *Studies in Social Interaction* (New York: Free Press, 1972).

25. Banks, *The Sociology of Education*, 178–187; Waller, *The Sociology of Teaching*, 104–106; Sergiovanni and Starratt, *Supervision: Human Perspectives*, 260–262.

26. From my field notes.

Chapter

8

Family Background and Academic Achievement

OBJECTIVES

In this chapter you will learn the answers to these questions:

- *How does family background affect the performance of students in classrooms?*

- *What role does socioeconomic background play?*

- *What other factors determine a student's success or failure in schools?*

- *Why do students drop out of school?*

- *What role does the father's occupation play in the academic success or failure of his children?*

- *What special gender problems exist in the selection processes of schools?*

- *How did the G.I. Bill allow students from diverse family backgrounds attend institutions of higher education?*

T he family is a child's primary group, the social arrangement wherein children learn who they are and where they fit into the social scheme of things. Not only does the family begin children's socialization and learning experiences, it also provides their perspective on society and schooling, creating an awareness of what to expect once classroom experiences begin. For these reasons, families exert a lasting influence on student self-perceptions throughout youth and adulthood.[1]

Some writers have suggested that certain family types contribute to or detract from the academic achievement of their children.[2] Mannheim[3] described three types of home environments that affected the academic success or failure of students: cooperative-to-school families, antagonistic-to-school families, and average families that were between these two extremes.

Cooperative-to-school families tended to support the formal goals and purposes of schooling, sending their children to school on time, dressing them in appropriate ways, and providing them with the necessary school supplies. These families were concerned with what was happening in classrooms and interested in getting to know their children's teachers. They saw the school's reports as helpful comments on their child's progress and development and sought to help teachers whenever possible. If there were differences of opinion, the parents in these households felt these were usually the result of objective tests and standards and sought to work more closely with teachers. They thought of schools as partners in a common effort to educate their children properly.

Antagonistic-to-school families were seen as the exact opposite of cooperative ones. They tended to take the side of their children in disputes with the school, encouraging them to disregard the school's rules and requirements. Often children from such families were poor, punctuality was lax, and there were bad feeling between teachers and parents. The adults in these family groups had few, if any, common educational purposes.

Mannheim described these two types of home environments as polar opposites while admitting there was a wide range of attitudes in parental responses to schools. Some parents who seemed uninterested in what was happening in classrooms also thought of teachers as professionals who were primarily responsible for the academic and social development of their children. Mannheim pointed out that parents in antagonistic-to-school families often had little idea of what education should be or whether their children were getting a good education. They usually lived in poverty and moved about frequently, making schools less important than they might be to more stable families. In the average type of home, which was between these two polar opposites, parents had incomplete understandings of what education was because they did little to complement their children's experiences in the classroom.

Writing a decade later, Bernstein[4] distinguished between positional and person-oriented families. In positional families, the right to decide things resided in the formal role and status of parents, especially the father. Roles were clearly defined between father, mother, and child. In the person-oriented family, the right and power to decide things according to a family member's age, sex, or position was reduced, and individuals often discussed problems more openly. Bernstein pointed out that working-class families tended to be positional, with more traditional and formal orientations, whereas middle-class families were more person-oriented in their relationships.

Following up on these findings, Bernstein and his colleagues studied mothers in working-class and middle-class families to learn more about their child-rearing practices. They developed a model of motherly communication and discipline that seemed to confirm their original findings. The more open the level of communication in a family, the higher the mother's score. Mothers who relied on explanation rather than coercion and force as methods of control were categorized as being more person-oriented. Comparing these findings with the test scores of children in schools, they found a high correlation between these variables. Mothers who read to their children frequently and spoke to them about their problems and concerns were also seen to be more favorably disposed toward schools and teachers. When measured by this index, middle-class mothers tended to achieve higher scores on having more open communication and being more person-oriented than working-class ones.

Researchers have shown that working-class parents place less value on formal schooling, and they have less interest in their children attending and remaining in school. Ambition, an important value in middle-class families, is much less evident in these working-class parents. Their children tend to have lower aspirations, even when competencies and intelligence were controlled for statistical purposes. In a study of high school seniors in Wisconsin, Sewell and Shah[5] showed that when parental interest and encouragement were low, few students planned college careers, regardless of their family's status or their own intelligence. Conversely, when parental encouragement was high, the number of students planning to go to college was also high, regardless of the economic status of parents. Follow-up studies verified that support from parents, teachers, and friends, as well as the student's self-image and achievement levels, were variables that affected socioeconomic status, student ability, and aspirations.

The findings that working-class families limit the perspectives and ambitions of their children have been challenged by many. However, Bourdieu[6] showed that, in France, the selection of a school or course of study could be a retrogression or a progression, depending on the social status of the family. The social, economic, and emotional costs of advancement were more severe for working-class families that were striving to become something other than what they had been in the past.

Studies in Europe came to similar conclusions. Middle-class families who showed greater interest in their children's education had higher levels of academic achievement. They were more concerned with the day-to-day progress of their youngsters than were working-class parents, and they showed even greater interest as their children matured. Middle-class parents visited the schools more frequently, communicating face-to-face with teachers and administrators. They urged their children to stay in school longer, and they preferred private schools whenever possible.[7]

Investigations of equality of educational opportunity in the 1960s studied family background as a central variable in the success or failure of students in American schools. Coleman[8] pointed out that a family's social class was a determining factor in the student's success or failure in the classroom. The cultural background of students from poorer families was described as "deprived" and cited as a major reason for the high failure rates of minority and poor students.

Reviewing Coleman's data in the early 1970s, Jencks[9] agreed that the socioeconomic status of students was linked to student failure, but noted that this would not determine how much students would earn after entering the labor market. Jencks found that economic success depended on the ability of individuals to do their jobs well and on more capricious factors such as luck. Two decades later, however, Altenbaugh[10] found that this was no longer true and that school dropouts were returning to complete their education because they could not find work without a high school diploma.

The evidence that socioeconomic status is the single most important factor determining success or failure in school tells us little we did not already suspect. Such information only serves to divert attention from the important features of the schooling enterprise and the family structure as they now exist. Inequalities have existed from the beginning in public schools, and they persist despite efforts to eliminate them. Such studies, however, do provide ways of interpreting the effects of family background and culture on academic achievement. They constitute empirical and theoretical literature that describe the relationships between the child-rearing methods of families from different socioeconomic groups and the educational success or failure of their children.

Still, there are no easy approaches to these problems. We cannot base everything on the socioeconomic condition of families, as Jencks has shown.[11] Even in the same family there may be children with different levels of success and failure in school or different cultural values. While it seems evident that social status is important, it is never entirely clear how to transfer such ideas into operational terms or concepts. Child-rearing practices, language and cultural patterns, and value orientations toward schooling and learning have their consequences for academic success. Research has indicated that these factors are part of a complex socialization and learning process that has a profound effect on maturing children.[12] Yet it is impossible to determine precisely how these variables function in particular families to produce positive or negative results in schools. The concepts of working-class and middle-class families are not absolute. In reality, families tend to be a blend of these typological constructs. The definition of a family as middle-class, for example, often depends on the occupation of one working parent, yet it often fails to take into account other factors such as the other parent's cultural background and attitude toward education, which may or may not be middle class in orientation.

The ways that families earn a living has changed significantly during the past half-century. Mobility has been a source of productive efficiency but has also caused instability and disorganization in family life. Several generations may have passed since the movement from feudalism to industrialism, but the values of the past continue to have meaning for us. The attitudes of parents and grandparents toward factory-produced commodities as symbols of status and wealth still dominate our thinking. Their willingness to work long hours at meaningless tasks in order to purchase machine-made gadgets is still at the center of much that motivates family life today.

This transformation of work processes and values has brought with it an instability that is most severe for lower-class and lower middle-class families. These families have great difficulty adapting to the ever-changing conditions of urban industrial culture.[13] For middle-class families, the race for status and success has often meant two working parents and new adjustments for every member of the household. Homemaking is at best a part-time activity, and children spend much of each day with babysitters or in child care centers. Their education is in the hands of schools that deal with them along with many others who must be managed and moved about with care. Religious beliefs have also suffered, and individuals seem uncertain of what they should think or believe. The same can be said for educational values. In this sense, the **Gesellschaft relationships** first identified by Tonnies[14] at the end of the nineteenth century have become an overwhelming reality in our time.

But it is not only industrialism, urbanism, and bureaucracy that have influenced family life in the modern era. The Great Depression and two World Wars also have had their effect. In the case of the Depression, silent armies of unemployed men disrupted the mental health and economic security of families for generations. In the 1930s these conditions led to the industrial labor movement and the birth of the C.I.O., which seemed to promise families some protection from the problems of poverty and unemployment.[15]

As urban society grew, the religious, educational, and leisure activities of families changed. Education became an aspiration for people from all classes in mass society. Commercial ideas continued to control what was taught in public schools, emphasizing individualism and competition as the best way of organizing the affairs of schooling and society. The media became an important way for people to relax, providing entertainment at prices that put very little strain on family budgets. Church attendance appeared to decline for a time, but participation and religious values were still important parts of communal and family life.

It would be an oversimplification to say that the most important change that occurred during this period and after World War II was the women's liberation movement. Yet this transformation of the role of women has had a lasting effect on family life. The increased mobility of women had a decisive effect in changing sexual mores and responsibilities, while increasing the productivity and cost-effectiveness of labor in industry and commerce. Between 1940 and 1970, women broke many barriers as they entered most occupational categories of the mass labor market. Because of tradition as well as inadequate educational and work opportunities, they often found themselves at a disadvantage competing with men for better positions in the work force. As the number of working women increased, so did their demands for greater access and equity. While women had previously tended to lead sheltered lives at home, they could now take positions outside their homes and neighborhoods with the development of new job opportunities and transportation systems. Families with two working parents increased in number, and the scramble for machine-made goods and commodities quickened. Newly emancipated women workers demanded educational experiences that would increase their status and earning power in the world of work.[16]

Middle-class families adjusted to the new conditions more easily than their working-class counterparts, who emulated middle-class styles and values as best they could. Middle-class families were more accustomed to impersonal relationships with their children and more concerned with acquiring the goods and services that industrial production made available to them. Their membership in political, social, and athletic clubs increased as did their contacts with a wider variety of individuals. Mobility and adaptability became the keys to success, and the acquisition and display of wealth a universal goal.

CAUSES OF SCHOOL FAILURE

Along with studies of family background and social class, other inquiries have sought to discover causes of failure in school by looking at instructional practices. Stinchcombe,[17] for example, discovered that certain combinations of environment and circumstance tended to be more frequent in schools where a majority of children were failing than in those where this was not so. The finding that parental attitudes and interest were a significant feature of school success or failure was consistent with the findings of studies cited previously in this chapter. What was surprising, however, was Stinchcombe's conclusion that each case of academic failure was a story of personal tragedy, different from all others and requiring individual, intensive study. Following up on this idea, researchers have had difficulty defining the term *failure*, especially when understood as the variance between a student's actual and potential levels of achievement. Critical analyses of such variances have come to the conclusion that no test can reveal intelligence or innate abilities for mental development, because these concepts do not lend themselves to observations and measurement.[18] The employment of intelligence tests to measure such qualities is a poor use of these constructs since the tests were not designed to measure the genetic capabilities of students.[19] This argument has been excused by some because such measurements appear to be useful in predicting student levels of academic achievement. While most seem to agree that there is a hereditary factor in human ability, it is still difficult to separate from pervasive environmental influences.

A study of high school seniors in the United States[20] showed that youngsters with high ability test scores and high socioeconomic status had a 90 percent rate of attendance in college, compared with 69 percent for boys and 52 percent for girls with similarly high ability test scores but low socioeconomic status. Students with low ability test scores and low socioeconomic status displayed much lower levels of attendance in college (40 percent); only 10 percent of girls in this category attended college. These studies linked the likelihood of graduation from college and attendance in graduate schools to higher socioeconomic status, replicating the findings of Bourdieu in France.[21] In the highest socioeconomic class, 42 percent of men and 20 percent of women went on to advanced graduate study. In the lower socioeconomic classes, only 25 percent of men and 8 percent of women reached these levels of educational attainment.[22]

Studies of who attends institutions of higher learning reveal what previous studies would lead us to suspect. Most students are from affluent and middle-class families in both Europe and the United States. Public and educational planners appear to believe that working-class youth do not need a rigorous education because they will have little use for it in their adult lives. To the extent that this premise dominates the thinking of influential people, it tends to hold back research into the specific ways in which families and schools work together to delimit the aspirations and opportunities of lower-class children. More recent work has focused on the importance of familial and community ties as they provide youth with a linguistic and cultural background and identity that affects their success or failure in schools and in the work place. In the homes and neighborhoods where individuals live, personality and social perspectives develop as a normal consequence of intellectual and physical growth. Families, neighbors, and the surrounding communities all contribute to the early development of children. To the extent that youth learn to speak and understand their world, they become total and accepting members of their families and communities. In the schools, they learn to accept their place and identity in the institution and prepare for their life in the future workforce.[23] It must be apparent that poverty, poor wages, unemployment, size of the family, and the absence of a father are factors that affect the school performances of children, as are poor prenatal care and impoverished infancy experiences. Poverty can force youngsters into the workplace instead of college, and scholarships are often insufficient to change this. Poor housing can impair a child's ability to do homework, read, or engage in constructive play.

Still, there is no simple set of circumstances to point to. Rather there is an overwhelming rush of events and outcomes. Children from poor families suffer from malnutrition and poor health, poor living conditions, and negative attitudes toward schooling and life. Of course, individuals react differently to the conditions of their life. They define their personality according to their needs and understandings. Their consciousness is built on the insights and preoccupations of significant others as well as their own experiences, together with a sense of their ultimate fate and destiny as members of a family and group. Even though they may resist social influences and strive for success in school, the objective conditions of life work against their success.

The different stages of schooling provide students from poor families with neither the opportunity for individual insights and learnings about themselves nor the chance to learn completely the linguistic and cultural lore that are often second nature to children from affluent families. The standardization of curricula, pedagogies, and evaluation procedures has become a less-than-subtle way of casting out and failing the poorer individuals in society. The full implications of these findings have led to a stream of educational reforms, which have sought to ameliorate the worst excesses of segregation, hunger, and inadequate medical care for the poorest members of society.

Studies of students who dropped out of school found that only five percent had a clear and pressing economic need to do so.[24] However, such findings require a word of caution. Children who have left school at an early age are often undercounted, and some are counted as having transferred to another school even when the exact location of the transfer is unknown to school authorities. In studying why so many high school graduates failed to attend colleges, researchers assumed a scarcity of scholarships as an important reason. Yet despite increases in aid programs and loans, parents continue to be the most important source of tuition and support for college students. Students explained their failure to attend or remain in colleges by citing economic difficulties.

The "Crowther Report"[25] approached these types of problems in Great Britain by examining the role of financial problems in dropout rates in grammar and technical schools. Focusing on the effects of poverty on school attendance, the researchers measured the weekly income of each family's father. When the father's income exceeded a predetermined amount, dropping out was shown to be a negligible problem. As the father's income increased, the number of children mentioning a need or desire to earn money as a reason for leaving school declined. Only a tentative conclusion can be drawn from this study, however, since it did not measure the role of parents' and children's attitudes or of poverty in influencing decisions to drop out of school. New York City, for example, is reporting 75 percent dropout rates of African-American students, and southern California is reporting 41 percent failure rates for its Hispanic students. These reports, which appeared in the New York *Times* in 1991, lead to the conclusion that poverty is obviously a major part of the answer. Yet most researchers have continued to look for other conditions and attitudes that mitigate or affect the decision to drop out of school.

The authors of the "Plowden Report"[26] in Great Britain sought to clarify the effects of attitudes and socioeconomic conditions on the dropout and failure syndrome. They made considerable efforts to isolate home backgrounds and parental attitudes to trace their effect on academic achievement and student dropout rates. They used such factors as the physical living conditions, number of family members, presence of siblings, number of dependent children, father's occupation, and educational levels of parents as key variables. This report reaffirmed the importance of parental attitudes. As previous studies had shown, these attitudes were significantly linked to the academic achievement of children, and the relationship increased as students grew older.

Other studies have found that parental attitudes and maternal care were more important than the socioeconomic condition of the family. In these studies, however, it was not just the parents' orientation toward schooling that mattered, but rather their responses to society's demands that they remain upwardly mobile and ambitious despite their impoverished conditions. It is important to understand how poverty, poor housing, and other conditions affected children in ways that seriously limited their educational aspirations and achievements. Overcrowding was an important problem that was shown to have significant influence on school achievement. Children from poorer families had poorer health records and higher rates of illness and absenteeism. Again and again, reading levels were shown to be severely retarded in schools serving students from poor families. Many of these children moved frequently and missed more than half of a school-term's work.

Further studies in the United States revealed that the children of unskilled manual workers were afflicted with much higher levels of physical problems and deficiencies than were middle-class students. They tended to have greater incidence of problems such as stuttering, squinting, and visual and regressive behavior.[27] Such children had little or no medical care and were not immunized against many preventable childhood diseases.

Other writers have focused their studies on schools rather than unsuccessful students. These investigators wished to learn precisely how cultural and economic poverty handicapped youngsters from poorer families. They were able to show a conflict between the linguistic and cultural backgrounds of the children and the school's language and culture. While poverty and housing are important outside influences, these researchers found that failure in schools was more directly related to absence, neglect of schoolwork and homework, and an inability to pay the costs of schooling.[28]

From these studies, it seems clear that the culture and language of poverty affect every aspect of a child's life. Parents are less willing to support their children for long periods of time instead of sending them to work before age 16. They are less able to supply their children with books, toys, and experiences that will lead to a successful school experience. The strain and tension of poverty can make for an unhappy and frustrated environment in which parents fail to adequately play or talk with their children.

EUROPEAN PERSPECTIVES

The work of Bourdieu and Passeron approached the problem of selection in the primary and secondary grades in France by using enrollment figures in institutions of higher learning to learn the actual outcomes of selection in the lower grades.[29] They found that different social classes were not represented in colleges and universities according to their incidence in the lower grades. To solve the problem of how to operationalize the concept of social class, these researchers turned to a method commonly employed by census bureaus. They recorded the occupations of students' fathers as the primary indicator of a student's social standing, ranked these vocations, and calculated entrance possibilities from the ranked vocations. They found that less than 1 percent of children of farm workers attended universities and colleges, while the proportion of children of executives and professionals was just below 70 percent. They concluded that the French education system eliminated children from less privileged families from the higher reaches of learning during their years of training in primary and secondary schools.

In the same study, the authors found the selection of a high school resulted from a process of tracking that began in kindergarten and was felt unequally by children from different social origins. Those with fathers working in the lowest-ranked occupations suffered the most from this process of elimination, which occurred in every classroom in the nation. A senior executive's child was found to be eighty times more likely to enter a university than a farm worker's child, and so on. Bourdieu and Passeron mustered a great deal of statistical data to support the notion that a student's socioeconomic standing was one of the most significant indicators of these unequal opportunities and outcomes.

The authors used this data to identify ways in which higher education was using these socialization and selection processes. Children from deprived families had only the smallest opportunity to attend French universities (less than five percent), while those from the intermediate categories such as clerical workers, artisans, shopkeepers were becoming an increasing presence in the university population.

These attendance numbers increased according to socioeconomic status in a progression that was not surprising to those who have lived and studied in mass society. They indicated that higher education was an important determinant of a student's attendance in college and occupational status in later life. Those from the higher-ranked occupational categories had social experiences and a language that taught them to expect to go on to higher education once they finished high school. That was just the way things were in their families—they were destined to attend the university, while those from the lower occupational groups had none of these opportunities or understandings.

Bourdieu and Passeron also sought to clarify the effects of gender on this unequal distribution of educational opportunity. They found that lower-class women had a better chance of getting into the university than did lower-class men, while women from higher occupational ranks had the same opportunities as males. Further analysis showed a new form of discrimination. The choices that male and female students had once they entered the university were unequal and influenced by tradition and cultural understandings. Male and female students from upper occupational ranks had equal access, but they did not study the same subjects. Women from every social class were more likely to study the arts, while male students were more likely to study science. This appeared to follow the traditional division of labor in the workplace and was influenced by views of women as the more nurturing sex, better able to take care of children than do work in science, mathematics, or business. Women were more often trained for a career in teaching. Those from farm families entered this sheltered profession in overwhelming numbers (92 percent), whereas males from the same background were somewhat less likely to do so (81 percent). These figures held firm for sons and daughters of industrial workers and clerks, but decreased significantly as the father's occupation reached into higher income brackets. From this, the researchers concluded that females had more limited choices than males and that this difference was even greater by social class.

The spiraling costs of higher education were another element in denying access to students from the less privileged classes in French society. Most poorer students faced complete elimination from higher learning, and those that survived faced restricted choices. Children of senior executives had a much higher probability of getting into law schools (33 percent) compared to children of lower-ranked executives (23 percent), and the same was true for medical and other professional schools. Children of the lowest-ranked occupational groups, on the other hand, had elimination numbers in high school approaching an 85-percent dropout rate.

The arts, including the social sciences, was often a refuge for other social classes as well. Students who had been forced to attend college often chose these courses of study to gain some appearance of respectability. It came as little surprise, then, that the elite colleges and universities of France were heavily attended by students from the upper echelons of society.

Bourdieu and Passeron also found that students from lower-ranked occupational groupings did less well in their classwork, repeating grades and courses throughout their educational careers. The authors believed that economic determinants alone were insufficient to explain why educational success differed so widely between social classes. They found that linguistic and cultural experiences were crucial factors that could not be overcome easily. Differences in academic ability and attitudes toward schooling appeared to be part of the social and cultural background of students from every grouping. Students formed a significant set of ties and socialization experiences during the primary and secondary years of schooling that were important in setting the goals and possibilities of individual students. Of course, social origin was still the most important influence in these matters. But age and sex played important roles, as did religious affiliations. The distinction between "practicing" and "non-practicing" Catholics became an important way for the authors to classify students in reference to their educational and cultural values and culture. Religious affiliations provided students with opportunities to interact with one another in circles, clubs, and societies as an extension of familial and educational experiences. Also, Catholics (fifty-one percent, compared to non-Catholics) went to private or parochial schools with students from similar backgrounds. These students tended to be more personal in their thought patterns as opposed to the others who were more Marxist. Yet, in the final analysis, the researchers found that academic behaviors and attitudes in institutions of higher learning were not seriously influenced by religious backgrounds. The same was found to be the case for age variations. Seniority in years of tenure could be a plus or a minus in any given situation, depending on other variables.

But social background was another matter, defining living and working opportunities for students. It was the factor that determined where children lived and the language and culture they learned from parents and in neighborhood schools. The financial status of the family often decided what was realistic and possible for an individual student, acting either to stimulate or limit the child's aspirations. It created certain dependencies that were associated with loans and obtaining financial support for higher education. Even those few lower-class families (fourteen percent) who did maintain a student at the university could not do so without the youth working part-time to make ends meet. The less-privileged parents were not as aware of the importance or existence of certain disciplines, such as science, mathematics, or business, causing them to counsel their children into pursuits they considered more practical. There was unequal knowledge by social class about where different areas of study might lead. Abstract language and ideas were highly valued in the educational system, and those who studied the impractical subjects of Greek and Latin had an advantage that was not immediately apparent. These courses were seldom selected by students from the lower social classes, because they did not seem relevant to the needs and concerns of living and working in modern society. And the rising costs of higher education were already legendary in the French population.[30]

These findings were supported by studies in the United States that also focused on outcomes, using occupational categories to establish the social origins of students. These studies found that students from more privileged families obtained, from birth, a language and culture that gave them habits, skills, attitudes, and social ties they needed to pursue their academic interests effectively. These attributes are further supported by other inherited knowledge and practices that direct such students into the more elite universities and later occupational choices. There is an unequal distribution of academic culture and knowledge among students from different social origins, and inequality of income alone is not enough to explain these disparities. Language and culture play important roles that cannot be ignored. Visits to the theater, art galleries, and concerts give students experiences and insights not ordinarily provided by the schools. Those from more privileged backgrounds have had greater knowledge and understanding of the theater, music, painting, jazz, the cinema, and opera than those from the lower social classes. This includes the playing of musical instruments, which also appears to vary according to the class and habits of a particular family.[31]

THE G.I. BILL: A CASE HISTORY

Turning back to the schools themselves, we may ask: What is the relationship between the economy and educational success and mobility? Can we explain changes in schooling's outcomes by referring to economic determinants?

Many studies have tried to answer these questions, linking educational systems to society's need to train youth in particular skills. But there is insufficient proof that such training has actually occurred in the schools. In pre-industrial cultures, training took place in the home or in apprenticeship situations in the workplace. Even after the coming of high-speed machinery and the factory system, on-the-job training retained its importance. What characterized an advanced industrial society, however, was the degree to which occupational credentials and skills were increasingly available only in formal educational institutions.

The new conditions and technologies that changed nineteenth-century Europe and the United States into industrialized, urbanized, and bureaucratically organized cultures were only the beginnings of a process that has culminated in the computerized, mass society of the present. A second and third revolution in technology and knowledge has accompanied automation and the robot, and the knowledge base of society is progressing at an incomprehensible rate. Change has become the norm, and research in the physical sciences seems to promise ever higher levels of productivity. It is not surprising, then, that educational advances have often been dictated by the needs of the economy and the labor market.[32]

A good example of these two forces working together to influence education occurred as World War II was coming to an end. Following the decade of economic depression that had preceded the war, there was great concern that the return of 11 million American soldiers to civilian life would trigger another Great Depression. A *Washington Post* editorial in 1943 looked ahead to a "second Pearl Harbor of peace, not war." This disaster would be more devastating than any wartime battle, because the enemy would be the returning soldiers, the returning millions of unemployed workers. There were not enough jobs to go around, and a policy that guaranteed employment to returning soldiers was simply not possible. The Delano Committee, a presidential advisory group, was convinced that the postwar period would be one of recession or worse, with mass unemployment. To deal with this possibility, the committee recommended delaying the discharge of soldiers from service until jobs were available for them. This plan, however, was not acceptable to the Roosevelt administration. Servicemen and their families would never have agreed, and the committee members had to admit that they were unsure when jobs would become available for these men. Editorials in 1943 warned that returning veterans would not accept unemployment and poverty submissively, as their parents had done. Congressional committees and the President worried about what so many millions of Americans might do, especially since they now possessed military skills and training.

The congressional committees gathered as much data and statistical information as they could. Most of it pointed to decades of retooling and reconstruction in Europe and Asia, during which time economic depression was unlikely. But the memories and fears of the 1930s were too strong, and planners feared that a big dislocation during the changeover from a wartime to a peacetime economy might erode confidence and trigger a downturn.

The final recommendations were to send these returning veterans to school, keep them off unemployment lines, and pump millions of dollars into the economy as Keynesian economics advised. None of the political or lobbying groups that supported this plan were interested in education or how these veterans would fit into the institutions of higher learning. Their main concern was to ensure there would not be a return to the undesirable conditions of the 1930s. Only educators were worried about the impact this legislation would have on them. The planners decided to give all veterans four years of training in institutions of higher learning. Only after the bill was law and veterans were about to return did leaders in higher education begin to express concern about the educational reforms. James B. Conant, president of Harvard, was distressed because the new law gave support to all veterans, without trying to ascertain which of them could benefit most from higher education. His view was that the G. I. Bill should have been directed only at "a carefully selected number of returned veterans".[33] He warned that the new legislation would open a floodgate, and schools would be tempted to admit veterans who did not meet their standards just to earn the tuition. "Because of the G. I. Bill, we may find the least capable among the war generation . . . flooding the facilities for advanced education." In 1944, writing in Collier's Magazine, he warned that colleges and universities were in danger of being "converted into educational hobo jungles!" Yet the colleges were businesses, they needed students, and the new legislation meant they would have them in abundance. Larger universities had benefitted from the war, training personnel on their campuses and expanding to meet the needs of a massive armed services. Also, their research had provided the armed forces with much-needed weaponry, benefitting both parties. All institutions of higher learning actively prepared for the coming of G. I. students, with elite universities like Harvard getting more than their share of federal funds.

The decision to provide higher education for veterans was triggered not by a desire to establish more equitable relationships and opportunities for Americans, but by economic concerns that the returning soldiers would constitute an enormous economic burden. Institutions were ill-equipped to handle the millions who sought entrance after World War II. The comments of many educators showed their opposition to opening up higher education to prospective students who had little or no experience with colleges and universities. While most educational leaders advised against the four-year support program of the G. I. Bill, Congress left little doubt that returning American soldiers had to be kept off the unemployment lines and out of the labor market. They were to be given access to universities and colleges, which had excluded many in the past.

American educators were surprisingly negative in their response to the federal government's efforts to provide returning soldiers with educational opportunities. One of the most sweeping and important educational reforms of the century was accomplished by economic and political leaders who were concerned about economic, not educational, problems. American soldiers were given the economic support they needed to attend college, and millions took advantage of the opportunity and changed the face of higher education. They broke every conceivable enrollment record, more than doubling prewar numbers. And many proved educational experts wrong by taking rigorous academic courses and completing them successfully. The G. I. Bill democratized higher education by allowing veterans to sit next to students whose family background and income assured them a place in such classrooms. All this was done not with democracy and equality of opportunity in mind, but with the state once again using schools to solve social and economic problems. Education became a means to an end, keeping veterans off the streets and out of unemployment lines.

ⓖ *Summary*

The speech, language, and culture of the family profoundly influence a student's success or failure in schools. Socioeconomic background plays a profound part in the process. Students from poorer families have inferior prenatal care, and they suffer from many other liabilities associated with poverty. They come to school with fewer skills in language and mathematics and have difficulty with the competitive ethos they find in their earliest classrooms. Nevertheless, speech and language have great importance. Children from families who teach the speech and language closest to those of the schools succeed; other children fail. Students drop out of school because they do not see the relevance of schooling to their own lives. Many return to school later, when they have matured and need more skills and education to get ahead in the labor market. Studies in France indicate that the father's occupational role plays an important part in determining the academic success or failure of children. Recent research indicates that gender bias exists in the schooling experiences of young girls. However, elementary teachers who have viewed videotapes of this research do not agree with the researcher's conclusions. In the words of one teacher, boys are given more time and help because they need it. In recent times, the G. I. Bill has proven to be one of the greatest equalizers in American society, providing an educational opportunity for students who might otherwise never have attended college.

⑥ Projects

1. Write a detailed case history showing how your family background influenced your success or failure in school.

2. Inquire into the reasons people in your family attended college and graduate school. How many of them went to college to get a better job, and how many to improve themselves? What other reasons were given for choosing to delay their entry into the labor market?

3. Make a chart showing the family background of four or five students in your school or classroom. List factors that might affect their children's success in school, such as the parents' occupations, income, and number of years in school and the language spoken at home. Compare these with the educational attainment and prospects of the students.

⑥ Endnotes

1. Sewell, William H., and V. P. Shah, "Social Class, Parental Encouragement and Educational Aspirations," *American Sociological Review* XXII (1957); Warner, W. Lloyd, Robert J. Havighurst, and Martin B. Loeb, *Who Shall Be Educated?* (New York: Harper & Row, 1944); Sewell, William H., "Inequality in Opportunity for Higher Education," *American Sociological Review* XXXVI (1971): 794–795; Floud, John, A. H. Halsey, and I. M. Martin, *Social Class and Educational Opportunity* (London: Heinemann, 1956), 89–90; Parsons, Talcott, "The School as a Social System," in *Education, Economy and Society,* ed. A. H. Halsey, John Floud, and Charles A. Anderson, (Glencoe, Ill.: Free Press, 1961) 433–435; Greer, Colin, *The Great School Legend* (New York: Basic Books, 1972), 19–20; Gintis, Herbert, and Samuel Bowles, *Schooling in Capitalist America* (New York: Basic Books, 1976), 53–55; Katznelson, Ira, and Margaret Weir, *Schooling for All: Class, Race, and the Decline of the Democratic Ideal* (New York: Basic Books, 1985), 180, 221; Bernstein, Basil, *The Structuring of Pedagogic Discourse: Volume IV: Class, Codes and Control* (London and New York: Routledge, 1990), 63–93;

Rothstein, Stanley W., *The Voice of the Other* (Westport, Conn.: Praeger Publishers, 1993), chap. 3.

2. Bernstein, *The Structuring of Pedagogic Discourse*, 82–83, 96–97, 179; Aggleton, Peter, *Rebels Without a Cause? Middle Class Youth and the Transition from School to Work* (Lewes, England: Falmer Press, 1987); Coleman, James S., et al., *Equality of Educational Opportunity* (Washington, D.C.: Department of Health, Education and Welfare, U.S. Office of Education OE 38001, 1966), 302–303, 325; Jencks, Christopher, et. al., *Who Gets Ahead?* (New York: Basic Books, 1979).

3. Mannheim, Karl, and W. A. C. Stewart, *An Introduction to the Sociology of Education* (London: Routledge & Kegan Paul, 1962), 127–128.

4. Bernstein, *The Structuring of Pedagogic Discourse*, 96–97, 121. Coleman, et al., *Equality of Educational Opportunity*, 301–303, 318–321.

5. Sewell and Shah, "Social Class, Parental Encouragement and Educational Aspirations," *American Journal of Sociology* LXXIII (1957).

6. Bourdieu, Pierre, and Jean-Claude Passeron, *The Inheritors: French Students and Their Relation to Culture* (Chicago: The University of Chicago Press, 1979), 42–57.

7. Ibid., 12–19. See also Rothstein, Stanley W., *Identity and Ideology: Sociocultural Theories of Schooling* (Westport, Conn.: Greenwood Press, 1991), 13–15, for further discussion of women and their experiences in the schools and workplace.

8. Coleman, et al., *Equality of Opportunity*.

9. Jencks, Christopher, et. al., *Inequality: A Reassessment of the Effects of Family and Schooling in America* (New York: Harper & Row, 1972); Moynihan, Daniel P., "Sources of Resistance to the Coleman Report," *Harvard Educational Review* 38 (winter 1968): 26.

10. Altenbaugh, Richard J., "Families, Children, Schools and the Workplace," in *Handbook of Schooling in Urban America*, ed. Stanley W. Rothstein (Westport, Ct.: Greenwood Press, 1993), 19–42.

11. Jencks, et al., *Inequality: A Reassessment*, 8, 14.

12. Rothstein, *The Voice of the Other*, chap. 2.

13. Lynd, Robert, and Harriet Lynd, *Middletown in Transition* (New York: Harcourt Brace, 1937). See also Stein, Maurice, *The Eclipse of Community* (New York: Harper & Row, 1960), 47–55.

14. Tonnies, Ferdinand, *Community and Society* (New York: Harper & Row, 1957), 258–259, 240–242.

15. Nasaw, David, *Schooled to Order: A Social History of Public Schooling in the United States* (New York: Oxford University Press, 1979), 146–148.

16. Stein, *The Eclipse of Community*, 46–55.

17. Stinchcombe, A. L., "Environment: The Cumulation of Effects is Yet to Be Understood," *Harvard Educational Review* XXXIX (1969): 511–522. See also Craft, M., "Talent, Family Values and Education in Ireland," in *Contemporary Research in the Sociology of Education*, ed. John Eggleston (London: Methuen, 1974).

18. Glass, David V., ed., *Social Mobility in Britain* (London: Routledge & Kegan Paul, 1954), 291–307; Webb, Rodman B., and Robert R. Sherman, *Schooling and Society* (New York: Macmillan, 1989), 285–287. See also Lightfoot, Sara Lawrence, *Worlds Apart: Relationships Between Families and Schools* (New York: Basic Books, 1978).

19. Jencks, et al., *Inequality: A Reassessment*, 33–34, 88–89, 108–109.

20. Banks, Olive, *The Sociology of Education* (New York: Schocken Books, 1976), chap. 4.

21. Bourdieu and Passeron, *The Inheritors*, 1–28.

22. Vernon, Peter E., "Development of Current Ideas About Intelligence Tests," in *Biological Aspects of Social Problems*, ed. John E. Meade and A. S. Parkes (London: Oliver & Boyd, 1966), 4–7; Jenson, Arthur P., "How Much Can We Boost I.Q. and Scholastic Achievement?" *Harvard Educational Review* XXXIX, no. 1 (1969); Gintis and Bowles, *Schooling in Capitalist America*, 29–35, 110–114, 247–249.

23. Ashton, Patricia T., and Rodman B. Webb, *Making a Difference: Teachers' Sense of Efficacy and Student Achievement* (New York: Longman, 1986); Rothstein, Stanley W., "Orientations: First Impressions in an Urban Junior High School," *Urban Education* 14, no. 1 (April 1979), 91–116.

24. Banks, *The Sociology of Education*, chap. 4; Bernstein, *The Structuring of Pedagogic Discourse*, 70–71.

25. "Crowther Report," a governmental report discussed in Banks, *The Sociology of Education*, 51, 70–72.

26. "Plowden Report," a governmental study discussed in Banks, *The Sociology of Education*, 51, 70–72; Kohn, Michael L., "Social Class and Parent-Child Relationship: An Interpretation," *American Sociological Review* LXVIII (1963); Bernstein, *The Structuring of Pedagogic Discourse*, chap. 8; Nasaw, *Schooled to Order*, chap. 15.

27. Holland, James, "Social Class and Changes in Orientations to Meanings," *Sociology* 15, no. 1 (1981): 1–18; Rothstein, *The Voice of the Other*, 93–116.

28. Sewell, William H., "Inequality of Opportunity for Higher Education," *American Sociological Review* XXXVI (1971): 793–795; Banks, Olive, and D. Finlayson, *Success and Failure in the Secondary School* (London: Methuen, 1973), chap. 3.

29. Bourdieu and Passeron, *The Inheritors*, 12–19; Rothstein, *Identity and Ideology*, 13–15.

30. Bourdieu and Passeron, *The Inheritors*, 55–61.

31. Ibid., 54–67.

32. Nasaw, *Schooled to Order*, 173–177.

33. Ibid., 177–182.

Social Psychological Perspectives

⑥　⑥　⑥　⑥　⑥　⑥　⑥　⑥　⑥　⑥　⑥　⑥

OBJECTIVES

In this chapter you will learn the answers to these questions:

⑥　*What are the inescapable, universal conditions that all human beings share at birth?*

⑥　*How does the need for years of care and attention influence the psychological development of humans?*

⑥　*What role do speech and language have in establishing the identity of individuals in modern society?*

⑥　*What are some of the psychological effects of present-day educational practices?*

⑥　*How do teachers and students deal with the dominance-submission role set they encounter in classrooms?*

⑥　*Why do teachers control the movements and thoughts of students in mass schools?*

HUMAN NATURE AND THE SOCIAL ORDER

Human beings share some inevitable general conditions that educators should consider as they work with children. All are born into the world the most helpless of creatures, unable to feed or protect themselves in any meaningful way. Because of their dependent, defenseless circumstances, they are pathetically in need of recognition from others who can nourish and protect them from the dangers of nature. People are born with few instincts for survival and must depend on their ability to suck and cry out for their parents' attention. What instinctual drives they do possess can develop into socially positive or negative factors in their lives. These drives differ among individuals in levels of intensity and tenacity.

The unconscious, in the Freudian sense, seems to be alive and capable of development from the very beginning. However, the work of programmed instincts observed in other animals seems to be absent, and newborn babies learn what they need to survive over a long period of time. In the journey from the animal kingdom at birth to the world of humans at about age three, infants learn the speech, language, and culture of their parents. In this all humans are the same: they become primarily cultural animals who use speech and language to interpret and make sense of the world around them. Much of what other animals carry in their genes, human children learn from their environment, developing over a period of years from inertia to crawling and walking. The manner in which a child is taught to eat differs a great deal from culture to culture and according to the social class of the family.

Children thus need many years of care and education before they can take their place in the adult world. The prolonged childlike helplessness and subordination that follows birth is an inescapable biological reality that has variable but foreseeable psychological consequences for the individual. Human beings do have instinctual drives, though they may be flexible. Sexuality and aggression, the two most important drives, seem to dominate the early development of infants. As children grow older, they learn to disguise these drives, combining them and channeling them into other forms of behavior. Nevertheless, this theory never satisfied Freud. His observations indicated that infants were endowed with these biological drives, but that the drives varied in intensity from one child to the next. The extent to which a child was sensitive to sexual or aggressive stimulations or to anxiety depended on the particular predispositions of individual children. The drives were not single impulses or urgings that revolved around a simple, singular need or desire. Rather they appeared as clusters of complex urges that often consisted of conflicting desires striving for satisfaction at the same time. The defensive mechanisms that individuals developed in response to their world seemed to be a combination of flexibility and similarity, defying easy classification.

Human beings also share some inescapable universal cultural conditions. Before they are born they are often discussed by their parents as though they were objects in the real world. Many are given names before their birth, as well as racial, ethnic, religious, and social identities. In their first years they learn the speech, language, and thought processes of their parents, fitting themselves into family life. These early learnings structure the way infants see their world. The speech and language they learn allows them to become active participants in the world of humans. At first they are merely objects, with little ability to act. As they master language—or are mastered by it—by about age three, they begin to play their roles in the family.

These first years are sometimes called the "amnesia years" because so much of the emotions and experiences of this period seem beyond recall. Dependent and helpless infants respond to the world in ways that are more animalistic than human, sometimes experiencing extreme emotional responses to everyday happenings. The nourishing parent, who says "yes" and ministers to the infant's every need, will sometimes say "no" or be late in coming to the child's assistance. Infants may react in extreme ways that we do not fully understand, causing anxiety and guilt at later stages in their life. Human beings have a psychogenetic predisposition to learn the speech and language of their parents during these formative years, but they do this through a form of cultural osmosis. Speech and language are unconscious processes. We do not know how we speak or what we are going to say from one moment to the next. We do all this automatically in most instances. Even our planning for future events is done in language. Every aspect of our thought and sense of self is shaped by our speech and language, providing us with a system and rationale for living on a daily basis. Because these processes are unconscious, much of what is transmitted to newborns and infants is unknown, even to parents. The family's history, attitudes, religion, class, and world view are given to children over a period of many years, affecting the way they respond to their world both in and outside the home. Research has shown that schooling, as one example, is most effective when parents support the goals of educational institutions. Conversely, it is least effective when there is a conflict between the school's language and culture and those of the parents and students it serves.

A final, common experience of human beings is the oedipal triangle between mothers, fathers, children, and siblings, with its many variations. Such familial relationships have many purposes, but all point to civilizing children so they may take their rightful place in the family and society. This is a crucial psychosexual development that helps children establish and strengthen their conscience and the dominance-submission relationship they have with parents. The desire for exclusive relations with the parent of the opposite sex frightens and arouses children, forcing them initially to advance and retreat, and finally to accept the cultural taboos of modern culture. Fantasies play an important role in these processes of childhood socialization, forcing children to take into account the reactions of their parents if they persist in anti-social behaviors. Ambivalence, then, becomes a paramount response of children to their world, following them into adulthood and later life. Human beings are capable of loving and hating one another in the same moment, the same emotion, much as they did in their first years when they were in an extremely helpless and dependent condition.[1]

DOMINANCE AND SUBMISSION: THE PARAMOUNT RELATIONSHIP

Dominance and submission characterize the social relations between parents and children and between teachers and the students they serve in mass schools. Simmel argued that this was the paramount relationship in society, and that, without it, social life was not possible. The oneness of groups and their ability to do sustained work together required a socialization process centered on the individual's need to submit to the power and authority of others. At first glance, the superordinate-subordinate relationship appears to be one-sided, giving an advantage to the party that holds the superior position. But subordinates are not without power in this relationship, even when they appear to behave in passive or disinterested ways. This give-and-take is what makes the relationship, for one cannot take the position of superior without the other's willing subordination.[2]

Simmel argued that leaders are the products of a socialization process whose aim is to transmit ideas and values from one group of people to another. But in the interaction that occurs between leaders and followers, there is often a great deal of independent and spontaneous behavior on the part of subordinates. Even in the worst instances of despotism, subordinates have the choice of submitting to the power and authority of their tyrants or suffering the punishments for disobedience. There is a reciprocity that sustains the superior-inferior relationship. The active participation of both individuals is needed for the relationship to continue.

Simmel identified two ways in which authority is usually established for those in leadership positions. The first, which Weber called *charismatic leadership*,[3] is based on the extraordinary personality or message of the leader. Simmel indicated that such authority was founded both on the inspirational effect these superior individuals had on members and on the faith and confidence members had in the leader's opinions and decisions. Over time these forces became so powerful that they possessed, for the group, an objective validity that could not be challenged. A second form of authority came into being when the state, church, or educational system conferred on individuals the power of decision and the dignity of office, neither of which could be obtained without institutional appointments. This mirrored Weber's legal-rational authority and reflected the increasing influence of bureaucratic structures on the thought and social organization of European society. In the first instance, authority developed from the charismatic personality and message of the individual, while in the second, it came to the individual through the legal apparatus of the state or other corporate structures. In both instances, the transition could not occur without the active support and belief of those who had to submit to the new authority. Authority, then, is a sociological fact, in the Durkheimian sense, which requires the unrehearsed and dynamic participation of subordinates.[4]

Simmel's studies suggest that the subordination of a group to a single leader is one way of providing for a strong identity and unification of its group members. Although it is commonly held that such outcomes depend on harmony between leaders and followers, Simmel points out that the same effect occurs when there is opposition between members and superiors. When there is harmony, the group becomes aware of their unity and strength because their interests coincide with the leader's at crucial points. When there is opposition, members are forced to strengthen their unity so they can effectively oppose the policies and decisions of the leader. In schools and classrooms where the organization provides a single focus of authority and leadership, the common subordination of students leads to a strong unity whether there is harmony or opposition.[5]

The relationship between superiors and inferiors almost always combines submission and opposition at various times. Individual members seek a greater power that will provide them with protection and direction, not only against outside enemies but against their own antisocial inclinations. Members who feel a need for this power often place themselves in opposition to it, thus creating the social conflict that we frequently observe in corporate and institutional settings.

In the schooling situation, a different phenomenon often occurs. The hierarchical organization of educational systems forces individuals to accept the authority and control of board members, superintendents, administrators, and teachers, and they must often do so in spatial arrangements that accentuate the proximity of members. In this instance, the superior group is sometimes an imaginary, abstract entity or social structure that has a life and history of its own. The subordinate relationship of individuals loses its one-sidedness and develops a more mutual, cooperative quality in these circumstances. The emotions, attitudes, and feelings of individual students and teachers are ruled out of the decision-making process, and the relationships become less personal and more routine in nature. Relationships become more use-oriented and fragmented in their development.[6] This is especially evident in secondary schools, where teacher-student relationships manifest a certain detachment and impersonality.

The participation of teachers and students in schools represents a subordination to the objective principle of universal education in modern societies. The reciprocity involved in other such relationships does not exist here, and individuals submit to the rules and regulations of the educational system or the law of the state. Students who disobey the rules and regulations of the school are routinely punished, and most schools have a written list of disciplinary actions to take after each new offense. Students find their lives controlled by these rules and regulations and compulsory attendance laws, but they have little or no say in the origin or implementation of these controls. However, it is in the workplace that both superior and inferior members of an organization submit themselves to the objective principles of the social system. The personal relationship that employers and employees often develop is what was missing from the socialization process of schooling.[7]

Simmel noted that individuals are often forced to submit to more than one authority.[8] Such subordination can be confusing, as students who must adjust to several teachers each day can attest. If teachers or other superiors conflict with one another, the situation can become most unpleasant for students. Each teacher wants things done a certain way and holds the students responsible for what they do and say, even when these demands conflict with those of other teachers.

Simmel defines the conflicts that occur in social and organizational settings as a natural outgrowth of the diverse interests and concerns of subcultures and groups.[9] Societies and school systems need a certain balance between affinities and aversions, compatibility and discord, association and disassociation, integration and differentiation, cooperation and competition. Complete harmony among group members in their thoughts, emotions, and goals is not possible in the empirical world, because it runs counter to the varying emotional states of individuals and their differing interests. Conflict and opposition, along with relationships of dominance and subordination, form the core of human interaction in social institutions. These components of interaction are part of a common socialization function, which forces people to give up features of their individual personalities and interests so that the group can secure the continuation of civilization.

Simmel defines struggles and conflicts as positive factors in the social development of systems and organizations, in contrast to the negative responses of dissolution and repudiation.[10] An antagonism between teachers and students may arise because teachers are assigning too much homework or grading students too harshly. Once an open conflict erupts, it has the function of overcoming these difficulties to arrive at a more harmonious or reasonable way of doing things. The conflict between teachers and students is merely an attempt to resolve the tension that has developed between them. That it may end in a stalemate or in changed attitudes and behavior is only an obvious expression of the special synthesis that develops between these two groups. Nevertheless, the opposition to certain practices is balanced by the commitment of teachers and students to the classroom situation.

The study of conflict in the classroom must view conflict as a concept that contains and implies both union and opposition to existing authority. The termination of a conflict will differ considerably from the struggles that preceded it and from the actual conditions that will exist between teachers and students, for example. The end of a classroom conflict, or any social conflict, involves the development of more stable social relationships between groups or individuals. The actual forms of these new conditions will depend on what has happened during the conflict stage and how the struggle is resolved. The three ways of resolving a struggle are a victory of one group over another, a compromise, or some form of conciliation. In the classroom, the first form, victory, may lead to anarchy, autocracy, or worse; the second, compromise, may cause uneasy moments when the conflict seems to erupt again and again; and the third, conciliation, may result in an attempt to share the power and authority that were designated as the teacher's by state and educational authorities.

Victories are usually the outcome of such struggles in classrooms, with teachers achieving an absolute right to carry out their mandate with students. It has its counterpoint, of course. The peace that now descends on the classroom is gained at the expense of the liberty and autonomy of students and often results in psychological consequences, as we will discuss in the next section. Students are forced to confess or accept their inferiority, acknowledging that they cannot achieve their educational goals without the leadership and guidance of their teachers.

There will be variations in consequences whenever compromise is the way classroom conflict is resolved.[11] When compromise occurs after teachers have assumed complete control over classroom life, it often means a loosening of otherwise strict and unyielding disciplinary practices.

Conciliation too often shows itself only after a complete victory of the teacher. New teachers are often told to be tough at first so the students will know who is boss in the classroom. Later, they are told, they will be able to loosen up and adopt more friendly attitudes toward students.

Another factor in classroom conflict is that students are encouraged to compete with one another by teachers and parents, who accept the tracking system that dominates educational systems in modern society. Students thus find themselves caught up in a special form of unity and opposition to one another, indirectly struggling with one another to achieve better grades and move on to better classes.[12]

When teachers and students first meet, the struggle for control forces both to concentrate their energies on the conflict itself. Students who do not participate in the struggle form one subgroup, while those who focus on the conflict galvanize themselves as inharmonious elements in the classroom situation. When the struggle is over, these differences in student groupings often become less important as all adapt themselves to the regimentation of the learning situation.

PSYCHOLOGICAL CONSEQUENCES

Researchers have largely neglected the study of the psychological consequences of schooling in mass society. Studies of schooling's alienating effects have been left to psychologists and others, who focused only on how students might fit into the school's organization more efficiently. These studies ignored the social-psychological effects of the dominance-submission relationship between teachers and students, as well as the consequences of depersonalized learning experiences in huge, institutional settings.[13]

Some writers in Europe have pointed out that teachers and students often seemed unaware of the nature of their schoolwork. Teachers used ideologies to explain their impositional behavior, citing the commonly held belief that these were justified because they were in the best interests of the children. Problems developed most frequently in inner-city schools where a hidden curriculum existed, supported by the need of educators to maintain order and control in the most stressful of conditions.[14] There is some evidence that teachers tend to stress the group affiliations or differences that exist between themselves and their students. Darder,[15] for example, found that the cultural background of teachers influenced their ability to teach minority children effectively.

Moreover, research on the autocratic methods of classroom control and instruction has not adequately addressed the problems of student passivity and indifference, often mistakenly classifying such behavior as evidence of idleness or laziness. More recently, writers have tended to analyze such behaviors as regressive, describing students as using fantasies and past experiences to alleviate the frustrations associated with the unequal relations existing between them and their teachers.[16] These are not regressions in the clinical sense, of course. They can be viewed more as an attempt by children in inner-city schools to find safe havens and security in the infantile behaviors of the past, when parents controlled their every movement and thought. In their present relationships with teachers, students are allowed to respond in one of three ways. They may submit to their institutional role, they may withdraw into themselves, or they may lash out against those in authority.

It seems evident, then, that the educational experiences of teachers and students may often be misleading for them. Not only can their words be misunderstood, but the emotional force behind those words may likewise be misinterpreted. The struggle for dominance in classroom life often precludes close relationships between teachers and students, since both must attend to the state curriculum that separates them in the first instance. Teachers who take the deference and obedience of students at face value often tend to forget their own reactions to classroom life when they were children. Real contact between teachers and students was rare, and teachers were often unaware of what was happening to students once they left the classroom. This had unintended effects on teachers and children, clouding their relationships with repressed emotions and resistances. Teaching has not changed that much from what it was in the pre-industrial period, and innovations have been very slow to take effect.[17] Remembering and reciting facts from an arbitrary curriculum have remained the norm, and the grading and selecting of successful and unsuccessful students is still an educational aim in itself. Coercion maintains its primary role in classroom life because students are forced to learn in mass institutions where order and control are essential.

The consequences of such educational conditions have been noted by Goodlad and others. Teachers have become drill masters, preparing students for the ever-expanding array of standardized tests. Children have become enmeshed in a depersonalized educational experience that prepares them for the adult world of commerce and competition. Schoolwork has become even less interesting than it was in the past. Teachers, students, and parents seem to have little power to change things. The conditions of classroom life seem more suited to the factory and workplace of the past than to an educational system preparing youth for the twenty-first century.[18] Student obedience is essential, and the idea of instructional methods that emphasize inquiry and thought are subverted by the structural conditions of the mass school. Students often sit quietly in overcrowded inner-city classrooms and listen to lessons that have little to do with their lives now or in the future.

Undoubtedly some reasons for these change-resistant practices arise from overcrowded conditions in mass schools. But another factor seems to be the failure of schoolteachers to remember their own educational experiences as students. One way to improve things would be for teachers to put themselves in the student's place, recalling what they were thinking and feeling when they were students themselves. Teachers might then get a better idea of the reality that hides behind the bland and disinterested expressions of students. Increased listening and attending skills might help teachers to learn more about the youngsters they teach. But if such changes did occur, new questions about what and how students are learning would inevitably come to the fore as demands for accountability increased.[19]

Without the appropriate conditions, teachers cannot listen to or empathize with their students. They must rely instead on their observational powers and what has worked for teachers in the past. When students seem uninvolved, when they are unprepared, when they are late or absent, teachers must try to understand what children are experiencing at home. Otherwise they will find themselves facing students who are incompletely involved in their classroom work. Their efforts will be met by muffled or muted responses, and they will never know whether they are reaching their students. For teachers, there is no other way to learn about students in today's overcrowded classrooms, no other way to learn about their secret fears, hopes, and aspirations.[20] Students will seldom commit themselves to a learning experience that ignores their individual needs and concerns. The teachers' words will have less and less value for students as well as teachers because those words will be confounded by transferences of which teachers are often unaware. Too many of the psychological and cultural factors of classroom interaction are ignored because of the demands of the mass school for order and control. Teachers may think their primary role is to teach and to socialize, as they have always done, but such actions may force inner-city students to defend their heritages and personal identities against constant rejection. Teachers may believe that their role is to correct and amend the behavior and character of their students, but such approaches sometimes force youngsters to adopt defensive postures against the hidden messages of such actions. These messages say to the student, "You are not okay the way you are. Otherwise, there would be no reason to change you."

A STRUGGLE FOR DOMINANCE

We have already discussed the struggle for dominance that characterizes most classroom settings. Teachers must assert their authority from the first, and in some cases this authority is tested by students for a variety of reasons. An unpleasant moment may occur when students decide they have little to lose by defying educational authorities.[21] As Simmel has shown, without the consent of students, no instructional situation can be constructed or maintained. Teachers have the decisional rights over students because of the legal-rational authority conferred on them by the state, but they exercise that power only as long as students are willing to concede it to them.

It is against this background that we must understand the power and authority of teachers in mass schools. To do this, we must pay attention to the consequences of traditional practices, since so many students now come from cultural, linguistic, and socioeconomic backgrounds that have suffered discrimination in the past. Darder's study, for example, drew attention to the ambivalence that students often feel toward mentors who do not share or understand their linguistic and cultural backgrounds.[22] The work of some psychologists has also suggested that many frustrations and animosities in classrooms operate below the surface.[23] Still the teacher's authority rests on a fragile social compact, and such an agreement can come apart under the conditions of extreme stress and tension that characterize many inner-city schools. As long as students accept schooling as a worthwhile enterprise and renounce their right to move or speak without constraints, the authority and power of the teacher is secure. Once they feel the effects of years of failure and frustration, however, many inner-city students withdraw or act out, often dropping out of school as soon as they are able to do so.[24]

There is little evidence of change in the teacher-dominated classroom of the past century despite a great deal of dissatisfaction expressed by people in business and scientific circles. Until changes are initiated, schoolwork will be dictated by the traditions and overcrowded conditions of mass schools. Students will remain deeply troubled and confused by their educational experiences and by the conflict that develops between the teachers' need for order and control and their own need for more relevant learning experiences. Nominally, teachers may appear to be in control of every facet of classroom life. But they have little control over which students they teach and the overcrowded conditions that exist there. They teach materials that Goodlad has described as boring or busy work because children need to be prepared for tests and because such practices work in public schools. The methods of mass education require discipline and a set of routines that allow teachers to control and move about large batches of students on command. Students often fail to see how such practices relate to their needs or interests. They wait for the end of their compulsory schooling so they can regain their personal identities, so they can forget the years of dependency and failure that marked their educational experiences.

The idea that students participate and learn in different ways is no surprise to educators. Differences in learning and teaching styles alone, however, cannot account for the complex relations that exist in the classroom. The causes of student behavior, even uncomplicated behavior such as idleness, are not easy to understand or identify. Observers have suggested that such behavior may be caused by complex mental processes. The student's ego may outflank its superego in order to maintain some scrap of self-esteem in the face of constant scholastic failure.

At the same time, many students desire to gain acceptance from sometimes mercurial pedagogues, submitting deferentially to constant corrections of their thoughts and actions. Goffman, for example, has argued that these adaptations to institutional life help individuals make sense out of their roles in state institutions. In schools, both teachers and students, from their first meetings, seek to come to terms with one another, assuaging the fears and anxieties they both bring to the learning situation. For students, this takes the form of assuring teachers, again and again, that they are harmless and pose no threat to the teachers' power and authority.[25]

In the struggle to force students to learn what educators and the state say they must learn, the seeds of constant conflict are sown. Studies of schooling in the early grades suggest that open resistance by students is common in the beginning, as children seek to maintain their personal identity and familial associations. They yearn for the nurturing parent and the familiar environment of their first years of life. At first they openly resist the schooling situation and the demanding adult. Later they come to accept their new student role and the other children in the classroom. Gradually they become one of the many students competing for the recognition and approval of the teacher. They often transfer emotions and insights from the past to their teachers, who, in turn, are unaware of the counter-transferences that dominate their behavior. It is not surprising, then, that the school's initial effects are seen as bewildering and deeply disturbing experiences.

Students in these early grades are still dominated by egocentric attitudes and wish to be recognized as unique individuals. They have learned to move freely at home and in their neighborhood and express their feelings and attitudes openly. Prior to beginning interaction in classrooms, children have learned to distinguish themselves from others, establishing the uniqueness of individuals around them. They understand that they have become an object that others can talk about and that they are like the others in one important respect: they can initiate action whenever they wish to. Once they enter the classroom, however, children are deprived of this right to move or express themselves freely. They must remain silent and control their bodily movements. They must concern themselves with the precise demands of the teacher and the constant fear of shame and failure. The opportunities of children to initiate actions are severely limited by the large number of students in the classroom.

Ethnographers of inner-city schools have described the regressive and defensive behaviors that students develop once classroom interaction begins. When students are not doing well in school, they may want to strike out at their teacher or simply leave the classroom. They must defend themselves against being considered a failure, along with the potential and daily conflicts that characterize so much of classroom life. Yet they must do this while trying to fit into the educational system itself. They cannot realistically reject these educational experiences or evaluations without drawing the disfavor of their parents and teachers. They cannot reject or criticize the instructional practices of teachers in traditional classroom settings, because such practices are supported by the ideologies and myths of mass society. They cannot turn away from education or tell adult mentors that what they teach is meaningless and unworthy of study, because they are mandated by law to listen to and obey the dictates of schoolteachers. And finally, withdrawal from school at an early age would simply validate the educational system's function as an agency of social selection in the larger society.[26]

Waller has described the relationship between teachers and students as one of struggle and acceptance, especially as youngsters come to embrace the teachers' need and right to control their movements and thoughts in mass classrooms. The relationship is always characterized by the dominance of teachers because of their legal-rational authority and their desperate need to maintain order and control inside the classroom. Traditional instructional methods are also dictated by overcrowded conditions, closing off communication channels and leading to distortions and misunderstandings between teachers and students in many classrooms. Teachers usually refuse to think about their role as the cultural agent of adult society. They usually dislike thinking about themselves as martinets or drill masters, and they often refuse to accept part of the blame for the failure of their students. The cultural and spoken folklore of schooling in mass society absolves them of these responsibilities, citing the incredibly difficult task they have been asked to perform. In this ideological justification of schooling's current practices, it is the students who are responsible for failing grades, not their teachers. The entire blame for a student's failure is laid at the doorstep of family background or poor work habits in the classroom.

Students need and desire the good will and social approval of teachers to progress through the grade system, even as teachers need the students' acceptance of their authority in the classroom to construct meaningful learning environments. From the need to establish rigid disciplinary practices in mass schools comes part of the distrust that characterizes relations between these groups. Teachers use their power to punish as an instrument of social control, and students respond to such practices with only a part of their personality.

To summarize, then, the teacher-student relationship is one of dominance and submission. Teachers are in the dominant role. They can decide and tell students what to do while they are in the classroom. They are the arbiters of all differences and destinies during the school day. They have an exclusive presence in the learning situation, commanding the attention of students. Their rights and powers are derived from education's legal mandate in the modern world and from the speech and language that teach youth to accept adult domination as a necessary element in their socialization. With teachers in complete control of the classroom, communication patterns are one-sided and filled with psychological distortions. Teachers define what the learning situation is, who is doing well and poorly, and why they are ethically and morally bound to evaluate students' efforts. By the fact of their legal-rational authority and the traditional understandings associated with their profession, they talk and command throughout the school day, imposing their will through a stream of continuous discourse.[27]

Students often display their resistance in gestures and disinterested stares. They cannot criticize the teacher's practices because teachers are supported by the full force of the laws and customs of society. They cannot say what is on their minds unless they are willing to deal with the inevitable punishments and humiliations. The unequal status and power of teachers and students has its roots in the precommercial era and in society's need to subordinate the desires of the individual to its own will and desires. This can lead to misunderstandings in the earliest grades. Some students may seek to turn their teachers into substitute parents, transferring previous thoughts, feelings, and behaviors to them. Children may give to this new, powerful adult the attributes of others they have dealt with in the past. Without being aware of it, they may substitute these images for those that are in front of them, determining their behavior by using behaviors that worked well for them in the past. At the same time, teachers may also use counter-transferences to govern their responses to students, thus confounding classroom communication even further. Teachers and students may appear to be speaking to one another, even though the students are limited by their lower status and often cannot initiate conversations. Teachers seem unaware of their own defensive reactions and unable to grasp how their students really feel about what is happening to them. Studies have also shown that teachers are unaware of their prejudices toward children from diverse backgrounds and tend to deny negative feelings by saying, for example, that they treat all their children the same way.[28]

Moreover, both teachers and students seem blissfully unaware and unconcerned about the power and influence of individuals and groups outside their classrooms. Their failure to grasp the political and social functions of schoolwork compounds the difficulties that teachers and students experience as they work with one another in the classroom. They accept at face value the words that define the structures and relational conditions of their situation, viewing them as immutable givens that cannot be changed. Through speech and language, an imaginary authority is given to the classroom itself, and teachers and students come to believe that in the learning situation, they are at the center of what is happening. The social status and socioeconomic position of individuals are ignored, even though these deeply influence the success and failure of many students.[29]

Industrial society has long been obsessed with efficiency, punctuality, competition, order, and predictable worker behavior. Bureaucratic and corporate structures have used methods of social order and control to ensure the continuation of their own structures and status systems. Schools have imitated the structural and relational features of the workplace and government in their attempt to reproduce the knowledge and social relations of production.[30] It seems probable, as Durkheim argued, that every social system in history has confronted this problem of sustaining itself in the face of human aging and mortality. Mass schools in modern society have attempted to achieve these goals of reproduction by using five specific methods: (1) obtaining power and control over youth by referring to traditional values, beliefs, and heritages; (2) erecting school buildings and classrooms separate and apart from the view of outsiders and community agencies, minimizing resistance from students and parents by citing the democratic goals of education; (3) bringing the effects of educational authority and power into play through routines that structure each school day; (4) constantly justifying coercive and controlling actions as necessary to meet the overall educational objectives of schools; and (5) increasing through training the usefulness and pliability of students so they could perform more effectively in the mechanistic world of work.[31]

Braverman and others have suggested that the aims of school discipline coincide with those of business and industry in the modern age.[32] One consequence of the industrial revolution and world trade has been the enormous rise in world population. Individuals also move about the world much more freely than in the past, thwarting to some extent the aims of social forces that would otherwise keep them in their places. The magnitude of these changes has caused many educational systems to enforce even stricter discipline to manage and control the ever-increasing numbers of students they serve. Six billion people now live on the earth's surface, and the number continues to grow rapidly. In addition, problems of economic production and distribution have forced social institutions of all types to turn to bureaucratic methods. Many view such methods as the best way to prepare students and workers for the types of rationalized work that await them in the labor market. The maintenance of nineteenth-century discipline systems is no doubt linked to these new conditions and the rise of legal-rational authority in a society in which all the old traditions and estate variations have seemingly vanished.

⑥ Summary

All human beings are born and live out their first few years as the most dependent of creatures. They have a primal need for recognition in familial groups, developing in settings that are characterized by stages of emotional and educational development. This need for care and attention influences the psychological lives of all people, reaching far into their adulthood. The speech and language that children learn from their parents establish their identity at home, in school, and later in the adult world. Present-day practices in overcrowded schools often cause teachers and students to transfer past attitudes and behaviors onto one another, further confounding their interpersonal relationships. Teachers tend to ignore their coercive behaviors in classrooms, justifying them when confronted by the obvious need for order and control in mass institutions. Students often adopt many of the responses of inmates and prisoners in other state institutions. Still the need to manage hundreds and thousands of students in confined spatial areas seems reason enough for teachers to seek control over the movement and thoughts of students.

⑥ Projects

1. Observe a classroom in your school. Chart the communication patterns that emerge and the kind of behavior exhibited by the students and the teacher. Are there evidences of regressive student behaviors? If so, what are they and how does the teacher respond to them?

2. Chart the interpersonal relations that you observe in another teacher's classroom. How do students and teachers show feelings (love, hatred, fear, confidence, mistrust, rebellion), as opposed to thoughts? Analyze the personalities of two different classrooms and see if you can discover why they differ. How is the tone set by the actions of the teacher? the students?

3. Interview some teachers about their grading policies. How do these policies influence the way they interact with students? How do the teachers develop good rapport in the classroom? Give examples of remarks or gestures that you think are significant and analyze their meaning as best you can.

⑥ Endnotes

1. Gay, Peter, *Freud: A Life for Our Time* (New York: Anchor Books, Doubleday, 1989). See especially discussions on human nature and the drives.

2. Simmel, Georg, *The Sociology of Georg Simmel*, trans. Jurt Wolff, (Glencoe, Ill.: Free Press, 1950), 181–182, 190–191.

3. Durkheim, Emile, *Moral Education: A Study in the Theory and Application of the Sociology of Education* (New York: Free Press, 1961), 7–10.

4. Simmel, *The Sociology of Georg Simmel*, 192–194; Rothstein, Stanley W., "Orientations: First Impressions in an Urban Junior High School," *Urban Education* 14, no. 1 (April 1979): 91–116.

5. Tonnies, Ferdinand, *Community & Society* (New York: Harper & Row, 1957), 258–259.

6. Bowles, Samuel, and Herbert Gintis, *Schooling in Capitalist America: Educational Reform and the Contradictions of Economic Life* (New York: Basic Books, 1976), 18–25, 53–58.

7. Simmel, *The Sociology of Georg Simmel*, 224–229.

8. Ibid., 273–276.

9. Ibid., 300–306.

10. Waller, Willard *The Sociology of Teaching* (New York: Russell & Russell, 1961), 279–292.

11. Clarke, S., Victor J. Seidler, Kenneth McDonnell, K. Robins, and T. Lovell, *One Dimensional Marxism: Althusser and the Politics of Culture* (London: Allison & Busby, 1980), 204–207.

12. Wilson, John, "Power, Paranoia, and Education," *Interchange: A Quarterly Review of Education* 22, no. 3 (1991): 43–54; Johnson, David, *Reaching Out: Interpersonal Effectiveness and Self-Actualization* (Englewood Cliffs, N. J.: Prentice-Hall, 1981), 171–194; Peters, R. S., "Reason and Passion," in *Education and the Development of Reason*, ed. R. F. Dearden, Paul H. Hirst, and R. S. Peters (London: Routledge & Kegan Paul, 1972); Freud, Anna, *Normality and Pathology of Development in Childhood: Assessments of Development* (New York: International Universities Press, 1965); Jersild, Arthur T., *When Teachers Face Themselves* (New York: Teachers College Press, 1955), 11–19.

13. Cummins, John, "Empowering Minority Students: A Framework for Intervention," *Harvard Educational Review* no. 56 (1986): 18–36; Kozol, Jonathan, *Savage Inequalities* (New York: Harper Perennial, 1991); Nasaw, David, *Schooled to Order* (New York: Oxford University Press, 1979); Cardenas, J., and J. M. First, "Children at Risk," *Educational Leadership* (September 1985).

14. Darder, Antonia, "How Does the Culture of the Teacher Shape the Classroom Experience of Latino Students? The Unexamined Question in Critical Pedagogy," in *Handbook of Schooling in Urban America*, ed. Stanley W. Rothstein (Westport, Conn.: Greenwood Press, 1993), 195–222.

15. Rothstein, Stanley W., *The Voice of the Other: Language as Illusion in the Formation of the Self* (Westport, Conn.: Praeger Publishers, 1993), 117–124.

16. Waller, *The Sociology of Teaching*, 108–109, 453; Rothstein, Stanley W., *Schooling the Poor* (Westport, Conn.: Bergin & Garvey, 1994), chap. 1.

17. Tyack, David, "Bureaucracy and the Common School: The Example of Portland, Oregon, 1851–1913," in *Education in American History*, ed. Michael Katz (New York: Praeger Publishers, 1973), 166–167.

18. Rothstein, Stanley W., "Building and Maintaining High Trust Climates: Training the New Administrator in Feeling Expression and Inquiry Skills," *Education and Urban Society* IX, no. 1 (November 1976): 81–102.

19. Webb, Rodman B., and Robert R. Sherman, *Schooling and Society*, 2nd ed. (New York: Macmillan, 1989), 11–18; Waller, Willard, "What Teaching Does to Teachers," in *Identity and Anxiety: Survival of the Person in Mass Society*, ed. Maurice Stein, Arthur J. Vidich, and David Manning White (Glencoe, Ill.: The Free Press, 1962), 329–250.

20. Rist, Ray C., *The Urban School: A Factory for Failure* (Cambridge, Mass.: MIT Press, 1973), 184–191: Ogbu, John U., and Signithia Fordham, "Black Students and the Burden of Acting White," *The Urban Review* 18, no. 3 (1986): 176–206.

21. Darder, Antonia, *Culture and Power in the Classroom: A Critical Foundation for Bicultural Education* (Westport, Conn.: Bergin & Garvey, 1991), 43–44.

22. Wilson, "Power, Paranoia, and Education," 43–54; Jersild, *When Teachers Face Themselves*, 44–64.

23. Greer, Colin, *The Great School Legend* (New York: Basic Books, 1972), 105–129; National Center of Education Statistics, *Dropout Rates in the United States: 1989* (Washington, D. C.: Government Printing Office, NCES 89–609, 1990).

24. Rothstein, Stanley W., "The Ethics of Coercion: Social Control Practices in an Urban Junior High School," *Urban Education* 22, no. 1 (April 1987): 53–72.

25. Webb and Sherman, *Schooling and Society*, 13–15; Seeman, Melvin, "On the Meaning of Alienation," *American Sociological Review* 24, no. 6 (December 1959): 783–791.

26. From my notebooks.

27. Katznelson, Ira, and Margaret Weir, *Schooling for All: Class, Race, and the Decline of the Democratic Ideal* (New York: Basic Books, 1985), 20–22, 46–51; Bowles and Gintis, *Schooling in Capitalist America*, 53–55.

10

Urban Education and the Significance of Race

⑥   ⑥   ⑥   ⑥   ⑥   ⑥   ⑥   ⑥   ⑥   ⑥   ⑥   ⑥

OBJECTIVES

In this chapter you will learn the answers to these questions:

⑥   *What are the problems associated with studying urban education?*

⑥   *Why has urbanization become such a dominant social form in schools and society?*

⑥   *Why were African-Americans segregated in the North and West prior to the Civil War?*

⑥   *What was the condition of African-Americans in the South during the slavery period?*

⑥   *How did the Hayes-Tilden compromise affect the segregation system that grew up in the South after 1876?*

⑥   *How did the "separate but equal" decision of the Supreme Court make Jim Crow and segregation the law of the land?*

⑥   *How did Brown v. Board of Education in 1954 lead to the integration of public schools in the 1950s, 1960s, and 1970s?*

⑥   *Why are big-city school districts today more segregated than those in smaller cities?*

DEFINITIONS

Many educators have studied urban education and the effects of urbanization on the school system.[1] Studies have connected recurring themes of crowded schools and cities with the technological innovations, world trade, and expanding commerce of industrial society.[2] The need to understand these educational trends remains. Some researchers, however, have begun to examine the processes of urban education as more than an unfortunate imbalance or natural consequence of progress.[3]

Altenbaugh,[4] for example, has defined urban educational systems in terms of their development over more than a century and a half, while Katznelson[5] has described them as a commitment to equality and democratic citizenship in American society. Rothstein[6] has viewed urban schools as state institutions whose practices and use of space cannot be explained without relating them to the needs of commercial and industrial society. Durkheim[7] pointed to the socializing functions of schooling in modern society, wherein children find their places in an increasingly impersonal and mechanistic world. Schooling sends messages that reinforce the ideological position of important state agencies such as churches, the media, and the state itself.[8]

For some, the expanding urban school system is a natural consequence of modern society.[9] In this line of reasoning, the problems associated with urban schools are related to overcrowded conditions. Space and its attributes are presumed to have the power to cause the social contradictions and impersonal relationships observed in inner-city schools. These arguments seem persuasive because they are affirmed by common sense and everyday experiences. Overcrowded, underfunded, dysfunctional schools are most often seen in urban centers. The problems associated with these schools are almost always found in the inner cities of urban areas.

This approach, however, is a partial denial of American educational history. In particular, it ignores the reasons why urban schools have been host to large and diverse populations for more than a century. Studying the development of education in the United States, Tyack[10] showed that state governments have always had difficulty dealing with immigrant and poor families, which flocked to the country's largest cities. A shrinking tax base and a commitment to educate the increasing numbers of students requiring education forced state agencies to severely reduce their financial support for schooling and other governmental services.

The term *urban school* has itself been difficult to define, although most Americans believe they know when they are in an urban school. More and more, the characteristics typically associated with urban schools are found not only in inner-city schools but also in suburban schools. A somewhat distinct approach to the term *urban* is provided by Castells,[11] who argues that the word cannot be understood by giving spatial arrangements the power to affect the social relationships that form in society and the workplace. He suggests that the common-sense view of urban life, with its emphasis on the mass nature of modern society and its effects on human behavior, helps legitimize a way of thinking that ignores the economic and historical considerations that caused these specific social and educational formations to take hold. In this approach, however, we are back to looking at state schools as institutions of socialization and control, accepting the history of their arbitrary teachings and disciplinary practices as though they were the consequences of interests groups alone. Following these structuralist perspectives, Althusser[12] developed theoretical understandings of the individual that were anti-humanistic and anti-empirical. Individuals were no longer seen as subjects in control of their lives, nor could their experiences be understood through empirical validations. Althusser insisted that only a theoretical understanding of social relationships in schools and society could provide an adequate explanation for modern state apparatuses. His attempt to develop an approach that dealt with the structures of such agencies, however, paid insufficient attention to their historical development. Bourdieu,[13] on the other hand, began his study of urban educational systems by focusing on the instructional act as inculcation. From this, he developed an elaborate theory of pedagogic work and the ways authority and control develop in urban educational systems. Both authors believed urban schools were essentially agencies of inculcation and reproduction. Yet they began by choosing different features of urban schooling as their basis of investigation. Althusser was more interested in society as an entity, whereas Bourdieu focused more on urban educational systems and their practices. Neither attempted to reduce everything to an economic explanation, although they did recognize its intrinsic importance. Both were concerned with the linguistic and cultural characteristics of urban educational systems and the economic conditions that those characteristics sought to validate and reproduce.

The problems of studying urban educational systems in cross-cultural ways are formidable. Attempts to do so have been marked by some success, but they have been accompanied by significant misunderstandings. The specific nature of an urban educational system can express itself in differing forms of curriculum, pedagogy, and evaluation practices, in differing forms of symbolic violence and control. But educational production will always express, in one way or another, the needs of the society that supports it. Typically there will be some interplay of influence, as Weber has suggested,[14] since urban educational systems sometimes appear to change or affect social and economic institutions. Richard Johnson, writing about urban educational policy in Victorian England, maintained that problems of authority and control could best be recognized as a reflection of the tensions and conflicts that existed in society at the time.

Educational historians in the United States have generally accepted these explanations of urban educational systems, emphasizing the social needs and ideas of particular classes during different periods in American history.[15] Such approaches help us to see how and why urban, charity schools were first established after the Revolutionary War. The ethical and economic reasons for their creation are uncovered, and education comes to be viewed as a struggle between status groups for control of the minds and bodies of children from the poorer classes. Religious and democratic values were used by advocates to justify these pauper schools, and Americans appeared to accept them at face value until the 1830s. They were presented as a humane response to the social and economic problems of urban crime and poverty, as a more civilized way of dealing with these persistent social evils.[16]

The evolving dominance of urban educational forms has been a constant and persistent social phenomenon existing across historical periods. In fact, the size and density of urban areas and educational systems have been increasing in recent history, especially in the past century.[17] Our incapacity to control or deal with their worst excesses has been a continuing concern, especially now that inner cities have become nearly uninhabitable wastelands where the poorest of our citizens live. Rising levels of lawlessness, **normlessness**, and social isolation in the midst of ever-increasing populations and the movement of millions of people to the suburbs are just some of the more obvious consequences of our use of space in the twentieth century.[18] Most studies of these problems have provided only a quantitative basis for describing and analyzing urban education and the urbanism phenomenon itself. The real problems of qualitative changes and deteriorating life-styles have been either ignored or left to the media.

Apart from its obvious population density and bureaucratic structures, urban education has its own forms and practices. In many instances, the grimness of urban schools and classrooms has evolved naturally from their internal structures and historical traditions, as has their rigid pedagogical style.[19] These include the use of partitioned classrooms to divide students into smaller, more manageable groups; the grade system with its graduated curricula and tracking mechanisms; the interdependency of the state and economy; and the need to prepare urban youth for the future in an increasingly competitive labor market.

In almost all urban schools, two activities are found consistently: an overly corrective pedagogy of inculcation and a bureaucratic impersonality that often deadens the curiosities of young minds.[20] Urban schools are involved in maintaining the social relations of schools and providing the labor market with replacement workers. They are responsible for sorting out and evaluating the merits of students and assigning them to various tracks in the higher reaches of learning and earning. These activities can be seen more clearly in inner-city schools, where children attend state institutions with a history and culture of failure. But they are found in the outer rings of the urban setting and in the suburbs, where urbanism has made significant inroads. In all these state schools, there is a similar organizational ethos and structure: bureaucratic and hierarchical lines of communication facilitate the reproductive functions of schooling in mass society. Urban schools bring together licensed teachers and educational buildings belonging to the state. Some schools are more successful than others, depending on the socioeconomic class of the students. The more successful schools cater to middle-class students and organize themselves around college-bound curricula and standards of discipline. Other urban schools are characterized by educational practices that are much less successful than those of their suburban counterparts. Their location in the inner city causes them to reflect some of the worst aspects of urban blight as it is developing in the United States at the end of the twentieth century.

THE AFRICAN-AMERICAN EXPERIENCE: A SPECIAL CASE

Race relations in the United States have been characterized by segregation in the North and slavery in the South. During the earliest days of the republic, segregation practices in the North were recorded in both the legislative demands of free African-Americans and the schooling experiences of their children. Litwack described the ways in which African-Americans were refused admission to free schools in the North in 1787 and how these exclusionary policies were still being practiced forty years later.[21] African-Americans were usually assigned to segregated schools, no matter where they lived or how they made a living. As new states entered the Union, most established separate instructional sites for African-Americans. By 1850 most states outside the South followed these practices. Litwack quoted a citizen of Indiana in 1850 to show an attitude that was prevalent at the time: " . . . whites rose en masse, and said, 'Your children shall not go to schools with our children,' and they were consequently expelled. Thus, then, we see that in this respect, there is a higher law than the Constitutional law."[22] Some said the admission of African-Americans to white schools would result in social anarchy and violence, proving a disaster for public education. A common stereotype of African-Americans was that they were less intelligent than whites and incapable of doing academic work beyond an elementary school level. The strength and security of Ohio, according to one politician, was thought to reside in the education of its white citizens. Other segregationists said that providing equal educational opportunities for African-Americans would encourage them to migrate to the western states, antagonizing southern-born residents and their kinfolk. Litwack quoted an Iowan who said of African-Americans, "They are not by nature equal to whites, and their children cannot be made equal to my children."[23] Throughout the West, delegates and representatives spoke out against educational measures that might encourage African-Americans to migrate to their states. These exclusionary policies forced African-Americans to develop their own institutions across the country while still paying taxes for public schools.

As early as 1831, however, abolitionists began encouraging free African-Americans to educate themselves and supporting their inclusion in the free school movement. They were forced to accept segregated schools in Cincinnati, however, while other communities found themselves unable to support even segregated schools. Litwack described the struggle between African-Americans seeking an education and segregationists who discouraged them as one that occurred throughout the nation. Racial prejudice, which had developed during three hundred years of African-American slavery, seemed to permeate the American experience.

Segregated schools were inherently unequal. At African-American schools, staff members were less qualified, and the curriculum was less demanding, arousing the anger of African-American parents. Officials expected little from students at these schools, and they voiced their attitudes publicly and without shame. Classes took place in poorly equipped, poorly ventilated facilities. In urban centers such as Rochester and New York, Frederick Douglass, the preeminent African-American of this period, condemned the conditions of the school buildings that African-American children were forced to attend. Douglass argued that the cities collected taxes from both blacks and whites but did not provide equally for their children.

In the South before the Civil War, the vast majority of African-Americans lived as slaves. Their particular situation differed from state to state and plantation to plantation, but the conditions of servitude never varied. Family members were routinely sold to different buyers in an effort to make slaves more manageable.[24] Teaching a slave to read was a criminal offense punishable by death. By the 1830s the abolitionist movement was gaining strength, and people in the North and West were beginning to question whether slavery was justified in light of the Bible, the Constitution, and the Bill of Rights. Finally, the issue of slavery was decided during the Civil War, when President Lincoln issued the Emancipation Proclamation in January of 1863, freeing all slaves. Two hundred thousand African-Americans fought in the Union armies. Laws passed during the Reconstruction period gave African-Americans many of the same legal rights as other Americans, although few were actually put into effect.[25]

A new system of segregation became widespread in the South after the Hayes-Tilden compromise of 1876, which called for the withdrawal of Union soldiers from southern states and permitted white southerners to reassert local autonomy. By the 1890s the system dominated Southern life, allowing whites to enjoy power and authority while blacks were shunted into the background of American political life.[26] Those in power ignored the Fourteenth and Fifteenth Amendments to the Constitution and routinely denied African-Americans their citizenship and voting rights. This so-called Jim Crow system was officially sanctioned by law in 1896, when the Supreme Court of the United States accepted the proposition of "separate but equal" as the law of the land.

From 1880 to 1920, African-Americans moved to northern cities in large numbers to escape the poverty and degradation of life in the South. Wherever they went, however, they found the pernicious segregation system. This affected where they went to school, where they worked, and the type of employment they were able to obtain. Rates of unemployment among blacks were officially listed as twice that of whites, and these statistics have hardly changed since then. Franklin Roosevelt's New Deal program brought African-American citizens more equality and opportunity, and coalitions tried to gain fairer treatment for them. A million African-Americans joined the armed forces during World War II, even though the army and navy segregated members along racial lines. The armed forces were not integrated until 1948, and not until the Korean War four years later was integration actually implemented. During and after World War II African-Americans began a second mass migration to northern and western cities, often lured by work in the defense industry, which had sprung up during that period.

INTEGRATING URBAN SCHOOLS

In May of 1954, the United States Supreme Court unanimously struck down the "separate but equal" doctrine that had ruled the land for more than half a century.[27] In *Brown v. Board of Education* the Court ruled that public schools had to be integrated with "all deliberate speed." After many years of struggle, the coalitions of whites and blacks who sought to implement the Court's decision began to erode in the 1970s and 1980s. Black citizens turned to other, more ethnocentric political leaders to improve their terrible conditions in the urban centers of the United States.

One reason for the change was the racial segregation black Americans encountered when they moved to the larger cities of the United States after World War II. Big-city school districts enrolled more and more nonwhite children and assigned them to schools and classrooms on the basis of aptitude and achievement tests. The tracking and segregation of students followed the residential patterns of the United States, as well as the further divisions along socioeconomic class lines implied by those patterns. During the fifty-year period following World War II, the number of white students enrolled in schools in major cities has declined steadily. In 1940, whites accounted for 17 percent of the school-age population in major cities. The figure dropped consistently each decade until by 1970, only 10 percent of students attending schools in big-city districts were white. The number of nonwhite children who entered these same urban schools steadily increased during this period. In 1940, schools reported 13 percent of their students were nonwhite; in 1950, 18 percent; in 1960, 26 percent; in 1970, over 30 percent. These demographic changes were also seen in the nation's major metropolitan areas, where, by 1970, eight out of every ten black children in the country lived in big-city school districts. This compared with only four out of ten white students. More recent numbers suggest that big cities and their schools are more segregated today than ever before.[28]

As early as 1966, the nation's largest cities were reporting a steady increase in nonwhite enrollment. More than sixty percent of students enrolled in elementary schools in Washington, D. C., were African-American. Baltimore, St. Louis, Philadelphia, Detroit, and many other cities were reporting enrollments between fifty and sixty percent. The rate of nonwhite enrollment has increased during the past twenty-five years, while the white student population has decreased dramatically. Conditions in the inner cities deteriorated and social discontent and riots erupted during the 1960s and periodically afterwards. The division of America into two societies, separate but unequal, was forecast by the Kerner Commission in 1967 and has come to fruition in our own times.[29] As early as 1967, the U. S. Commission on Civil Rights concluded that the racial separation and isolation of African-Americans was increasing at an alarming pace. School segregation was most severe in the big cities of America, where two-thirds of the nation's population now lived. Seventy-five percent of African-American students attended classes that were severely segregated, and these patterns could not be explained by the location of the cities or other demographic data.

Segregation has persisted and grown in spite of legal restrictions against it, and the numbers of African-American and other minority students attending urban schools have risen sharply.[30] Nevertheless, Webb and Sherman reported that there have been some gains as well and that attitudes of white Americans are changing, with increasing levels of acceptance toward the idea of integration. The authors cited opinion polls in the late 1980s, which reported seventy-five percent of African-Americans said they had never suffered discrimination in "getting a quality education." Seventy-three percent said they had not been discriminated against in "getting decent housing," and sixty percent said they had never experienced discrimination in "getting a job." Webb and Sherman also found increases in the number of African-Americans and Hispanic Americans graduating from high school from 1968 to 1985, citing the Bureau of the Census. This has led to significant gains in the number of minority students enrolling in institutions of higher learning, giving blacks, as one example, greater access to middle-class and professional jobs.[31] Average income levels among blacks has increased significantly during the four decades since the end of World War II but still lags behind those of whites doing comparable work. In spite of these improvements, discrimination has persisted, and a large inner-city class of unemployed and unskilled black citizenry has developed alongside these gains. Moreover, a pattern of growth in the enrollment of blacks in higher education from 1960 to 1980 has since reversed, and black enrollment figures have declined somewhat. Meanwhile, progress toward a more integrated educational system has virtually ceased, and educators and the American public seem unwilling to do much about it. Inner-city schools are still the shame of the nation, and day-to-day experiences in these depressed communities affect every aspect of a youngster's life there. Family structures have been severely distorted, and single-parent families living below the poverty level have become widespread. The population of urban poor families is growing faster than that of any other segment of American society, and these individuals remain isolated and out of sight in segregated communities and schools.

HISPANIC AMERICANS: A BRIEF SKETCH

Hispanic Americans come from many places but are identified in schools under a single category, usually classified as "Spanish-surname" or Hispanics. This diverse group includes people from the Philippines, Latin and Central America, Mexico, the Caribbean area, and other places. Hispanic Americans are thus a multi-group minority, which includes many people who settled in the southwestern United States after the Mexican-American War. At the turn of the century, Mexican laborers and field workers began to cross the border to work in factories, mills, and farms in California, Texas, and Arizona. Many moved to other states, where they were welcomed as cheap and dependable labor. Even though the United States passed restrictive immigration laws during and after World War I, millions of Mexican continued to migrate from Mexico from 1910 to 1930. Many of these migrant families lived and worked in the United States, and some of their children became citizens and gained greater entry into mainstream society. Most, however, found their opportunities for success hindered by racial and ethnic prejudice. Mexicans were seen as individuals who were ideally suited for "stoop labor," so-called because it referred to stooping over to pick strawberries or cotton, and should be relegated to menial and field work whenever possible.[32] These attitudes caused southwesterners to adopt educational and social welfare systems that hindered the social mobility of Mexican-Americans. Widespread slums, or *barrios*, were created in cities such as El Paso, San Antonio, Los Angeles, San Diego, and Tucson, Arizona. Labor camps and rural shantytowns dotted the well-to-do valleys of California. They housed the "wetbacks," a derogatory term for those who illegally entered the country in search of work by crossing the Rio Grande, and the "braceros," who entered legally as contract laborers. This bracero program was curtailed at first and finally eliminated in 1970 when new immigration laws took effect. Mexicans were now refused entry unless they met the requirements of the revised Immigration and Nationality Act, and many millions were forced to enter illegally if they wished to work or reunite their families.

Much of anti-Mexican prejudice developed from fearful and resentful attitudes among some white Americans, or *Anglos*, as they were often called in the Southwest. Many saw Mexican-Americans as an economic threat to employment opportunities, for example, because of their willingness to work at menial jobs for low wages. In response to their undesirable working and living conditions, Mexican-Americans organized themselves into unions in the vineyards, lettuce fields, and orange groves where they worked. They sought to raise the level of employment for their workers, made new demands for political power, and started a movement stressing cultural self-pride for the more than eight million Hispanic Americans.

The term *Chicano*, formerly used by non-Hispanics in a derogatory way, now became a designation of self-satisfaction and unity. New leaders—Cesar Chavez, Corky Gonzalez, Ries Tijerina—found their voices, and Americans across the nation began to listen to them. Stereotypical attitudes began to change, as did the lives of many Mexican-Americans. Still, Mexican-Americans were categorized as nonwhite by schools and other governmental and private agencies. They represented another minority seeking a place in an increasingly pluralistic America. They continued to suffer from racial and ethnic prejudices. In the 1990s, California's governor became increasingly upset with the large number of migrants who were crossing the Mexican border illegally. He demanded that the federal government pay for the costs of these illegal immigrants, citing welfare and educational services the state government provided them. Others who crossed the border between Mexico and the United States came from Central America because they found it difficult to enter legally.

Educational systems in the Southwest have had great difficulty teaching children from migrant families, and the failure rates reported by school districts have been very high. Children from these families must move frequently because their parents move to find work as the seasons change. Many find the public schools an unpleasant and frustrating experience, even though many programs have been put in place to ease their transition problems. Such programs as "English as a Second Language" and bilingual education have had some success, but students from impoverished families have continued to fail in great numbers.

Another group of Spanish-speaking people migrated to this country from Puerto Rico. Puerto Ricans have been citizens of the United States since 1917. Puerto Rico has been under American control since the Spanish-American War of 1898. Migration began almost at once after that war, and Puerto Ricans have moved back and forth between the United States and Puerto Rico according to economic conditions. After World War II, the number of people migrating to the United States climbed dramatically as job opportunities increased. A desire for a better life, along with improved methods of transportation, led many Puerto Ricans to leave their impoverished island and settle in urban centers of the eastern states. New York City was usually the gateway for these new arrivals, who found menial jobs in the garment industry and elsewhere in the city. A million Puerto Ricans continued to live in New York City, while another million migrated to other parts of the country in search of economic opportunity.

In urban centers, Puerto Ricans were often forced to live in the worst slums, where rents were unreasonably high. Their children attended inner-city schools that seemed unable to educate them effectively, and failure rates remained very high into the 1990s. Their attempt to climb the socioeconomic ladder in the United States was hindered by the attitudes of other citizens and the difficulty they encountered once they were in a strange new environment. Some suffered racial discrimination because of their African or Indian heritage. Others found that language barriers were very difficult to overcome and sought barrios where Spanish was widely spoken. Data from the Census Bureau indicated that Puerto Ricans lived and worked in the most difficult of conditions and that many were unprepared for life in the urban centers of the United States. Their incomes on the mainland were found to be slightly higher than what they had received on the island, but living expenses were high in both places. According to the 1990 census, nearly a third of Puerto Rican families live beneath the official poverty level, and there is reason to believe this estimate may not be high enough.[33]

Many other people have immigrated to the United States from Asia and elsewhere seeking greater economic opportunity and political freedom. In this brief sketch we have not been able to describe the problems encountered by other immigrants, such as the large numbers of Asian immigrants before and after the Vietnam War, Cuban immigrants moving into Florida and other areas after the Cuban Revolution, and European immigrants at various times. What unites all these immigrants is the racial, ethnic, and socioeconomic discrimination they encountered once they began to live in the urban centers of the nation. All suffered from patterns of segregation, and their children attended schools that were ill-equipped to teach them effectively.[34]

⑥ Summary

The problems of studying education are formidable. They require a multidisciplinary approach that includes sociology, psychology, anthropology, and economics. Certain common themes such as urbanization have become central because they focus everyone's attention on a dominant force in commercial society. Other phenomena, such as racial segregation outside the South, had to do with the attitudes that many Americans developed to justify the slavery that lasted three hundred years. By segregating African-Americans in northern and western cities, commercial interests were able to keep them separate, identifiable, and exploitable. A new segregation system developed in the South after the Civil War, especially following the Hayes-Tilden compromise of 1876. This was followed by Supreme Court decision that affirmed the constitutionality of "separate but equal" facilities for blacks and whites. The *Brown* case in 1954 led to school integration efforts in the 1960s and 1970s. Nevertheless, the big-city school districts are more segregated today than ever before.

⑥ Projects

1. Make comparative observations of a classroom in an inner-city school and another in a suburban school. Describe the physical and educa-

tional experiences of students and relate these to their racial or social class standing. Are students in both classrooms getting a good education? What problems exist in the inner-city school but not in the suburban one?

2. Study the official records of students in an inner-city school that is segregated along racial or ethnic lines. What types of incidents are recorded? How well are students doing on their standardized test scores? Talk to some of the teachers in the school. What attitudes do they seem to have toward their students?

3. Interview some teachers whom you know well about their attitudes toward children from different racial or cultural backgrounds. How do they feel about teaching students who are racially or culturally different from them? Are they willing to speak openly about their feelings? How well are these teachers doing with minority and poor children in their classrooms, and why?

⑥ *Endnotes*

1. Cremin, Lawrence A., *The Transformation of the School: Progressivism in American Education, 1876–1957* (New York: Knopf, 1961); Cohen, Sol, *Progressives and Urban School Reform: The Public Education Association of New York: 1895–1954* (New York: Teachers College, Columbia University, 1963); Greer, Colin, *Cobweb Attitudes* (New York: Teachers College Press, 1970); Gintis, Herbert, and Samuel Bowles, *Schooling in Capitalist America* (New York: Basic Books, 1976); Katznelson, Ira, and Margaret Weir, *Schooling for All: Class, Race, and the Decline of the Democratic Ideal* (New York: Basic Books, 1985), especially 3–27.

2. Lazerson, Marvin, *Origins of the Urban School: Public Education in Massachusetts, 1870–1915* (Cambridge, Mass.: Harvard University Press, 1971), 105–106; Braverman, Harry, *Labor and Monopoly Capital: The Degradation of Work in the Twentieth Century* (New York: Monthly Review Press, 1974), 297–8; Tyack, David, *The One Best System: A History of American Urban Education* (Cambridge, Mass.: Harvard University Press, 1974), 262–266; Nasaw, David, *Schooled to Order: A Social History of Public Schooling in the United States* (New York: Oxford University Press, 1979), 236–237.

3. Ogbu, John U., and Signithia Fordham, "Black Students and the Burden of Acting White," *The Urban Review: Issues and Ideas in Public Education* 18, no. 3 (1986): 176–206; Rothstein, Stanley W., *Identity and Ideology: Sociocultural Theories of Schooling* (Westport, Conn.: Greenwood Press, 1991), 45–51.

4. Altenbaugh, Richard J., "Teachers and the Workplace," *Urban Education* 21 (January 1987): 365–389.

5. Katznelson and Weir, *Schooling for All*, 4–7, 5–8.

6. Rothstein, Stanley W., *The Voice of the Other: Language as Illusion in the Formation of the Self* (Westport, Conn.: Praeger, 1993), 69–74.

7. Durkheim, Emile, *Education and Sociology*, trans. Sherwood D. Fox (New York: Free Press, 1956).

8. Althusser, Louis, *For Marx*, trans. Ben Brewster (London: New Left Books, 1970), 229–236.

9. Hummel, Raymond C., and John M. Nagle, *Urban Education in America: Problems and Prospects* (New York: Oxford University Press, 1973), 23–32; Sarason, Seymour B., *Schooling in America: Scapegoat and Salvation* (New York: Free Press, 1983), 11–27.

10. Tyack, David, *Turning Points in American Educational History* (New York: John Wiley, 1967).

11. Castells, Manuel, *The Urban Question: A Marxist Approach* (Cambridge, Mass.: MIT Press, 1980), 75–85.

12. Althusser, Louis, *Reading Capital*, trans. Ben Brewster (London: New Left Books, 1970), 199–308; See also Benton, Ted, *The Rise and Fall of Structural Marxism* (New York: St. Martin's Press, 1984).

13. Bourdieu, Pierre, and Jean-Claude Passeron, *Reproduction in Education, Society and Culture* (Beverly Hills, Calif.: Sage, 1977), 56–67.

14. Weber, Max, *Protestant Ethic and the Spirit of Capitalism* (New York: Charles Scribner's Sons, 1958), 183.

15. Katz, Michael, *The Irony of Early School Reform: Educational Innovation in Mid-Nineteenth-Century Massachusetts* (Boston: Beacon, 1968); Lazerson, Marvin, "Revisionism and American Educational History," *Harvard Educational Review* no. 43 (1973): 269–283; Cremin, Lawrence, *Traditions of American Education* (New York: Basic Books, 1977), 37–39; Tyack, David, *The One Best System: A History of American Urban Education* (Cambridge, Mass.: Harvard University Press, 1974), 9–11.

16. Edwards, Nathan, and Harold G. Richey, *The School in the American Social Order* (Boston: Houghton-Mifflin, 1963), 237–238; Trollope, F., *Domestic Manners of Americans* (New York: Knopf, 1949), 212–213.

17. Hummel and Nagle, *Urban Education in America*, 212–219; Levine, Daniel, and Robert J. Havinghurst, "Negro Population Growth and Enrollment in Public Schools: A Case Study and Its Implications," *Education and Urban Society* I (November 1968): 24–25.

18. Castells, *The Urban Question*, 79–81.

19. Bourdieu, Pierre, and Jean-Claude Passeron, *The Inheritors: French Students and Their Relation to Culture* (Chicago: University of Chicago Press, 1979), 3–12.

20. Altenbaugh, Richard J., *The Teacher's Voice: A Social History of Teaching in Twentieth-Century America* (London: Falmer Press, 1992), 1–4; Webb, Rodman B., and Robert R. Sherman, *Schooling and Society*, 2nd ed. (New York: Macmillan, 1989), 299–306.

21. Goodlad, John I., *A Place Called School: Prospects for the Future* (New York: McGraw-Hill, 1984).

22. Litwack, Leon, *North of Slavery: The Negro and the Free States, 1790–1860* (Chicago: University of Chicago Press, 1961), 113–152.

23. Ibid., 116.

24. Litwack, Leon, "Education: Separate and Unequal," in *Education in American History: Readings on the Social Issues*, ed. Michael B. Katz (New York: Praeger, 1973), 255.

25. Grant, Madison, *The Passing of the Great Race* (New York: Scribner, 1944), 87–92.

26. Rose, Peter I., *They and We: Racial and Ethnic Relations in the United States* (New York: McGraw-Hill, 1990), 22–24.

27. Ibid., 24–25.

28. Kromkowski, John A., ed., *Race and Ethnic Relations 93/94* (Guilford, Conn.: Dushkin Publishing Group, 1993), 21–23.

29. Hummel and Nagle, *Urban Education in America*, 102–104.

30. Gresham, Jewell Handy, "The Politics of Family in America," in *Race and Ethnic Relations 93/94*, ed. Kromkowski, 148–149.

31. Levine, Daniel, and Robert J. Havinghurst, *Society and Education* (Boston: Allyn & Bacon, 1992), 302–303.

32. Webb and Sherman, *Schooling and Society*, 538–540.

33. Rose, *They and We*, 46–48.

34. Parillo, Vincent N., *Strangers to These Shores* (Boston: Houghton-Mifflin, 1980), 416–418.

11

Possibilities

Ⓖ　Ⓖ　Ⓖ　Ⓖ　Ⓖ　Ⓖ　Ⓖ　Ⓖ　Ⓖ　Ⓖ　Ⓖ

OBJECTIVES

In this chapter you will learn the answers to these questions:

Ⓖ　*Why should more of the nation's economic resources be placed at the disposal of teacher-training programs and schools?*

Ⓖ　*How can instructional practices be changed to make them more interesting and relevant to students?*

Ⓖ　*What is activity-based education, and how could it improve educational practice today?*

Ⓖ　*What type of education is needed for students as they approach adulthood in the information age?*

Ⓖ　*Why must teachers begin to think about helping students through every stage of their social development?*

Ⓖ　*Why must the relationships between teachers and students become more cooperative and friendly?*

t is easier to talk about the problems of schools than to solve them. It is easier to criticize educational systems that are trying to educate everyone than to suggest remedies for their worsening problems. It is also easier to use scientific data and theory in evaluative studies than to go into a classroom and teach children who are poorly prepared to meet the requirements of the traditional educational agenda. Most remedies we can suggest do not rest on facts we can depend on. The consequences of humanistic innovations and activity-based education remains largely unknown and untried. Nevertheless the need to reconstruct our schools is universally accepted by Americans of every political persuasion.

Certain innovations seem desirable in and of themselves. It is in our power to insist that more of the nation's economic resources be placed at the disposal of teacher-training programs and schools. However, a cynic might say, this might have unintended and undesired results. More money might simply pay for more programs to train new generations of teachers who teach students only to take tests, as teachers have done for more than a century. So more will be needed if schools are to provide our children with a future. Perhaps the money could be spent at first on down-sizing public schools so that teachers and students could work in less crowded conditions. Teachers might then be able to focus less on problems of order and control and more on the needs and concerns of individual students.

Alleviating the crowded conditions of schools would only be a beginning. It would not solve the many social and economic problems plaguing the children of our republic, but it would show a desire to put the wealth of the nation at the service of its educational system. What would such a change mean in practical terms?

It would mean that educators would have to accept the idea that education is an individual experience that has to grow out of the needs and concerns of students. Insights, skills, and understandings would be developed in situations that occurred every day in the school, and these would have more relevancy for students growing up in our increasingly troubled and violent society. The power of the school would lie in the social insights and situations it provided for students. For students, a sense of their own education would depend on their ability to be active participants in the learning situation and not robots who are moved about at the whim of the teacher. What students need to know as they grow and develop into adulthood is what schools should be teaching them. Without this initial thrust toward relevancy the best-laid plans of school reformers will go astray. This must come about in smaller classrooms, as we have shown, where teachers, students, and parents interact with one another in a more cooperative, empathetic way. In the past schools chose certain goals devised by politicians and educators and then developed instructional methods to deal with those goals. This approach has not worked, as anyone who has studied the schools can see, for education must concern itself with the social and economic reality of the children if it is ever going to regain some semblance of respectability and strength.

Schools still base their practices on ideas that were popular more than a hundred years ago. These assert that children are idle and incompetent individuals who need to be trained in certain important habits and understandings. This is the education that exists outside the mind and body of the learner, and that is why it fails to produce educated citizens and workers. We know better than to believe that the training of youth to obey authority and to learn predigested lessons and knowledge will result in an educated citizenry. Students must learn to be inner-directed if they are to assume responsible positions in families and the workplace of the future. We need to address the conflicts that arise between individuals from diverse backgrounds, along with the social and economic reasons for those conflicts. Thus no textbook should be read for content alone. The teacher must help students assume a critical attitude in their readings, searching for the author's biases and distortions.

JOHN DEWEY'S LEGACY

Student behavior today is a response to the dictatorial methods teachers use in overcrowded, underfunded schools. Such behavior could change significantly with better funding, especially if accompanied by staff development programs. Teachers should be encouraged to use more individualized, experiential learning methods. Early primary students should be presented with situations that mirror the problems they face in their childhood world. Differing forms of adjustment should be explored, with children deciding on adaptations that need to be made in each situation. Youngsters should be encouraged to explore the consequences of their decisions, along with the unintended outcomes that might occur.

These concepts are part of a doctrine advocated by John Dewey and others for many years. It now has the support of researchers who have studied human personality and its behavior in complex organizations like schools.[1] Children must be able to see the usefulness of their educational experiences and how they relate to their everyday lives outside school. Learning and instruction should be linked to the needs and concerns of individuals and groups of students rather than to bureaucratic goals and outcomes. When this is done, interest and application usually follow, and teachers no longer have to drive their students to learn. Books should still be a central instrument of instruction. However, there should be other materials and technologies in classrooms that engage youngsters on many levels and help open them up to the enormous world of knowledge that exists in the outside world. The teaching of reading should remain a paramount and personal experience that does not begin until the child expresses a desire or need to do so. This would eliminate the undue eye strain and emotional trauma that sometimes accompany this learning experience. This method of instruction would allow some students to acquire reading skills with much less difficulty and greater ease at a later time in their physical and mental development. Reading should be taught as part of the teacher-learner relationship, and that relationship should be a cooperative one. It should be part of learning experiences in science, mathematics, and history rather than a subject of and by itself. Texts should be discouraged because they would only serve to re-create the uniformity and regimentation that now persist in classrooms across the country. Students come to depend on these books that talk a little bit about many things without focusing deeply on any of them. Children assume passive attitudes toward their learning experiences and a reliance on those who are in a position of higher authority. Texts have children doing the same thing at the same time, which may be good for order and control in mass schools. Important information is imposed, and students do not have to think much or solve problems. Inquiry is often stifled or discouraged. Such methods serve to produce the factory worker of the early twentieth century, even though we are on the threshold of the information age and the twenty-first century.[2]

The schools of the future will have to provide students with individual instruction. They will have to place small groups of children under the care of large numbers of teachers and aides. A systematic instructional approach that includes an awareness of the diverse cultures and language backgrounds of children needs to be worked out. Relationships between adults and students need to be democratized and placed on a more scientific basis. Practices could then be subjected to ongoing and cumulative evaluations and placed on a firm footing. The observed laws of nature and child development would assure a personal and individualized instructional experience for students while providing guidance for new approaches to teaching and learning.

Punishment should be much less evident in these schools of the future, as should the fear and anxiety it produces in children. However, these practices will continue to exist as long as schools act as selection agencies for the labor market and society. They will continue to exist as long as teachers and other adults use sarcasm and ridicule without thinking about the trauma they create in students. To eliminate such destructive practices, classrooms of the future must exist in some zone between competition and cooperation, and boys and girls must receive an equal opportunity to prepare for their future roles as adults. John Dewey championed this activity-based educational program many years ago, but it has never been adequately used in the public schools. Initial experiences in cooking, sewing, carpentry, and metal work would introduce elementary school students to many of the tasks parents perform in their homes. This could lead to a curriculum that provides hands-on experiences and insights into the development and growth of important inventions that have changed modern society. Greater emphasis should be placed on the relations between humanity and nature and between different social, cultural, and racial groups in the surrounding community.[3] Diverse cultures can be explored by studying the way in which they gather food, live their daily lives, dress themselves, and work in agrarian or industrial settings. Children could learn about the world of work by going into the community to observe different occupations. Younger students could be taught about the occupations in the home, by not only reading about it but also performing the work itself. Such experiential learnings could then become the subject of deeper study and insight. Students could trace the progression of many occupations from ancient times to the present. Learning pre-digested knowledge and the diligence and discipline of the factory age would become less important. Teachers would have to stop thinking about preparing students for the world of work alone and start thinking about helping them through the problems they are having at every stage of their social development. The rote remembrance of unrelated facts, which so bored generations of students, would no longer be the primary feature governing relationships between teachers and students. Children would be freed of the severe discipline needed in mass schools. Together with their teachers and other adults in the room, they could develop knowledge and insight in a learning environment more in harmony with scientific and humanistic ideas. Anxiety would exist only in the minds of individual students who share responsibility for much of their education and in the group pressures that would remain unavoidable. Students would no longer be viewed as ignorant since the learning situation would begin developmentally with the things they know. However, their apprehensions would grow out of their new relations with teachers. In other words, by this freedom students would become responsible individuals in the learning situation, often with inadequate training and insight. Their educational experiences would now be planned by teams of teachers and students, and they would be asked to operate as responsible people in the learning situation. Obviously, they would need supportive supervision to operate more effectively as individual learners and as members of the group.

The old habits will be difficult for teachers and students to break. This doctrine can furnish teachers and students with a new basis for working together. Teachers would have to give up their right to decide everything in the classroom and to teach in the old-fashioned way. Students would have to learn to take more responsibility for their own education and for their behavior toward others around them. Research has indicated that the habits and knowledge of traditional education have not been retained by students. A set of facts that will be outdated by the time the student finishes high school is hardly the way to educate the next generation of Americans. More needs to be done. The personalities and behaviors of teachers and students have to become more cooperative and adventurous before we will see any improvement in our schools. Children are not automatons, and all attempts to treat them as such will only create the hostility and hatred of learning that characterizes so many of our people today. When things are imposed on students by dictatorial teachers, they are not retained or fitted into any meaningful scheme of a student's life. Children toss such baggage over as soon as they can and search in other places for insights and understandings that will help them to get on with their lives. So school reformers will have to think about individual students first and specific information second. It is only when relationships between learners and teachers are secure that students can develop deeper insights, knowledge, and understanding. Such habits as punctuality, neatness, diligence, and the like can be taught indirectly once the teacher and student have developed good communications. It is then that teachers can raise moral questions and teach students the processes of problem-solving and knowledge development. Whatever makes students more sensitive and aware of their environment and the people in it should become the center of educational reform movements.

SOCIAL AND EDUCATIONAL KNOWLEDGE

We must alleviate crowdedness in schools, then, so teachers and students can work out their attitudes together, so they can meet with one another as individuals worthy of interest and respect. This personalized education can happen only when students are allowed to become active participants in situations that require their attention and concern.[4] Only then can they become part of an educational training that prepares them for more complex social situations and for adult life. Two features of such training seem central. First, schools may use family and neighborhood surroundings to reproduce situations that students are experiencing at different moments in their emotional and physical development. This kind of education can only occur in classrooms where communication is a two-way street and high levels of trust have developed between students and teachers. Nevertheless, teachers will have to be trained to understand the emotional life of children at different ages and the way that personality develops in different classroom situations. This is the activity method. When students become involved and active in their own learning, they like it better and learn more. Such participation helps students learn more about one another and about the teacher who is acting as their guide in the classroom.

Second, as relationships between teachers and students improve, a method of presenting social and educational knowledge can be used. If it is done in the old-fashioned way, however, it will do no better than in the past. An experiential method of learning must be incorporated into every educational experience so students can actually see and feel what they are studying. A difficulty that comes to mind immediately is that teachers generally do not have the training to introduce such lessons into the classroom curriculum.

We must organize teacher training and development so that children are given many opportunities to undergo actual learning experiences. This activity method can progress only when children are brought face-to-face with the elements from the past that bring it to life. A situation might include, for example, the songs Americans sang as they moved across the continent, so that children become a part of the westward movement and more interested in other features of life on the frontier. The songs and dances of the past are fun and can help students master many skills while developing more supportive relations with their teachers. Youngsters can learn to read, since the songs have words that need to be memorized. Dances need choreography before they can be done well.

Elementary school teachers may attempt to reproduce the way weather is predicted in their city or town by constructing weather instruments from scrap. Students could use these instruments to measure the weather and compare their findings with those in daily newspapers. They could predict the weather, learn to read weather maps, do mathematical problems, and so on. Information would be developed in the context of actual experiences, and they would be retained for use in other circumstances.

The list of possibilities is endless, but it all begins with a commitment by teachers to do something to change our antiquated schools. Whatever methods they use, teachers must create learning situations for students that permit them to solve the problems associated with their own educational development and training. They must develop new and more sophisticated forms of discipline to replace much of the regimentation in public school classrooms today and substitute inner controls in the youngsters themselves. The school should become less an agent of the state and labor market and more a place for personal growth and development.

Children would still give up their personal identities to assume those of students in modern schools. However, classroom life would make more sense to them, and their subordinate status would be warranted by a more interesting and meaningful learning experience. At first, the external restraint of the teacher would be replaced with group norms and peer pressures. Later these would be reinforced by the development of inner controls in youngsters that would help them motivate themselves in their educational work. Children would be made more aware of their own needs in school and later in the workplace, and this would spur them to greater interest and effort. Certainly the pressure of the group will be very strong. If schools are integrated along cultural, racial, and economic lines, they will prove a stimulus to greater understanding between children from diverse backgrounds.

REFORMING THE SCHOOLS

It would hardly be novel to say that education can only succeed in our own time if it is firmly tied to the economic needs of the nation. The attempt to build such an educational system would mean creating schools concerned with individual children and with their future as citizens and workers. Present-day relationships between teachers and students will have to be set aside so they can both work together as co-learners in our changing technological society. Schools will have to be thoroughly reorganized and dedicated to more rigorous studies of mathematics and science, in the first instance.

The reforming of school becomes a problem of getting and keeping good teachers who can lead students into a new world of technology. Schools must hire teachers who are able to derive authority from their own personal qualities as well as by the bureaucratic organization of schools. Teachers will have to modify their instructional methods and curriculum fast enough to keep pace with an ever-changing world, and they will have to be literate in the latest technologies. No educational system will succeed if it does not inspire students to seek out and master the rapidly expanding knowledge base of our information age.

Reforming schools is also a problem of getting and keeping good administrators who can work with teachers as co-professionals. Such administrators will rely on their supervisory skills and their ability to work with teachers as professionals in search of educational excellence. Supervisory methods will have to be modified so that more open forms of communication can take place in classrooms and schools.[5] No supervisory method will succeed if it does not include this emphasis on co-professionalism and open communication. Only teachers are in a position to know what is really happening in their classrooms each day.

The reformation of schools becomes a problem of higher administration also. Schools must find board members who are able to encourage these new forms of teaching and learning, who have no need to hold on to practices that create barriers between themselves and educators, as in the past. They must be more knowledgeable about the actual conditions of mass education and how they must be modified over time. Board members must be willing to use democratic decision-making processes whenever possible so that the people most affected by policies are given a chance to shape them. If such board members are found, they can begin to initiate a problem-solving mentality in their organizational ethos. No educational system can succeed without this focus on problem identification and resolution. Nor can it succeed if the people in the organization who are having these problems are not involved in solving them. This is the crux of educational leadership in American schools. We can accomplish little until we support teachers and administrators in their search for new ways of doing things, new ways that do away with many of the behaviors that have closed down communication in the educational hierarchy.

These suggestions have been made time and again by many groups of people, and yet the schools have remained pretty much the way they were during the early years of this century. The question is how to get our best and brightest people to take up teaching. This leads to a second question: How can we improve the working conditions and salaries of teachers so they will be competitive with other occupational opportunities today? The answer given most often is that teachers need to be paid better and that their class sizes and relationships with students and administrators need to be changed substantially. Certainly better salaries are needed, as President Reagan's Commission on Education found in 1981, but that will not be enough to attract the types of individuals we need to the teaching profession.

Educators need to be freed from many clerical and monitoring tasks they are asked to perform so they can focus more attention on the teaching and learning situations that develop between them and the students they serve. It is these tasks that must be eliminated from the job description of educators if we want to encourage sincere and open-minded persons into the profession. Persons of strong character are likely to move away from occupations that demand so much deference and subservience to those in positions of higher authority. They are likely to reject teaching as a poorly paid, sheltered profession, preferring to try their hand at more competitive, more rewarding occupations.

Contact with the outside world might also further the educational advancement of many of our children. It would provide them with opportunities to think about the good and bad things that are happening in their immediate community and suggest ways to improve things. If community leaders could be drafted into schools and classrooms, the cause of relevancy in education would be greatly enhanced. This resource would represent an army of amateur teachers who could acquaint youngsters with the many possibilities existing in the adult world. Perhaps as assistant teachers, they could bring their knowledge of the information age into the classroom. If some of the instructional tasks were performed by business and community groups themselves, this might make it possible for teachers to individualize their work with students. We need to develop new ways of connecting students in classrooms with the men and women who are actually running the government and business organizations in our society. Nevertheless, we should have the instruction of our children in the hands of a professional staff, with members who are paid well and given reasonable working conditions as we try out new ways of doing things in classrooms, schools, and district offices.

Further suggestions could be debated and modified to meet the needs of teachers and students in particular schools. They would pertain to the use of psychoanalytic methods and insights to identify the normal development of youngsters and the needs and concerns associated with individual children during these different phases of emotional life. Professional psychological personnel could play an important role in identifying why teachers and students act as they do in mass schools and what might be gained by changing these educational conditions. Such training would allow educators to become more aware of their own impulsive systems. They could learn more about the way in which they influence their relationships with students and with one another. Most attempts to reform the schools have floundered on teacher resistance and the bureaucratic tendency of administrators to protect their turf against changes that might adversely affect their power and authority. But if mass schools are to change, educators and others must learn more about them and about the informational age that we are now living in. Only then can the task of reforming the schools be taken up with enough energy and concern. It is to this goal that this book has tried to make a beginning, confident that insights into the nature and social functions of schooling are imperative if we are to make the changes that the future demands.

ⓖ *Endnotes*

1. Dewey, John, *Experience and Education* (New York: Macmillan, 1938), 66–67; Cohen, Sol, *Progressives and Urban School Reform: The Public Education Association of New York City: 1895–1954* (New York: Teacher College, Columbia University, 1963), chap. 3.

2. Dewey, John, *Democracy and Education* (New York: Macmillan, 1933), 225–230.

3. Dewey, John, "An Undemocratic Proposal," in *American Education and Vocationalism: A Documentary History, 1870–1970* (New York: Teachers College Press, 1974), 142–148.

4. Rothstein, Stanley W., "Conflict Resolution in a Supportive Environment," *Education and Urban Society* VII, no. 2 (February 1975), 193–206.

5. Rothstein, Stanley W., "Building and Maintaining High Trust Climates: Training the New Administrator in Feeling Expression and Inquiry Skills," *Education and Urban Society* IX, no. 1 (November 1976), 81–102.

Glossary

ⓖ   ⓖ   ⓖ   ⓖ   ⓖ   ⓖ   ⓖ   ⓖ   ⓖ   ⓖ   ⓖ   ⓖ

alienation   estrangement of human beings from themselves and from others

anomie   a sense of normlessness

authority   three types: traditional, charismatic, and legal-rational

bureaucrats   characterized by Weber by these criteria: (1) they were personally free of all servitude to others and appointed to their position on the basis of a contract; (2) they exercised their authority in accordance with the impersonal rules, and their loyalty was enlisted on behalf of their faithful execution of official duties; (3) their appointment and placement in the organization depended on their technical qualifications; (4) administrative work was their full-time occupation; and (5) their work was rewarded by a regular salary and the prospects of advancement in a lifetime career

burgher   mercantile

collection-type of curriculum   characterized by a separation of information from its contexts and a competitive ethos that pitted students against one another in the classroom

curriculum   usually includes: (1) aims that specify why this body of knowledge is being validated by school authorities; (2) content that delimits what will and will not be included; (3) technique that explains how things will be taught and why; (4) timing that explicates the order in which material will be presented to children progressing through the grade system; (5) evaluation of the level of success achieved in transmitting knowledge to students

dysfunctional not functional

elitist ideology a system that limits education to a small number of people and stresses the exclusivity of formal schooling, emphasizing the knowledge and ties of the traditionally select few rather than those of the common people

feudalism a system based on patronage and estate classes
functionalism a theory whose proponents analyzed the functions of social institutions in industrial culture and viewed the social system as an organism in the Darwinian sense, possessing many of the same needs and concerns as living things
functionaries bureaucrats

Gemeinschaft community - where family and community values were cherished - people were born, lived, and died within a twenty-mile radius, centering their lives around families and communities
Gesellschaft society - where family and community values were not cherished - estranged from family and friends and at home in urban communities - rampant individualism and cosmopolitanism - of the contractual relationships entered into with prior calculation for the attainment of mutual ends
Gesellschaft relationships relationships outside the family and lifelong friends

habitus culture

ideologies associations or systems of ideas - the language-based thought of people living and working together in the real world - the way human being make sense of their lives
indoctrination coercive teaching or education; propagandizement

Kurwille will shaped by rational weighing of means and ends associated with contractual or Gesellschaft relationships

legitimate used in a Weberian way, emphasizing the traditional and legal-rational authority on which modern educational systems depend
looping effect term used by Goffman to describe how individuals are deprived of their ability to defend themselves against assaults on their self-concepts. They have no right to protest effectively or to appeal decisions.

modern state described by Weber as having four characteristics: (1) administrative apparatuses that were formed by legislated laws; (2) a set of organizations that performed the official acts demanded by such legislative acts; (3) actual power and authority over all citizens and over most happenings that occurred within a certain bounded area; and (4) the right to use police and military action to force people to behave in accordance with legal prescriptions and statutes

normal schools   non-four-year college schools, usually two years
normlessness   lawlessness

organic solidarity   the division of labor that accompanied the Industrial Revolution

pedagogic act   instructional practice seen as a cluster of habits and routines that reproduce the culture and social relations of schools and society
pedagogic authority   authority derived from instructional position in modern schools
people's colleges   high schools
psychic state   mental condition
psychoanalysis   the study of unconscious mental processes
psychogenetic   refers to innate mental abilities

received perspective   one of Bernstein's message systems, described as strongly moral and normative in its orientations and mirroring the thought and attitudes of traditionalists
reflexive perspective   one of Bernstein's message systems, described as new, insisting that the new technologies of modern society demanded a more flexible and inquiry-based method of instruction

stratified labor market   pyramidal structure of labor market

total institutions   all-encompassing bureaucratic organizations where inmates spend all their time

warrior aristocrats   in ancient Greece, needed for the city-states to survive against the invasions of larger empires and the internal struggles for supremacy on the peninsula
Wesenwille   natural or integrated will associated with Gemeinschaft relationships
Wettkampf   German word used in Nazi schools, which called upon the youth to struggle, fight, and prepare for the inevitable military combat that would give meaning to their lives. All sports led finally to Wettkampf, and military training began with guns or shooting at an early age.

Selected Bibliography

A

AAUW. *How Schools Shortchange Girls*. New York: American Association of University Women Educational Foundation.

Abbot, Edith. *Truancy and Non-Attendance in Chicago's Schools*, 82–86. Chicago: University of Chicago Press, 1917.

Abbott, Max G. "Hierarchical Impediments to Innovation in Educational Organizations." In *Change Perspectives in Educational Administration*, edited by Max G. Abbott and John Lovell, 43-45. Auburn, Ala.: Auburn University School of Education, 1965.

Adler, Louise, and Kip Tellez. "Curriculum Politics in Urban Schooling." In *Handbook of Schooling in Urban America*, edited by Stanley W. Rothstein, 91-111. Westport, Conn.: Greenwood Press, 1993.

Aggleton, Peter. *Rebels Without a Cause? Middle Class Youth and the Transition from School to Work*. Lewes: Falmer Press, 1987.

Alexander, Jeffrey C. *The Classical Attempt at Theoretical Synthesis: Max Weber*. Berkeley and Los Angeles: University of California Press, 1983.

Altenbaugh, Richard J. "Teachers and the Workplace" in *Urban Education* 21 (January 1987): 365-389.

Altenbaugh, Richard J., ed. *The Teacher's Voice: A Social History of Teaching in Twentieth Century America*. London: Falmer Press, 1992.

Altenbaugh, Richard J. "Families, Children, Schools, and the Workplace." In *Handbook of Schooling in Urban America*, edited by Stanley W. Rothstein. Westport, Conn.: Greenwood Press, 1993.

Althusser, Louis. *For Marx*, 71-6. New York: Vintage Books, Random House, 1970.

Althusser, Louis. *Reading Capital*. Translated by Ben Brewster, 199-308. London: New Left Books, 1970.

Anderson, C. Arnold. "Successes and Frustration in the Sociological Study of Education." *Social Science Quarterly* 55 (1974): 286-287.

Apple, Michael W. "Regulating the Text: The Socio-Historical Roots of State Control." In *Textbooks in American Society*, edited by Philip G. Atbech. Albany, N. Y.: State University of New York Press, 1991.

Apple, Michael W. "Cultural Form and the Logic of Technical Control." In *Culture and Economic Reproduction in Education*, edited by Michael W. Apple, 250-257. London: Routledge & Kegan Paul, 1982.

Ashton, Patricia T., and Rodman B. Webb. *Making a Difference: Teachers' Sense of Efficacy and Student Achievement*. New York: Longman, 1986.

Ayers, W. "Teaching and the Web of Life: Professional Options and Folk Alternatives." *Holistic Education Review* 3 (1990): 19-21.

B

Bamford, Theodore W. *The Rise of the Public Schools*, 118-121. London: Nelson, 1967.

Banks, Olive. *Parity and Prestige in English Secondary Education*. London: Routledge & Kegan Paul, 1955.

Banks, Olive. *The Sociology of Education*. New York: Schocken Books, 1976.

Banks, Olive, and D. Finlayson. *Success and Failure in the Secondary School*, Chap. 3. London: Methuen, 1973.

Becher, Tony, and Stuart Maclure. *The Politics of Curriculum Change*. London: Hutchinson, 1978.

Becker, Howard S. "Schools and Systems of Social Status." In *Sociological Work*, edited by Howard S. Becker. Chicago: Aldine, 1970.

Becker, Howard S. "Social Class Variations in the Teacher-Pupil Relationship." *Journal of Educational Sociology* 25 (April 1952): 451-465.

Ben David, J. "Professions in the Class System of Present-Day Societies." *Current Sociology* XII (1963-4): 294-295.

Bendix, Reinhard. "Bureaucracy and the Problem of Power." In *Reader in Bureaucracy*, edited by Robert Merton, Asa Gray, B. Hockey, and H. Selvin. New York: Free Press, 1967.

Bendix, Reinhard. *Max Weber: An Intellectual Portrait*. New York: Doubleday, 1962.

Benedict, Ruth. "Continuities and Discontinuities in Cultural Conditioning." In *A Study of Interpersonal Relations*, edited by Patrick Mullahy. New York: Hermitage Press, 1949.

Bensman, Joseph, and Bernard Rosenberg. "The Meaning of Work in Bureaucratic Society." In *Identity and Anxiety: Survival of the Person in Mass Society*, 181-197. Glencoe, Ill.: Free Press, 1962.

Benton, Ted. *The Rise and Fall of Structural Marxism*. New York: St. Martin's Press, 1984.

Bernstein, Basil. *The Structuring of Pedagogic Discourse, Volume IV Class, Codes and Control*. London and New York: Routledge, 1990.

Bernstein, Basil. "Class, Codes and Control." Vol. 1 of *Theoretical Studies Towards a Sociology of Language*, 121-122. London: Routledge & Kegan Paul, 1975.

Bernstein, Basil. "Code, Modalities and the Process of Cultural Reproduction: A Model." In *The Structuring of Pedagogic Discourse*, edited by Basil Bernstein. London and New York: Routledge & Kegan Paul, 1990.

Bernstein, Basil. "Language and Social Class." *British Journal of Sociology* no. 11 (1960): 271-6.

Blanck, Gertrude, and Rubin Blanck. *Ego Psychology: Theory and Practice*. New York: Columbia University Press, 1974.

Boneparth, Ellen, ed. *Women, Power and Policy*, 55-62. New York: Pergamon, 1982.

Bourdieu, Pierre. "Cultural Reproduction and Social Reproduction." In *Knowledge, Education, and Cultural Change*, edited by Richard Brown. London: Tavistock, 1973.

Bourdieu, Pierre. *Distinction: A Social Critique of Judgement of Taste*. Translated by Robert Rice. London: Routledge, 1986.

Bourdieu, Pierre. *Outline of a Theory of Practice*. Translated by Richard Nice. Cambridge: Cambridge University Press, 1977.

Bourdieu, Pierre. "Systems of Education and Systems of Thought." In *Readings in the Theory of Educational Systems*, edited by Edward Hopper. London: Hutchinson, 1971.

Bourdieu, Pierre, and Jean-Claude Passeron. *Education, Society and Culture*. Translated by Richard Nice. Beverly Hills: Sage, 1972.

Bourdieu, Pierre, and Jean-Claude Passeron. *The Inheritors: French Students and Their Relation to Culture*. Chicago: University of Chicago Press, 1979.

Bourdieu, Pierre, and Jean-Claude Passeron. *Reproduction In Education, Society and Culture*. London and Beverly Hills: Sage, 1976.

Bowlby, J. *A Secure Base*, Chap. 1. New York: Basic Books, 1988.

Bowles, Samuel, and Herbert Gintis. *Schooling in Capitalist America: Educational Reform and the Contradictions of Economic Life*. New York: Basic Books, 1976.

Boyer, E. L. *High School: A Report on Secondary Education in America*. New York: Harper & Row, 1983.

Brady, Robert A. *The Spirit and Structure of German Fascism*, 78-87. London: Victor Gollancz, 1937.

Braverman, H. *Labor and Monopoly Capital: The Degradation of Work in the Twentieth Century*. New York: Monthly Review Press, 1974.

Brophy, James E., and T. L. Good. *Teacher-Student Relationships*. New York: Holt, Rinehart & Winston, 1974.

Byrne, Edwin M. *Planning and Educational Inequality: A Study of the Rationale of Resource Allocation*, 12-17. Slough: N. F. E. R., 1974.

C

Callahan, R. D. *Education and the Cult of Efficiency: A Study of the Social Forces That Have Shaped the Administration of the Public Schools*. Chicago: University of Chicago Press, 1962.

Callahan, Raymond E. *An Introduction to Education in American Society*. New York: Alfred A. Knopf, 1960.

Cardenas, J., and J. M. First. "Children at Risk." *Educational Leadership* (September 1985).

Castells, Manuel. *The Urban Question: A Marxist Approach*. Cambridge, Mass.: MIT Press, 1980.

Clarke, S., V. J. Seidler, K. McDonnell, K. Robins, and T. Lovell. *One Dimensional Marxism: Althusser and the Politics of Culture.* London and New York: Allison & Busby, 1980.

Clignet, Robert. *Liberty and Equality in the Educational Process,* 183. New York: Wiley, 1974.

Cohen, Sol. *Progressives and Urban School Reform: The Public Education Association of New York: 1895-1954.* New York: Teachers College, Columbia University, 1963.

Coleman, James S., et al. *Equality of Educational Opportunity,* 302-303, 325. Washington, D.C.: Department of Health, Education and Welfare, U.S. Office of Education OE 38001, 1966.

Corwin, Ronald. *A Sociology of Education,* 275. New York: Appleton-Century-Crofts, 1965.

Cosin, Bernard R., ed. *Education: Structure and Society.* Harmondsworth, Middlesex: Penguin, 1972.

Cox, Oliver Cromwell. *Caste, Class and Race: A Study in Social Dynamics.* New York: Modern Reader Paperbacks, 1970.

Craft, M. "Talent, Family Values and Education in Ireland." In *Contemporary Research in the Sociology of Education,* edited by John Eggleston. London: Methuen, 1974.

Cremin, Lawrence. *American Education: The National Experience, 1783-1876.* New York: Harper & Row, 1980.

Cremin, Lawrence. *Traditions of American Education.* New York: Basic Books, 1977.

Cremin, Lawrence. *The Transformation of the School: Progressivism in American Education.* New York: Knopf, 1961.

Crozier, M. *The Bureaucratic Phenomenon,* chap. 7. Chicago: University of Chicago Press, 1964.

Cuban, Larry. *How Teachers Taught: Constancy and Change in American Classrooms 1890-1980,* 22-27. New York: Longman, 1984.

Cubberley, Ellwood P. *The History of Education.* Cambridge, Mass.: Houghton-Mifflin, 1920.

Cubberley, Ellwood P. *The Portland Survey: A Textbook on City School Administration.* New York: World Book, 1916.

Cubberley, Ellwood P. *Public Education in the United States.* Cambridge, Mass.: Houghton-Mifflin, 1934.

Cummins, John. "Empowering Minority Students: A Framework for Intervention." *Harvard Educational Review* no. 56 (1986): 18-36.

Cusick, Philip A. *The Educational System: Its Nature and Logic,* 41-59. New York: McGraw-Hill, 1992.

D

Darder, Antonia. *Culture and Power in the Classroom: A Critical Foundation for Bicultural Education.* Westport, Conn.: Bergin & Garvey, 1991.

Davidson, Harold, and George Lang. "Children's Perceptions of Their Teachers." *Journal of Experimental Education* (1960-1961).

Dewey, John. *Democracy and Education.* New York: Macmillan, 1933.

Dewey, John. *Experience and Education.* New York: Macmillan, 1938.

Dewey, John. "My Pedagogic Creed 9." In *Dewey on Education: Selections,* edited by M. S. Dworkin, 19-42. New York: Teachers College Press, 1897.

Dewey, John. "An Undemocratic Proposal." In *American Education and Vocationalism: A Documentary History, 1870-1970*. New York: Teachers College Press, 1974.

Dreeben, Robert. *The Nature of Teaching*. Glenview, Ill.: Scott, Foresman, 1970.

Drew, David. "Mathematics, Science, and Urban Education." In *Handbook of Schooling in Urban America*, edited by Stanley W. Rothstein, 297-315. Westport, Conn.: Greenwood Press, 1993.

Durkheim, Emile. *The Division of Labor in Society*. Translated by George Simpson. New York: Free Press, 1964.

Durkheim, Emile. *Education and Sociology*. Translated by Sherwood D. Fox. New York: Free Press, 1956.

Durkheim, Emile. *Moral Education: A Study in the Theory and Application of the Sociology of Education*. Translated by Everett K. Wilson and Herman Schnurer. New York: Free Press of Glencoe, 1961.

Durkheim, Emile. "On Anomie." In *Images of Man: The Classical Tradition in Sociological Thinking*, edited by C. Wright Mills. New York: George Braziller, 1960.

E

Edwards, Nathan, and Harold G. Richey. *The School in the American Social Order*, 237-238. Boston: Houghton-Mifflin, 1963.

Eggleston, John. "Decision-Making on the School Curriculum: A Conflict Model." *Sociology* VII (1973).

Eggleston, John. *The Sociology of School Curriculum*. London: Routledge & Kegan Paul, 1977.

Elsbree, W. S. *The American Teacher: Evolution of a Profession in a Democracy*. New York: American Book, 1939.

F

Floud, John, A. H. Halsey, and I. M. Martin. *Social Class and Educational Opportunity*, 89-90. London: Heinemann, 1956.

Freire, Paulo. *The Pedagogy of the Oppressed*. New York: Seabury Press, 1970.

Freud, Anna. *Normality and Pathology of Development in Childhood: Assessments of Development*. New York: International Universities Press, 1965.

Freud, Sigmund. *Civilization and Its Discontents*. Translated by James Strachey. New York: W. W. Norton, 1961.

Freud, Sigmund. *The Ego and the Id*. New York: W. W. Norton, 1989.

Freud, Sigmund. *The Interpretation of Dreams*. Translated by James Strachey. New York: Avon Books, 1965.

Freud, Sigmund. *Introductory Lectures on Psychoanalysis*. Translated and edited by James Strachey. New York: W. W. Norton, 1977.

Fuchs, Estelle. "How Teachers Learn to Help Children Fail." In *Children and Their Caretakers*, edited by Norman K. Denzin. New Brunswick, N. J.: Transaction Books, 1973.

Fuchs, Estelle. *Teachers Talk: Views From Inside City Schools*. Garden City, N. Y.: Doubleday, 1969.

G

Gallup, Alec M., and David L. Clark. "The 19th Annual Gallup Poll of the Public's Attitudes Toward Public Schools." *Phi Delta Kappan* 69 (September, 1987): 26-27.

Gay, Peter. *Freud: A Life for Our Time*, 415. New York: Anchor Books, Doubleday, 1989.

Geuss, Raymond. *The Idea of Critical Thinking*. Cambridge: Cambridge University Press, 1981.

Gilligan, Carol. *In a Different Voice*, 151-174. Cambridge: Harvard University Press, 1982.

Ginsburg, Morris. "Durkheim's Ethical Theory." In *Makers of the Modern World: Emile Durkheim*, edited by Robert Nisbet, 142-155. Englewood Cliffs, N. J.: Prentice-Hall, 1965.

Gintis, Herbert and Samuel Bowles. *Schooling in Capitalist America*. New York: Basic Books, 1976.

Glass, David V., ed. *Social Mobility in Britain*, 291-307. London: Routledge & Kegan Paul, 1954.

Goffman, Erving. *Asylums: Essays on the Social Situation of Mental Patients and Other Inmates*. New York: Doubleday-Anchor, 1961.

Goodlad, John I. *A Place Called School: Prospects for the Future*. New York: McGraw-Hill, 1984.

Goodlad, John I. *What Schools are For*. Bloomington, Ind.: Phi Delta Kappa, 1979.

Graham, Patricia A. *Community and Class in American Education, 1865-1918*. New York: John Wiley & Sons, 1974.

Greer, Colin. *Cobweb Attitudes*. New York: Teachers College Press, 1970.

Greer, Colin. *The Great School Legend*. New York: Basic Books, 1972.

H

Halsey, A. H., J. Floud, and C. A. Anderson, eds. *Education, Economy and Society*, 23-25. Glencoe, Ill.: Free Press, 1961.

Hargreaves, David H. *Social Relations in a Secondary School*, 214-215. London: Routledge & Kegan Paul, 1967.

Hawley, William. "The Importance of Minority Teachers to the Racial and Ethnic Integration of American Society." *Equity and Choice* 5, no. 1 (1989): 31-36.

Heritage, John. *Garfinkel and Ethnomethodology*. Cambridge, UK: Polity Press, 1984.

Herrick, Mary J. *The Chicago Schools: A Social and Political History*. Beverly Hills, Calif.: Sage, 1971.

Hirst, Paul. "Althusser and the Theory of Ideology." *Economy and Society* 5, no. 4 (November 1980): 385-412.

Hodgkinson, Harold. *Institutions in Transitions: A Profile of Change in Higher Education*, 16-18. New York: McGraw-Hill, 1971.

Hodgson, George. "Inequality: Do Schools Make a Difference?" In *Equal Opportunity in Education*, edited by H. Silver. London: Methuen, 1973.

Holland, James. "Social Class and Changes in Orientations to Meanings." *Sociology* 15, no. 1 (1981): 1-18.

Holly, David. *Beyond Curriculum*. London: Hart-Davis McGibbon, 1973.

Hummel, Raymond C., and John M. Nagle. *Urban Education in America: Problems and Prospects*. New York: Oxford University Press, 1973.

Hyman, Harold H. "The Value System of Different Classes." In *Class, Status and Power*, edited by Reinhard Bendix and Seymour Lipset. London: Routledge & Kegan Paul, 1954.

I

Irvine, Jacqueline Jordan. *Black Students and School Failure: Policies, Practices, and Prescriptions*. Westport, Conn.: Greenwood Press, 1990.

J

Jackson, Peter W. "The Student's World." In *The Experience of Schooling*, edited by M. Silberman. New York: Holt, Rinehart & Winston, 1971.

Jencks, Christopher, et. al. *Inequality: A Reassessment of the Effects of Family and Schooling in America*. New York: Harper & Row, 1972.

Jencks, Christopher, et. al. *Who Gets Ahead?*. New York: Basic Books, 1979.

Jenson, Arthur P. "How Much Can We Boost I.Q. and Scholastic Achievement?" *Harvard Educational Review* XXXIX, no. 1 (1969).

Jersild, Arthur T. *When Teachers Face Themselves*. New York: Teachers College Press, 1955.

Johnson, David. *Reaching Out: Interpersonal Effectiveness and Self-Actualization*. Englewood Cliffs, N. J.: Prentice-Hall, 1981.

Johnson, Donald. "Althusser's Fate." *London Review of Books* (April 16-May 6 1981): 13-15.

Joseph, Pamela Bolotin, and Gail E. Burnaford, eds. *Images of Schoolteachers in Twentieth Century America: Paragons, Polarities, Complexities*, 40-44. New York: St. Martin's Press, 1994.

Joyce, Bruce, Richard H. Hersh, and Michael McKibbin. *The Structure of School Improvement*, 23-35. New York: Longman, 1983.

K

Kaestle, Carl F. *Pillars of the Republic: Common Schools and American Society, 1780-1860*. New York: Hill & Wang, 1983.

Karabel, Jerome. "Community Colleges and Social Stratification." *Harvard Educational Review* 42, no. 4 (November, 1972): 541-542.

Katz, Michael B. *The Irony of Early School Reform: Educational Innovation in Mid-Nineteenth Century Massachusetts*. Boston: Beacon, 1968.

Katz, Michael B. *Class, Bureaucracy and Schools: The Illusion of Educational Change in America*. New York: Praeger, 1971.

Katz, Michael B. *A History of Compulsory Education Laws*. Bloomington, Ind.: Phi Delta Kappa Educational Foundation, 1976.

Katz, Michael B. "The New Departure in Quincy, 1873-1881." In *Education in American History*, edited by Michael B. Katz, 68-71. New York: Praeger, 1973.

Katznelson, Ira. *City Trenches: Urban Politics and the Patterning of Class in the United States*. New York: Pantheon, 1981.

Katznelson, Ira, and Margaret Weir. *Schooling for All: Class, Race, and the Decline of the Democratic Ideal*. New York: Basic Books, 1985.

Kohn, Michael L. "Social Class and Parent-Child Relationship: An Interpretation." *American Sociological Review* LXVIII (1963).

Kojeve, Alexandre. *Introduction to the Reading of Hegel*. Edited by Allan Bloom. Translated by James H. Nichols, Jr. New York: Basic Books, 1969.

Kozol, Jonathan. *Savage Inequalities: Children in America's Schools*. New York: Harper Perennial, 1991.

Kromkowski, John A., ed. *Race and Ethnic Relations 93/94*, 21-23. Guilford, Conn.: Dushkin Publishing Group, 1993.

L

Lacan, Jacques. *The Seminar of Jacques Lacan Book II.* Edited by Jacques-Alain Miller. Translated by Sylvia Tomaselli. New York: W. W. Norton, 1991.

Lacan, Jacques. *Speech and Language in Psychoanalysis.* Translated by Anthony Wilden. Baltimore and London: Johns Hopkins University Press, 1989.

Laing, R. D. *The Divided Self.* Harmondsworth: Pelican Books, 1965.

Laquer, Thomas W. "Working Class Demand and the Growth of English Elementary Education." In *Schooling and Society: Studies in the History of Education,* edited by Lawrence Stone. Baltimore: Johns Hopkins University Press, 1976.

Lazerson, Marvin. *Origins of the Urban School: Public Education in Massachusetts, 1870-1915.* Cambridge, Mass.: Harvard University Press, 1971.

Lazerson, Marvin. "Revisionism and American Educational History." *Harvard Educational Review* no. 43 (1973).

Lazerson, Marvin, and W. Norton Grubb. *American Education and Vocationalism: A Documentary History, 1870-1970.* New York: Teachers College Press, 1974.

Levine, Daniel, and Robert J. Havinghurst. "Negro Population Growth and Enrollment in Public Schools: A Case Study and Its Implications." *Education and Urban Society* I (November 1968): 24–25.

Levine, Daniel, and Robert J. Havinghurst. *Society and Education,* 302–303. Boston: Allyn & Bacon, 1992.

Levi-Strauss, Claude. *The Elementary Structures of Kinship.* New York: Beacon Press, 1969.

Lightfoot, Sara Lawrence. *The Good High School: Portraits of Character and Culture.* New York: Basic Books, 1983.

Lightfoot, Sara Lawrence. *Worlds Apart: Relationships Between Families and Schools.* New York: Basic Books, 1978.

Litwack, Leon. "Education: Separate and Unequal." In *Education in American History: Readings on the Social Issues,* edited by Michael B. Katz. New York: Praeger, 1973.

Litwack, Leon. *North of Slavery: The Negro and the Free States, 1790-1860,* 113-152. Chicago: University of Chicago Press, 1961.

Lortie, D. C. *Schoolteacher: A Sociological Study.* Chicago: University of Chicago Press, 1975.

Lukes, Steven. *Emile Durkheim: His Life and Work.* New York: Harper & Row, 1972.

Lutz, Frank, and Carol Mertz. *The Politics of School/Community Relations.* New York: Teachers College Press, 1992.

Lynd, Robert, and Harriet Lynd. *Middletown in Transition.* New York: Harcourt Brace, 1937.

M

Machlup, Fritz. *The Production and Distribution of Knowledge in the United States,* 155-156. Princeton, N. J.: Princeton University Press, 1962.

Mahler, M. S. "Thoughts About Development and Individuation," In *The Psychoanalytic Study of the Child.* New York: International Universities Press, 1963.

Mannheim, Karl, and W. A. C. Stewart. *An Introduction to the Sociology of Education.* London: Routledge & Kegan Paul, 1962.

Moynihan, Daniel P. "Sources of Resistance to the Coleman Report." *Harvard Educational Review* 38 (winter 1968): 26.

N

Nadal, Antonio, and Milga-Morales Nadal. "Multiculturism in Urban Schools: A Puerto Rican Perspective." In *Handbook of Schooling in Urban America,* edited by Stanley W. Rothstein, 145-160. Westport, Conn.: Greenwood Press, 1993.

Nasaw, David. *Schooled to Order: A Social History of Public Schooling in the United States.* New York: Oxford University Press, 1979.

National Center of Education Statistics. *Dropout Rates in the United States: 1989.* Washington, D. C.: Government Printing Office, NCES 89-609, 1990.

O

Ogbu, John U., and Signithia Fordham. "Black Students' School Success: Coping With the 'Burden' of 'Acting White.'" *The Urban Review: Issues and Ideas in Public Education* 18, no. 3 (1986): 176-206.

Ogbu, John U. *Minority Education and Caste.* New York: Academic Press, 1978.

P

Pappenheim, Fritz. *The Alienation of Modern Man.* New York: Monthly Review Press, 1959.

Parillo, Vincent N. *Strangers to These Shores,* 416-418. Boston: Houghton-Mifflin, 1980.

Parsons, Talcott. "The School as a Social System." In *Education, Economy and Society,* edited by A. H. Halsey, J. Floud, and C. A. Anderson. Glencoe, Ill.: Free Press, 1961.

Peters, R. S. "Reason and Passion." In *Education and the Development of Reason,* edited by R. F. Dearden, Paul H. Hirst, and R. S. Peters. London: Routledge & Kegan Paul, 1972.

R

Radin, Paul. *The World of Primitive Man,* 106, 126, 130. New York: Henry Schuman, 1953.

Ravitch, Diane. *The Great School Wars.* New York: Basic Books, 1974.

Ravitch, Dianne. *The Troubled Crusade: American Education 1945-1980.* New York: Basic Books, 1983.

Rice, Joseph M. *The Public School System of the United States.* New York: Century, 1893.

Rist, Ray C. *The Invisible Children: School Integration in American Society.* Cambridge, Mass.: Harvard University Press, 1978.

Rist, Ray C. "Sorting Out the Issues and Trends in School Desegregation." In *Schools and Society,* edited by J. H. Ballantine, 330-337. Palo Alto, Calif.: Mayfield, 1985.

Rist, Ray C. *The Urban School: A Factory for Failure.* Cambridge, Mass.: MIT Press, 1973.

Rose, Peter I. *They and We: Racial and Ethnic Relations in the United States.* New York: McGraw-Hill, 1990.

Rothstein, Stanley W. "High Trust Climates: Training the New Administrator in Feeling Expression and Inquiry Skills." *Education and Urban Society* IX, no. 1 (November, 1976): 81-102.

Rothstein, Stanley W. "Conflict Resolution in a Supportive Environment." *Education and Urban Society* VII, no. 2 (February 1975): 193-206.

Rothstein, Stanley W. "The Ethics of Coercion: Social Control Practices in an Urban Junior High School." *Urban Education* 22, no. 1 (April 1987): 53-56.

Rothstein, Stanley W. *Identity and Ideology: Sociocultural Theories of Schooling.* Westport, Conn.: Greenwood Press, 1991.

Rothstein, Stanley W. "Orientations: First Impressions in an Urban Junior High School." *Urban Education* 14, no. 1 (April 1979): 91-116.

Rothstein, Stanley W. "Schooling in Mass Society." *Urban Education* 22, no. 3 (October 1987): 267-285.

Rothstein, Stanley W. *Schooling the Poor.* Westport, Conn.: Bergin & Garvey, 1994.

Rothstein, Stanley W. "A Short History of Urban Education." In *Schooling in Urban America: A Handbook,* edited by Stanley W. Rothstein. Westport, Conn.: Greenwood Press, 1993.

Rothstein, Stanley W. "The Sociology of Schooling." *Urban Education* 21, no. 3 (October 1986): 295-315.

Rothstein, Stanley W. "Symbolic Violence: The Disappearance of the Individual in Marxist Thought." *Interchange: A Quarterly Review of Education* 22, no. 3 (1991): 28-42.

Rothstein, Stanley W. "Theory and Schooling." *Urban Education* 23, no. 3 (October 1988): 294-315.

Rothstein, Stanley W. *The Voice of the Other: Language as Illusion in the Formation of the Self.* Westport, Conn.: Praeger, 1993.

S

Salzberger-Wittenberg, Henry I., and X. Osborne. *The Emotional Experience of Learning and Teaching,* 57-59. London: Routledge & Kegan, 1983.

Sarason, Seymour B. *Schooling in America: Scapegoat and Salvation,* 109-111. New York: Free Press, 1983.

Seeman, Melvin. "On the Meaning of Alienation." *American Sociological Review* 24, no. 6 (December 1959): 783-791.

Sergiovanni, Thomas J., and Robert J. Starratt. *Supervision: Human Perspectives.* New York: McGraw-Hill, 1988.

Sewell, William H. "Inequality in Opportunity for Higher Education." *American Sociological Review* XXXVI (1971): 794-795.

Sewell, William H., and V. P. Shah. "Social Class, Parental Encouragement and Educational Aspirations." *American Sociological Review* XXII (1957).

Shakeshaft, Charol. "Meeting the Needs of Girls in Urban Schools." In *Handbook of Schooling in Urban America,* edited by Stanley W. Rothstein. Westport, Conn.: Greenwood Press, 1993.

Shipman, Martin. "Curriculum for Inequality." In *The Curriculum: Context, Design and Development,* edited by R. Hooper, 104-106. Edinburgh: Oliver & Boyd, 1971.

Simmel, Georg. "The Metropolis and Mental Life." In *Images of Man: The Classical Tradition in Sociological Thinking,* edited by C. Wright Mills. New York: George Braziller, 1960.

Simmel, Georg. *The Sociology of Georg Simmel.* Translated by Kurt H. Wolff. New York: Free Press, 1950.

Smith, David. "Codes, Paradigms and Folk Norms." *Sociology* X (1976).

Smith, Joan K., and L. Glenn Smith. *Education Today: The Foundations of a Profession,* 128-129. New York: St. Martin's Press, 1993.

Smith, Steven. *Reading Althusser: An Essay on Structural Marxism.* Ithaca and London: Cornell University Press, 1984.

Stein, Maurice. *The Eclipse of Community.* New York: Harper & Row, 1960.

Stinchcombe, A. L. "Environment: The Cumulation of Effects is Yet to be Understood." *Harvard Educational Review* XXXIX (1969): 511-22.

Sudnow, David. *Studies in Social Interaction.* New York: Free Press, 1972.

T

Thabault, Rene. "The Professional Training of Teachers in France." In *Year Book of Education,* 242-245. London: Evans Brothers, 1963.

Tonnies, Ferdinand. *Community and Society.* New York: Harper & Row, 1957.

Touraine, Alain. *The Academic System in American Society,* 43-45. New York: McGraw-Hill, 1974.

Tracy, D. *Plurality and Ambiguity: Hermeneutics, Religion and Hope,* 43-46. New York: Harper & Row, 1987.

Trollope, F. *Domestic Manners of Americans,* 212-213. New York: Knopf, 1949.

Tropp, Andrew. *The School Teachers,* 6-9. London: Heineman, 1957.

Tyack, David. "Bureaucracy and the Common School: The Example of Portland, Oregon, 1851-1913." In *Education in American History,* edited by Michael Katz, 166-167. New York: Praeger, 1973.

Tyack, David. *The One Best System: A History of American Urban Education.* Cambridge, Mass.: Harvard University Press, 1974.

Tyack, David. *Turning Points in American Educational History.* Waltham, Mass.: Blaisdell, 1967.

W

Waller, Willard. *The Sociology of Teaching.* New York: Russell & Russell, 1961.

Waller, Willard. "What Teaching Does to Teachers." In *Identity and Anxiety: Survival of the Person in Mass Society,* edited by Maurice R. Stein, Arthur J. Vidich, and David Manning White. Glencoe, Ill.: Free Press, 1962.

Warner, W. Lloyd, Robert J. Havighurst, and Martin B. Loeb. *Who Shall Be Educated?* New York: Harper & Row, 1944.

Warwick, David. "Ideologies, Integration and Conflicts of Meaning." In *Educability, Schools and Ideology,* edited by M. Flude and J. Ahier. London: Croom Helm, 1974.

Webb, Rodman B., and Robert R. Sherman. *Schooling and Society,* 2nd edition. New York: Macmillan, 1989.

Weber, Max. "Bureaucracy." In *From Max Weber,* edited by Hans Gerth and C. Wright Mills, 212-213. New York: Oxford, 1946.

Weber, Max. *Essays in Sociology.* Translated by C. W. Gerth and C. W. Mills. London: Routledge & Kegan Paul, 1952.

Weber, Max. *Protestant Ethic and the Spirit of Capitalism.* Translated by Talcott Parsons. New York: Charles Scribner's Sons, 1958.

Weber, Max. *Theory of Social and Economic Organization.* Translated by A. M. Henderson and Talcott Parsons, 332-335. New York: Oxford, 1947.

White, Dana. "Education in the Turn-of-the-Century City: The Search for Control." *Urban Education* IV (July 1969): 170-172.

Whitty, Geoff. *Sociology and School Knowledge: Curriculum Theory, Research and Politics.* London, Methuen, 1985.

Wilson, John. "Power, Paranoia, and Education." *Interchange: A Quarterly Review of Education* 22, no. 3 (1991): 43-54.

Winnicott, D. W. "Transitional Objects and Transitional Phenomena." *International Journal of Psychoanalysis*, 34 (1953): 89-97.

Wirt, Frederick, and Kirst Michael. *Politics of Education: Schools in Conflict*. Berkeley, Calif.: McCutchan, 1989.

Y

Young, M. F. D., ed. *Knowledge and Control: New Directions for the Sociology of Knowledge*. London: Collier-Macmillan, 1971.

Young, M. F. D. "On the Politics of Educational Knowledge." In *Economy and Society, Vol. I*, Chap. 1. London: Collier-Macmillan, 1971.

Index

AAUW, 185
Abbot, Edith, 26, 185
Abbott, Mac G., 102, 185
Abolitionists
 and the free school movement, 161–162
Academic achievement
 and family background, 121–135
 and poverty, 128–130
Activity schools, 173–176
 and punishment methods, 174
Adler, Louise, 62, 94, 101, 185
African-American experience
 a special case, 161–163
Aggleton, Peter, 137, 185
Aggression
 as a human trait, 11–12
Alienation, 2, 181
 and industrialized communities, 9–10

Alexander, Jeffrey C., 185
Altenbaugh, Richard J., 44, 63, 84, 85, 118, 137, 158, 168, 169, 185, 186
Althusser, Louis, 25, 159, 169, 186
 and cultural communications, 51
American Federation of Teachers (AFT), 78, 79
 and teacher militancy, 79–81
Americanization
 and the immigrant experience in schools, 22–24
Amnesia years
 in human development, 141
Anderson, Charles, 32, 43, 136, 186, 190
Animalism
 and human nature, 10–11
Anomie, 1, 9–10, 181
 and normlessness, 9
Antagonistic-to-schools families, 122

Apple, Michael, 64, 186
Ashton, Patricia T., 138, 186
Assimilation
    and social control, 21–24
Authority, 181
    legal rational, 89
Ayers, W., 70, 83, 84, 186

Banks, Olive, 43, 45, 46, 62, 85, 101, 102,
    119, 120, 138, 186
Becher, Tony, 186
Becker, Howard S., 85, 186
Ben David, J., 46, 186
Bendix, Rinehardt, 101, 186
Benedict, Ruth, 63, 186
Bensman, Joseph, 101, 186
Benton, Ted, 25, 169, 186
Bernstein, Basil, 39, 41, 43, 48, 49, 51, 54,
    62, 64, 65, 119, 122, 133, 137, 138,
    186, 187
Blanck, Gertrude, 187
Blanck, Rubin, 187
Bourdieu, Pierre, 25, 39, 40, 41, 44, 45,
    50, 53, 54, 63, 64, 65, 123, 127, 130,
    131, 137, 138, 159, 169, 187
    and achievement of women, 40
    and culture of the school, 50
Bowlby, J. A., 68, 83, 187
Bowles, Samuel, 25, 43, 44, 63, 64, 65,
    118, 136, 138, 154, 155, 168, 187
Boyer, Ernest L., 44, 101, 187
Brady, Robert A., 25, 102, 187
Braverman, Harry, 26, 44, 152, 168, 187
Brophy, James E., 119, 187
Brown v. Board of Education, 163
Bureaucracy
    characteristics, 92–93
    and cumulative school files, 113–114
    as an ideal type, 89, 91
    and industrialism and urbanism, 125
    as a rational response to modern life,
        89
    as a total institutional type, 93–94
    the school as, 87–95, 91–95
Bureaucratic structures
    and personal needs, 95–100
Bureaucrats, 181
    defined, 89–90

Burgher class, 18, 181
Burnaford, Gail E., 83, 119, 191
Byrne, Edwin M., 53, 64, 187

Callahan, R. D., 187
Callahan, Raymond E., 26, 43, 44, 187
Cardenas, J., 154, 187
Carter, Patricia, 84, 85
Castells, Manuel, 158, 169, 187
Charismatic leadership, 142
Chase, Phyllis McGruder, 85, 118
Chavez, Cesar, 166
Clark, David L., 84, 189
Clarke, Simon, 42, 44, 154, 188
Classroom life
    communication problems in, 115–117
    and conflicts, 144–145
    and conditions of, 147–148
    framework of, 106–108
    and psychological effects on students,
        112–113
    rituals of, 109–110
    social relations of, 103–117
    as a struggle for dominance, 148–152
Classrooms
    and order and control problems, 68–69
    and overcrowding, 68
    and the teacher's authority, 104–105
Class systems (socioeconomic)
    based on ability, 82
Client culpability syndrome
    and school failure, 54
Clingnet, Robert, 101, 187
Cohen, Sol, 168, 180, 188
Coleman, James S., 102, 124, 137, 188
Collection-type curriculum, 47–49
    as socially constrcuted knowledge, 48
Communication problems
    in classroom life, 115–117
    and the language of devaluation, 111–
        113
    and the looping effect, 97–98
    and school administrators, 97
Community, 1
    and the individual, 10–12
    and society, 2
Compulsory education in the United
    States, 22–23

Conflict
  in the classroom, 144–145
Cooperative-to-school families, 122
Corwin, Ronald, 101, 188
Cosin, Bernard R., 188
Crowther Report, 138
  in Great Britain, 128
Cox, Oliver Cromwell, 43, 188
Craft, M., 188
Cremin, Lawrence A., 26, 43, 168, 169, 188
Crozier, M., 82, 86, 188
Cuban, Larry, 62, 84, 112, 114, 119, 188
Cubberley, Elwood P., 26, 43, 44, 84, 188
Cultural backgrounds
  and the language of poverty, 129–130
  and socialization of youth, 51
  of students, 47
  and subcultures of teachers and students, 114–117
Cultural communications, 51
  and the struggle for dominance in classrooms, 148–152
Culture of the school
  as a habitus, 50
  and hierarchy of educators, 52
  and knowledge, 51–52
Cummins, John, 154, 188
Curriculum, 181
  as a syllabus in schools, 60–61
  collection type, 47, 181
  development and reform, 56–58
  hidden, 54
  integrated model, 49–50
  official and unoffical, 48
  sociology of, 47
  and speech and language, 53–54
Cusick, Philip A., 69, 73, 83, 84, 101, 188

Darder, Antonia 63, 85, 118, 148, 154, 155, 188
Darwin, Charles
  and social system as an organism, 17–18
Davidson, Harold, 119, 188
Depression (Great)
  and effects in 1930s, 125–126
Devaluation

the language of, 111–113
Dewey, John, 61, 84, 180, 189
  and activity-based education, 173–176
Discipline
  and teacher-student relationship, 69–70
Discrimination
  according to race, culture, and gender, 53
  and cultural systems, 54
Dominance and submission
  and cultural determinants, 148
  in the pedagogic act, 38
  as a relationship, 142–143
  as a struggle for control in the classroom, 148–152
Dreeben, Robert, 85, 189
Drew, David E., 118, 189
Drop-out rate
  and family background, 128–129
  and spiraling costs of higher education, 131
Durkheim, Emile, 1–2, 9–10, 13, 16–18, 24–25, 49–51, 53, 62, 63, 65, 81, 86, 94, 101, 143, 152, 154, 158, 169, 189

Economic systems, 32
Education Act in England, 31
Educational production, 34–37
  defined, 35
  and schools' responsibilities in modern society, 34
  and speech and language of students, 36
Educational systems
  and the collectivity, 16–17
  and division of labor, 52
  and socializing youth, 15
  and student failure rates, 21–24
Edwards, Nathan, 84, 169, 189
Egalitarianism
  as an ideology in schools, 32–33
Eggleston, John, 45, 51–53, 56–57, 59, 63, 64, 65, 137, 189
Elitist ideology, 30–31, 181
  and common schools, 31–32
  in England, 31
Elsbree, W. S., 44, 189
Emancipation Proclamation

and President Lincoln, 162
Ethnographic research
 of an inner city school, 108–110, 150
Evaluation
 of educational organizations, 52

Family
 as child's primary group, 122–125
 middle class in Europe, 123
 and single parent homes, 164–165
 working class in France, 123–124
Family background
 and academic achievement, 121–135
 and drop out rate, 128–129
 and the influence of communities, 127–128
 effects of poverty on, 128
Feudalism, 182
 and Gemeinschaft, 3
 and movement toward mercantile
  economy, 29
 and pre-industrial period Christianity,
  10
First, J. M., 154, 187
Floud, J., 43, 136, 189, 190
Fordham, Signithia, 155, 168, 193
Freire, Paolo, 59, 65, 118, 189
Freud, Anna, 154, 189
Freud, Sigmund, 1–2, 10–12, 13, 45, 70
 and repression, 18, 140, 189
Fuchs, Estelle, 63, 84, 95, 102, 118, 189
Functionalism, 15, 17–19, 182
 and industrial society, 17
Functionaries, 182

Gallup, Alec M., 84, 189
Gay, Peter, 84, 153, 190
Gemeinschaft, 1–5, 6, 182
 and family and community values, 3
 and feudalism, 3
 and pseudo-Gemeinschaft associations,
  8
Gesellschaft, 1–5, 6, 182
 and educational values, 125
 as a contractual relationship, 4
 as a principal type of relationship in
  modern life, 4
Geuss, Raymond, 29, 43, 190

G. I. Bill programs, 80
 a case of educational policy making
  after World War II, 133–135
Gilligan, Carol, 84, 190
Ginsburg, Morris, 64, 190
Gintis, Herbert, 25, 43, 44, 63, 64, 65,
  118, 136, 138, 154, 155, 168, 190
Glass, David V., 138, 190
Goffman, Erving, 63, 93, 97, 102, 149,
  190
 and institutional identities, 50
Gonzalez, Corky, 166
Good, T. L., 119
Goodlad, John, 60, 65, 84, 118, 147, 149,
  169, 190
Graham, Patricia A., 26, 190
Grant, Madison, 170
Gray, Asa, 101
Greek schools, 41
Greer, Colin, 26, 136, 155, 168, 190
Gresham, Jewell, Handy, 170

Habitus, 182
Halsey, A. H., 43, 136, 190
Hargreaves, David H., 65, 190
Havighurst, Robert J., 136, 169, 170, 192
Hawley, William, 119, 190
Hayes-Tilden Compromise of 1876, 162
Henderson, A. M., 101
Heritage, John, 190
Herrick, Mary J., 85, 190
Hersh, Richard H., 85, 191
Higher education
 and expansion after World War II, 32–33
 and India, 33
 open to all in United States, 33
High schools,
 as people's colleges, 31
Hirst, Paul, 154 190
Hispanic Americans, 165–167
 and high levels of poverty, 166–167
 and stereotypical attitudes, 166–167
Hitler, Adolph, 95
Hockey, B., 101
Hodgkinson, Harold, 44, 190
Hodgson, George, 102, 190
Holland, James, 138, 190

Holly, David, 190
Human nature
and the social order, 140–142
Hummel, Raymond C., 169, 170, 190
Hyman, Harold H., 190

Iannaccone, Laurence, 94, 101
Identification
of students with teachers, 70
Ideology, 182
and class conflict, 35
and knowledge, 27–38
as beliefs and values, 29
as cement of social systems, 29
as explanation of teacher's behaviors,
146–147
as false consciousness, 29
defined, 28–30
elitist, 30–31
in schools, 30–34, 58
of students, 55
Immigrant children
and schools, 15
and student failure rates, 21–24
Immigration and Nationality Act of 1970,
165
India
and higher education, 33
Indoctrination, 182
or socialization, 19–21
Industrial culture, 15–17
and Emile Durkheim, 16–17
and obsession with efficiency and
order, 152
and state institutions, 17–18
Industrial Revolution
and rise of commercial society, 16–17
Inequality
problems of, 57–58
Inner-city schools
as depressed communities, 164–165
Instructional act
and speech, 113–114
and teacher attitudes, 108–109
Instructional situation
and subcultures of teachers and student, 114–117
Integrated curriculum model, 48–49

Integrating urban schools, 163–165
Intelligence tests
and role in tracking students, 127–128
Interaction systems
in schools, 54
Irvine, Jacqueline Jordan, 53, 63, 118, 119,
190

Jackson, Peter W., 191
Jencks, Christopher, 124, 137, 138, 191
Jensen, Arthur, P., 138, 191
Jersild, Arthur T., 154, 155, 191
Jim Crow, 162–163
as law of the land, 157
Johnson, David, 154, 191
Johnson, Donald, 191
Johnson, Richard, 159
Jospeh, Pamela Bolotin, 83, 119, 191
Joyce, Bruce, 73, 85, 191

Kaestle, Carl F., 191
Karabel, Jerome, 191
Katz, Michael B., 26, 43, 44, 45, 169, 191
Katznelson, Ira, 25, 35, 44, 45, 56, 63, 65,
136, 155, 158, 168, 191
Kerner Commission, 164
Kirst, Michael, 62
Knowledge
and culture, 51–52
and curriculum, 48, 59
and ideology, 27–38
social and educational, 176–177
Kohn, Michael L., 138, 191
Kojeve, Alexandre, 191
Kozol, Jonathan, 63, 154, 191
Kromkowski, John A., 170, 192
Kurwille, 182
as rational thought, 4

Lacan, Jacques, 43, 45, 119, 192
Laing, R. D., 192
Lang, George, 119
Laquer, Thomas W., 192
Lazerson, Marvin, 168, 169, 192
Legal-rational authority, 142–143
Latin schools, 41
Legitimate authority, 182
and Weber's thought, 38

Levine, Daniel, 169, 170, 192
Levi-Strauss, Claude 192
Lightfoot, Sara Lawrence, 119, 138, 192
Litwack, Leon, 161, 169, 170, 192
Loeb, Martin B., 136
Looping effect, 182
Lortie, Dan C., 44, 68, 73, 83, 84, 192
Lovell, T., 154, 188
Lukes, Steven, 192
Lutz, Frank, 94, 101, 192
Lynd, Harriet, 137, 192
Lynd, Robert, 137, 192

Mc Donnell, K., 154, 188
McGregor, Douglas
  and x and y theories, 55–56
McKibbon, Michael, 85, 191
Maclure, Stuart, 186
Machlup, Fritz, 44, 192
Mannheim, Karl, 119, 122, 137, 192
  and modern school systems, 19, 25
Marxian thought
  and false consciousness, 18
Mahler, M. S., 192
Martin, I. M., 136
Merton, Robert, 101
Merz, Carol, 192
Message systems
  in schools, 48
Modern culture
  and individual life, 5–8
  and money economy, 7
  and urban life, 6–7
Modern state, 182
Money economy
  and urban life, 6–7
Moynihan, Daniel P., 137, 193

Nadal, Antonio, 63, 193
Nadal, Milga Morales, 63, 193
Nagle, John M., 169, 170, 190
Nasaw, David, 43, 85, 137, 138, 154, 168,
  193
National Center of Education Statistics,
  155, 193
National Education Association (NEA),
  77–78
Nazi Germany, 20–21

and indoctrination, 20
and school systems, 94–95
Nelson, Margaret K., 85
New Deal, 163
Normal schools, 76, 183
Normlessness, 9, 160, 183

Oedipal triangle, 141–142
Ogbu, John, 64, 118, 155, 168, 193
Organic solidarity, 53, 183
Osborne, X., 70, 84, 194

Pappenheim, Fritz, 13, 193
Parents
  and influence on children, 29
  as first dispensers of ideologies, 29–30
Parillo, Vincent N., 170, 193
Parsons, Talcott, 9, 101, 136, 193
Passeron, Jean Claude, 39, 41, 44–45, 64,
  65, 130, 131, 137, 138, 169, 187
Pedagogic action
  and dominance and submission, 38
  and inculcation, 160–161
  and speech and language, 113–114
  as historical practices, 82–83
  as overly corrective methods, 55
Pedagogic authority, 27, 38–39, 183
Pedagogic work, 38–39
Peters, R. S., 154, 193
Plowden Report, 52, 138
  and drop-out and failure rates in
    England, 129
People's colleges, 183
Poverty
  and its effects on academic achieve-
    ment, 128–130
Powerlessness
  and new teachers, 96–97
Power systems
  in schools, 52–53
Psychic state, 183
Psychoanalysis, 10, 183
Psychogenetic abilities, 183
  and speech and language, 12
Psychological development
  and amnesia years, 141
  and human nature, 140–142
  and speech and language, 141–142

and oedipal triangle, 141–142
of human beings, 139
Psychological effects
of classroom life on students, 112–113
of classroom practices, 139
as consequences of classroom life, 145–148

Quantz, Richard A., 85, 118

Radin, Paul, 45, 63, 193
Ravitch, Dianne, 26, 193
Received perspective
in curriculum development, 56–57, 183
Reflexive perspective
in curriculum development, 56–57, 183
Reform
in the Information Age, 177–180
Reid, Robert, 77
Reproductive agencies
schools as, 27
Resistances and failures
in schools, 113–114
Rice, Joseph M., 193
Richey, Harold G., 84, 169, 189
Rist, Ray C., 102, 118, 119, 120, 155, 193
Robins, K., 154, 188
Roosevelt administration
and post-war plans for education, 134
New Deal, 163
Rose, Peter I., 170, 193
Rosenberg, Bernard, 101, 146
Rothstein, Stanley W., 13, 25, 41, 43, 44,
   45, 54, 55, 62, 63, 64, 84, 101, 102,
   118, 119, 137, 138, 154, 155, 158,
   168, 180, 193, 194

Salzberger-Wittenberg, Henry I., 70, 84,
   194
Sarason, Seymour B., 64, 169, 194
School administrators
and communication problems in
   schools, 97
School failure
and spiraling costs of education, 131
causes of, 126, 130
Schools
and ethnographic research, 108–110

and immigrant children, 15
and nineteenth century instructional
   methods, 37
and society, 60–61
and work in modern society, 37
as agencies of indoctrination, 19–21
as bureaucracies, 91–95
as ideological institutions, 58
communication patterns, 97
in totalitarian societies, 20–21
segregated and unequal, 161–162
Schoolteachers, 67–86
a feminized profession, 75–77
and choice of profession, 70–71
and disciplinary methods, 68
and equal rights campaign, 76–77
and professional organizations, 72–73
and public's perceptions of them, 69,
   70–72
and relations with students, 69–70, 73–75
and stereotypes, 72–73
elementary and secondary, 69
self-perceptions of, 68–70
status of, 70–73
Seeman, Melvin, 194
Segregated schools, 161–162
persistance of, 164–165
Seidler, Victor J., 42, 154, 188
Selvin, H., 101
Sergiovanni, Thomas J., 55, 56, 65, 84,
   101, 118, 119, 194
Sewell, William, 123, 136, 137, 138, 194
Shah, V. P., 123, 136, 137, 194
Shakeshaft, C., 40, 45, 64, 118, 194
Sherman, Robert R., 84, 93, 101, 119, 138,
   155, 164, 169, 170, 195
Shipman, Martin, 46, 194
Simmel, Georg, 1, 5–9, 13, 45, 85, 142–143, 148, 153, 154, 194
Smith, David, 43, 194
Smith, Joan K., 119, 194
Smith, L. Glenn, 119, 194
Smith, Steven, 25, 43, 63, 194
Social control
and assimilation, 21–24
and power systems in schools, 51–52
Socialization

and dominance and submission relationships, 142–144
in schools, 16–17
of teachers, 67–86
or indoctrination, 19–21, 81
Social psychological perspectives, 139
Social relations
of classroom life, 103–117
Society, 1
and community, 2–3
and educational systems, 59–60
and the individual, 10–12
and schooling's functions, 16–17
and triumph of industrialism, 2
as a control mechanism, 11–12
as a social organism, 17–18
Socioeconomic status of students
and resource allocations for schools, 53
as a definition of status, 125
as a determinant of success or failure in schools, 124–125
Soviet Union
and higher education, 32
Speech and language
and development of human nature, 141–142
and unconscious processes in the mind, 54
in school curriculum, 53–54
Starratt, Robert J., 84, 101, 118, 119, 194
Stein, Maurice, 118, 137, 155, 195
Stereotypes
of teachers, 71–75
Stewart, W. A. C., 137
Stinchcombe, A. L., 126, 137, 195
Stratified labor market, 183
Students,
and effects of race, gender, and culture, 53
and low test scores, 98–99
and responses to institutional identities, 50
and teachers, 104–105
assault on the self of, 98–99
cultural background of, 47
in classrooms, 107–108
Subcultures

and conflicts between diverse interests in society, 144
Sudnow, David, 120, 195

Teacher organizations, 77–79
and American Federation of Teachers (AFT), 78
and militancy, 79–81
and National Education Association (NEA), 77
Teacher-pupil relationship, 73–75, 104–105
and dominance and submission in classrooms, 139
Teachers
and autocratic instructional methods, 146–147
and control of students, 139
and students, 104–105
functions of, 105–106
new, 95–96
sense of powerlessness, 96–97
Teaching
and racism, 77
as a domestic occupation, 76
Teaching profession
and feminization of, 75–77
and first orientations, 108–109
and racism, 77
and state licensing, 82
Tellez, Kip, 62, 101, 185
Thabault, Rene, 84, 195
Tijerina, Ries, 166
Tonnies, Ferdinand, 1–5, 6, 13, 125, 137, 154, 195
Total institutions, 93–94, 183
Touraine, Alain, 44, 195
Tracking
in France, 130–133
Tracy, D., 69, 84, 195
Trollope, F., 169, 195
Tropp, Andrew, 84, 195
Tyack, David, 26, 43, 45, 154, 158, 168, 169, 195

University attendance
and economic systems, 32

Urban education
  and immigrant and poor families, 158
  and integration of schools, 163–165
  and the significance of race, 157–167
Urbanization
  as a problem of space, 158
  defined, 158–161

Vaughn-Roberson, Courtney Ann, 85
Vernon, Peter E., 138
Vidich, Arthur, 118, 155

Waller, Willard, 63, 64, 65, 71, 73, 84, 85,
  114, 118, 119, 120, 150, 154, 155,
  195
Warner, W. Lloyd, 136, 195
Warrior aristocrats, 183
  and ancient Greek education, 36
Warwick, David, 62, 195
Webb, Rodman B., 84, 93, 101, 119, 138,
  155, 164, 169, 170, 195
Weber, Max, 43, 65, 88, 91, 100, 101,
  142, 169, 195
  and typology of bureaucracy in the
    modern state, 88–89
Weir, Margaret, 25, 35, 44, 45, 63, 65,
  136, 155, 168, 191
Wesenwille, 183
  as natural will, 4
Wettkampf, 183
White, Dana, 195
White, David Manning, 118, 155
Whitty, Geoff, 62, 195
Wilson, John, 44, 154, 155, 195
Winnicott, D. W., 196
Wirt, Frederick, 62, 196
Women
  after World War II, 125–126
Women teachers
  and equal rights campaign, 76–77

York, Darlene, 63, 190
Young, M. F. D., 37, 44, 45, 62, 196